Fodor's

FOURTH
New
EDITION

Vacations on the Jersey Shore

Bill Kent

Fodor's Travel Publications, Inc.
New York and London

Fodor's Vacations on the Jersey Shore

Editor: Kathleen McHugh
Contributors: Bob Blake, Julie Tomasz
Art Director: Fabrizio La Rocca
Cartographer: David Lindroth
Illustrator: Karl Tanner
Cover Photograph: Lee Snider/Photo Images

Design: Vignelli Associates

Special Sales

Contents

Maps

Foreword

While every care has been taken to ensure the accuracy of the information in this guide, the passage of time will always bring change, and consequently, the publisher cannot accept responsibility for errors that may occur.

All prices and opening times quoted here are based on information available to us at press time. Hours and admission fees may change, however, and the prudent traveler will avoid inconvenience by calling ahead.

Fodor's wants to hear about your travel experiences, both pleasant and unpleasant. When a hotel or restaurant fails to live up to its billing, let us know and we will investigate the complaint and revise our entries where the facts warrant it.

Send your letters to the editors of Fodor's Travel Publications, 201 E. 50th Street, New York, NY 10022.

Highlights and Fodor's Choice

Highlights

The bad news is that a few months after James Florio was sworn in as New Jersey's governor, he raised the **state's sales tax to 7%.** The good news is that along the Jersey Shore at least, nobody seemed to care. Because, as the new decade begins, the Shore has made a much-needed comeback as a summer vacation destination.

Compared with the previous few summers, 1990 was a boom season along most of the 127-mile stretch of sandy beaches and protected bays: Hotel and motel room occupancies were up, restaurants were serving more meals, and few vacancies were found among rental properties on Long Beach Island, and in Ocean City and Avalon/Stone Harbor. And the beaches were jammed.

While a crowded, teeming beachfront may not be everyone's ideal getaway, it signals the Jersey Shore's return to health after three years of below-average summer business. From 1987 to 1989, waterborne pollution and garbage slicks forced local authorities to close numerous beaches along the coast for days during the high summer season. An unprecedented number of dolphins, whales, and sea turtles stranded themselves after suffering an unknown viral blight. These marine tragedies, along with escalating costs, caused many of the Shore's regular visitors to stay away.

Though there were a few beach and bay closings in 1990, most stayed open throughout the season. Improved sewage treatment facilities, vigorous enforcement of pollution laws, and a halt in seashore development seem to have been temporary, but effective, stopgaps to these problems.

You would think that with so many people depending on a happy, healthy, busy summer season, most seashore towns would welcome vacationers with open arms. Such was not the case in **Belmar,** a small, mostly residential Monmouth County Shore resort, which, following the lead of Bay Head, fought a statewide attempt to reduce beach-use fees along the Shore. Until 1990, local municipalities determined how much they would charge for beach tags—daily, weekly, or seasonal passes worn to gain beach admission. The proceeds were supposed to pay for lifeguards, beach cleaning, first-aid stations, and rest rooms. It was suggested that the inordinately high $50 seasonal fees some north Shore townships were demanding really served to limit visitors—and pad the municipal budgets—and the New Jersey Public Advocate sued Belmar, forcing the town and others in the county to offer beach tags at the more affordable daily rates of $3.25.

The best news in Monmouth County was the opening of the **Ocean Place Hilton Resort and Spa,** an ambitious business resort hotel with a genuine spa (not a room with a few exercise machines next to a pool) that may spearhead **Long Branch**'s revitalization.

The biggest news in 1990 came from **Atlantic City,** a town that can't seem to keep itself out of the headlines. The year began with Merv Griffin's Resorts, a casino owned by the former entertainer and TV talk-show host, slipping into Chapter 11 bankruptcy. Lower-than-anticipated gambling revenues, a soft market for Resorts' real-estate holdings, and costly casino renovations were among the reasons Griffin gave when he put his bondholders on hold. In April, casino entrepreneur Donald Trump opened the $1.3 billion Trump Taj Mahal Resort & Casino, the largest and most expensive gambling hall in the city. Though it did record business in the spring and summer, taking in more than $1 million a day, that wasn't enough to keep the Trump organization afloat. Other Trump holdings include the Trump Plaza and Trump Castle casino hotels, the Trump Regency, New York-to-Atlantic City commuter helicopter service, and a long-term lease on the city's marina. While not declaring bankruptcy, Trump struck an agreement with his creditors that suggests that some properties in his empire, including the Trump Shuttle, and real estate in New York, Florida, Connecticut, and Aspen might soon be sold. Construction was also halted on the Taj Mahal's 1,200-seat showroom, a health club, and a child-care center.

Trump and Griffin's financial woes were not good news for Atlantic City, though it forced the local government and the casino industry to bury the hatchet and cooperate in polishing the city's image. The year brought city-financed **refurbishment of the Boardwalk,** additional casino-financed **housing to the blighted Inlet district,** and a **new hydroplane service** from Long Island to Harrah's Marina Hotel and Casino. Meanwhile Governor Florio pledged to improve the International Airport in Pomona and speed development of a second Convention Center, adjacent to Atlantic City's Amtrak station. Among other possibilities being discussed are 24-hour gambling (casinos now close for four to six hours every night) and more efficient traffic routing.

The first casino-era bed-and-breakfast, **Inn at the Ocean,** debuted in Atlantic City. More of these small, intimate, alternative accommodations are built or restored in New Jersey every year, a welcoming trend. In addition to housing seasonal vacationers, Jersey Shore B&Bs are gaining favor as off-season meeting sites and executive retreats.

Cape May's many eccentric, informal, bistro-style restaurants have never been better. Led by the **Mad Batter, 410 Bank Street, Louisa's,** and **Maureen's,** the city is considered *the* place at the Shore for superb dining, outdistancing any of the so-called "gourmet rooms" in Atlantic City's casino hotels. Elsewhere along the Shore, international eateries are edging out the tried, true, but dull Italian restaurants and surf-and-turf houses. **Everybody's Cafe** in Sea Girt, the **Golden Pyramid** in Mays Landing, and **Sanna's Bay Club** in Margate feature cuisines from the Middle East, the Orient, Africa, and India.

In the 1970s, Cape May's Mid-Atlantic Center for the Arts **walking and trolley tours** of the historic center helped to spark interest in preservation along the Shore. Now the Long Beach Historical Society is conducting walking tours of **Beach Haven's historic district** and trolley tours of the island's other locales. The Society of Associate Performers in Asbury Park leads tours of sites made sacred by Bruce Springsteen, Southside Johnny Lyon, and other Jersey Shore musicians who came of age in that town. And the state is looking into linking all the Shore's historic sites into a vast **Heritage Trail,** a laudable concept. The Shore becomes more interesting when it is seen not as a crowded stretch of beaches, marinas, motels, and seafood restaurants, but as an evolving environment with unique folklore and traditions.

Fodor's Choice

No two people will agree on what makes a perfect vacation, but it's fun and helpful to know what others think. We hope you'll have a chance to experience some of Fodor's Choices yourself while visiting the Jersey Shore. For detailed information about each entry, refer to the appropriate chapter in this guidebook.

Special Moments

Dawn on the beach beside the lighthouse at Cape May Point

Saturday at 9 PM on Wildwood's boardwalk, between Morey's Pier and Mariner's Landing

Saturday at 11:30 PM at a Caesars high-limit craps table in Atlantic City

A spring Sunday morning in Ocean Grove

An evening Jersey Devil Hunt in the Pine Barrens, Ocean County

Hermit Crab Day, Ocean City

Christmas Day, Spring Lake

A Night in Venice Boat Parade along the canals of Ocean City

Taste Treats

The mole sauce at Taxco Village, Asbury Park

A steak sandwich at Harrigan's Pub, Sea Girt

David Brenner Special Sub Sandwich ("double meat, double cheese"), White House Subs, Atlantic City

Just-picked New Jersey white Silverqueen corn and beefsteak tomatoes from a farmer's stand

She-crab soup, Deauville Inn, Strathmere

Meatballs and homemade wine, Angelo's Fairmount Tavern, Atlantic City

Kimchi, Il Bon Gi, Atlantic City

Fralingers Saltwater Taffy, Atlantic City

Off the Beaten Track

Batsto in autumn
War games in the Pine Barrens, Ocean County
Higbee Beach, Cape May County

Sports

Shark fishing in the Hudson Canyon

After Hours

The Stone Pony, Asbury Park

Terrace Tavern, Long Beach Island

Ocean City Pops Evening Concert on the Music Pier

"An Evening at La Cage" revue, Bally's Park Place, Atlantic City

The Irish Pub, Atlantic City

King Edward Bar, Chalfonte Hotel, Cape May

Beaches

Sandy Hook, for its view of New York Harbor

Island Beach State Park, for scenic beauty, superb facilities, and smasher waves

The high dunes of Avalon

North Wildwood, because it's huge

Architecture

Sandy Hook and Navesink lighthouses
Convention Hall and the Casino Carousel, Asbury Park
Chalfonte Hotel, Cape May
Lucy the Elephant, Margate

Restaurants

Fromagerie, Rumson
Farmingdale House, Farmingdale
Romeo's, Long Beach Island
Knife & Fork Inn, Atlantic City
410 Bank Street, Cape May
The Mad Batter, Cape May

Hotels

The "Big Al" suite at the Trump Taj Mahal, Atlantic City
The Spa at Bally's Park Place, Atlantic City
Cashelmara, Avon
Normandy Inn, Spring Lake
Conover's Bay Head Inn, Bay Head
Golden Eagle, Avalon
The Berkeley-Cartaret, Asbury Park
The Mainstay, Cape May

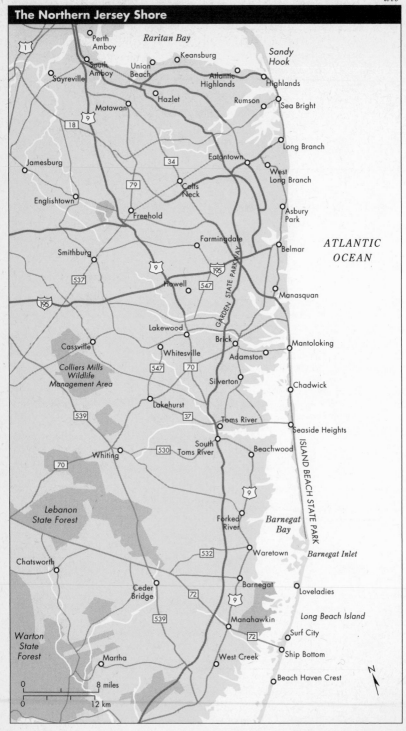

The Northern Jersey Shore

Raritan Bay

Perth Amboy

Keansburg

Sandy Hook

Union Beach

South Amboy

Sayreville

Atlantic Highlands

Highlands

Hazlet

Rumson

Sea Bright

Matawan

Jamesburg

Eatontown

Long Branch

West Long Branch

Englishtown

Colts Neck

Freehold

Asbury Park

Smithburg

Farmingdale

Belmar

ATLANTIC OCEAN

Howell

Manasquan

Cassville

Lakewood

Brick

Mantoloking

Colliers Mills Wildlife Management Area

Whitesville

Adamston

Chadwick

Silverton

Lakehurst

Toms River

Seaside Heights

Whiting

South Toms River

Beachwood

ISLAND BEACH STATE PARK

Lebanon State Forest

Forked River

Barnegat Bay

Waretown

Barnegat Inlet

Chatsworth

Ceder Bridge

Barnegat

Loveladies

Manahawkin

Long Beach Island

Warton State Forest

Martha

Surf City

West Creek

Ship Bottom

Beach Haven Crest

0   8 miles
0   12 km

GARDEN STATE PARKWAY

N

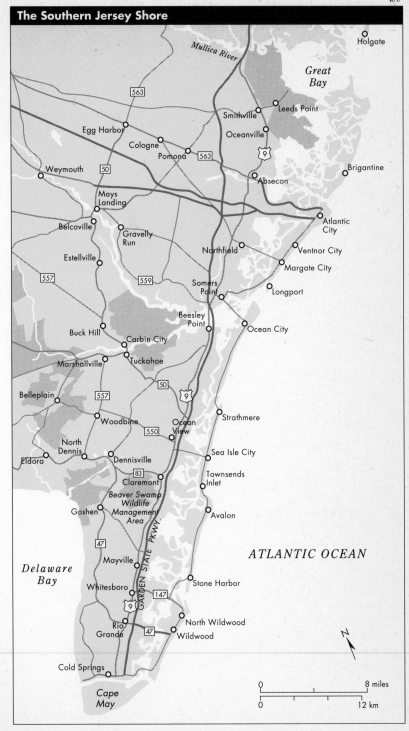

The Southern Jersey Shore

World Time Zones

MONDAY
SUNDAY

+12 +13 -9 -4

-3

3

International Date Line

7

-10 4 -5 -4

14 15
-8 -7 13
-11 5 8 9 16
-10 6 10 17
2 11 18
12

-5

19 22

-5 -4 -3

20

+11 23

+12 -3

1 21 24

+11	+12	-11	-10	-9	-8	-7	-6	-5	-4	-3	-2

Numbers below vertical bands relate each zone to Greenwich Mean Time (0 hrs.).
Local times frequently differ from these general indications,
as indicated by light-face numbers on map.

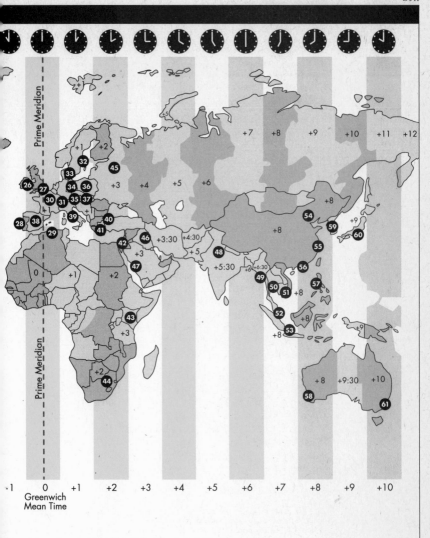

Introduction

J ust about everyone who ever ventured to the Jersey Shore was seeking a life that was better than the one they left behind.

The Leni-Lenape Indians were the first. They came not to splash in the ocean but to find food to get them through the winter. The Indians fished the ocean inlets, harvested marsh grasses and plants from the meadows, and collected cranberries and other berries. By merely standing and wiggling their toes in the soft mud at the entrance to streams and creeks, they could uncover oysters, which they smoked and stored for their winter sustenance. The Indians left huge circular piles of oyster shells all along the Jersey Shore. Later, ground oyster shells were used to pave the first roads in the American colonies.

As you walk along the beach, you'll notice several kinds of shells clinging to the tide line. Many of the smaller, smooth-surface clam shells found in shallow water have a deep-purple interior. When carved into beads and strung together, this became "wampum," an Indian name that doesn't mean money, as it has been assumed, but more a treaty, statement of value, or historical record.

The Leni-Lenape also hunted for wild game birds—turkeys, pheasants, ducks, geese—as well as rabbits, bears, deer, and other forest-dwellers. Anthropologists who studied the Indians believe that, though they left few artifacts and most of their folklore has been lost, the concept of private property was unknown to them—the beaches, bays, meadows, and forests were wild and free.

In the 1990s, however, only in the few relatively untouched wildlife refuges can you approach the image of the 127-mile Jersey Shore as wild or free. The Shore has been discovered, colonized, divided, subdivided, developed, renovated, and restored many times over. The few natural get-away-from-it-all places that remain are exceptions rather than the rule.

This conquering of nature occurred slowly. The Dutch and English explorers of the 16th century were followed by European settlers, who lived beside, and ultimately supplanted, the Indians. Some of these colonists built and furnished their first seaside dwellings from broken pieces of ships that had washed up on their sandy doorstep.

The first European settlers ate the clams, oysters, and wild game that fed the Indians, but the source of their livelihood was a few hundred yards offshore. Whaling was a growth industry from the late 16th until the mid-19th century, when the great herds almost died out, and gas and coal for heating and lighting replaced the need for whale oil. The barrier islands of the New Jersey Shore offered perfect bases for the rugged whalers. Shore whaling wasn't the lonely, long-distance adventure described in Herman Melville's *Moby Dick*. The first whalers boarded long, open boats that were never rowed out of sight of shore. Oil, whalebones, and other products from the catch were then loaded onto sailing ships that anchored in nearby inlets. These ships brought clothing, rum, and, occasionally, mail from Philadelphia, New Amsterdam (later New York), and other Colonial cities. The sea was the only route to and from the Shore until the 18th century, when stagecoach routes, following twisting Indian footpaths, linked the early whaling and fishing outposts to the emerging American nation.

With the whalers came pirates and privateers. (Pirates were self-employed nautical robbers; privateers were hired by one country to raid the ships of another country.) The early Jersey Shore pirates, using little more than whaling boats, waited until nightfall for a sailing ship to anchor, when they would row silently alongside the vessel, board it, and take it, sometimes without bloodshed. Some pirates didn't even use boats; by waving a lantern from the shore at night, they fooled ship captains into steering too close to dangerous shoals, where the ships would run aground and break apart. All the pirates had to do was to wait for the waves to wash anything of value into their hands.

Located between the ports of New York and Philadelphia, where pirates bought supplies, the Shore became a hiding place for booty. Blackbeard and Captain William Kidd are rumored to have buried treasure somewhere along the Jersey Shore. The Shore was also popular for smugglers in Colonial times, as well as during Prohibition. Virtually anyone with a fast, quiet boat could escape detection in the shallow, protected inlets.

As the tensions between the American colonies and England's King George III heated up, both the English and growing bands of revolutionaries hired pirates to attack and seize each other's ships. The British established a base at Sandy Hook—the northernmost landfall of the New Jersey Shore—to control the entrance to New York Harbor and raid privateer bases in Toms River and along the Mullica and Egg Harbor rivers. Though they were unsuccessful in controlling the area, the British led many bloody missions to stamp out opposition.

After the Revolutionary War, the Shore became a place to go to escape the hot, crowded cities of the East. Merchants who patronized privateers for stolen goods, as well as teamsters who drove flatbed wagons filled with oysters, spread the word about better weather and the delicious thrill of immersing oneself in the ocean, a novelty known as ocean bathing. Dr. Josiah Pitney, who lived near present-day Atlantic City, was one of several physicians who, in the mid-

1800s, lectured around the Eastern Seaboard on the health benefits of ocean bathing. No one seemed to question that Dr. Pitney's travel expenses were paid by the Shore's real-estate barons, eager to sell tracts of land at great profit.

What Dr. Pitney sold was a dream, that something as simple as a dip in salt water could be a cure for sickness and a return of youth. Extolling the healthful reputation of salt, the good doctor and others similarly employed claimed that the briny ocean water at the New Jersey Shore could cure just about anything. The ocean bathing he advocated was much different than taking a swim. Dr. Pitney's instructions called for wading into the surf until you were waist deep, and then letting the waves lift you gently off your feet. You wore a heavy cloth bathing costume, not merely because the moral climate prohibited gratuitous exposures of skin but because sunlight was perceived to be dangerous. (It turns out they were right on the last count.)

Bathing was meant to be done in the early morning hours under strict supervision. The bouncy effect of the ocean waves was known to produce a giddy sensation that was considered especially dangerous for women with weak constitutions. Indeed, women and men were not supposed to bathe together, for fear that the sensations it brought on would lead to, well, trouble.

That women—and men—could experience giddiness and be refreshed was ocean bathing's primary appeal. The Civil War, and America's steady development as an industrialized nation, created a large working class that, while never aspiring to wealth or distinction, looked to Europe's upper classes for guidance in living well. In 19th-century Europe it was fashionable for royalty and the landed gentry to "take the waters" at mountain spas and along the Mediterranean. Railroads linking Long Branch, Long Beach Island, Atlantic City, and Cape May to New York and Philadelphia made it possible for working-class people to put on their Sunday best and take the train to the Shore. Many "excursionists" stayed for at most a day, and a few were brave enough to duck into a bathhouse to change into a rented bathing costume and frolic in the waves. Just being in a new place, away from the smoke and summer heat of the city, was rejuvenating. Hotel owners, in an effort to wring some pocket money from the day-trippers, built boardwalks, beer gardens, theaters, museums, amusement rides for daytime fun; gambling dens, brothels, and nightclubs were constructed for nighttime naughtiness.

The latter gave rise to predictable castigation and condemnation, especially from church pulpits. But when religious leaders realized that they couldn't steer their flock away from the Shore's seductions, they built their own retreats. Ocean Grove, Ocean City, and Cape May Point sprouted up in the 19th century as Protestant tent villages, later religious communities. If life was indeed more healthful at the Shore, then God's children would get their share.

As America entered the 20th century, the New Jersey Shore became a place where the working and middle classes could pretend to royalty and a life of ease, if only for a day, or, as the hotels became more elaborate, a week and more. Just as religious congregations found their places in the sun, so did those from various ethnic groups. Long Branch and Wildwood attracted Italians; Spring Lake was called the Irish Riviera; and Bradley Beach and Asbury Park developed strong Jewish populations, which later moved to "suburban" Deal and Elberon a few miles north. Atlantic City had large populations of Quakers, Germans, Italians, Jews, Irish, and blacks.

An escape to a better life, even if it is no more than a fantasy, is still what brings most people to the New Jersey Shore. The varied seaside environment has given rise to many styles of vacationing. Children enjoy the beach, the simple joy of the sand and water, and the boredom of the occasional rainy day. The beach beckons teens in an athletic way: one can surf, sail, scuba dive, fish, or, in time, become a lifeguard-in-training. Then there is the allure of the carnival night—the loud and exciting amusement rides, first kisses under the boardwalk, rock-and-roll clubs that were training grounds for famous musicians and entertainers. Jon Bon Jovi and Bruce Springsteen emerged from the Asbury Park clubs; an earlier generation heard Dean Martin and Jerry Lewis in Atlantic City.

Young adults might take a romantic weekend in a bed-and-breakfast. Gourmands enjoy Cape May's eccentric, delightful restaurants, among the best in the state. Nature lovers visit the bird sanctuaries and wildlife refuges. Owners of Shore vacation homes are proud of the simplicity in "small town" Jersey Shore life, which is so different from that in the cities.

And, since the advent of gambling in Atlantic City in 1978, the casinos have created a big-spending, high-rolling lifestyle, with famous nightclub entertainers appearing every night in the summer season. Thanks to the casino industry, the southern half of the New Jersey Shore—from Long Beach Island to Cape May—has become even more developed, as former summer vacation homes are converted into year-round residences for casino employees.

Oh yes, the weather is nice, too—breezy and cool during the humid months of July and August, brisk and bright during spring and fall. Only from December to mid-March is the weather at the Shore a bit harsh, but that hasn't stopped Atlantic City from doing year-round business. (New Year's Eve is one of the casino city's busiest nights.) Nor has it prevented the restored, historic, atmospheric communities of Spring Lake and Cape May from starting Christmas tours in December, suggesting, quite correctly, that there are few pleasures more comforting than positioning your feet near a roaring fire in a beautiful Victorian guesthouse after a bracing winter's walk along a snow-shrouded beach.

With so many, many visitors—most from the New York and Philadelphia metropolitan areas, though some come from Washington, DC, and Canada, with an occasional high roller dropping into Atlantic City from Japan or Saudi Arabia—your best strategy for enjoying a visit to the Jersey Shore is to blend into the "scenes" and take from each the essence of the life well lived. You don't have to be a swaggering casino gambler, a rocking-and-rolling lifeguard, or a prim, respectful, churchgoing couple to sample the pleasures that each one finds at the Jersey Shore.

Some communities are more hospitable to visitors than others, and money tends to talk too loudly in Atlantic City, but the Jersey Shore still is what it has been since the Indians came: a place to escape to a different, possibly better life, if only for a few hours, days, or weeks.

1 Essential Information

Before You Go

Visitor Information

A variety of state, county, and city organizations have promotional brochures, booklets, events calendars, and additional data about their corner of the New Jersey Shore. The chambers of commerce for various municipalities are useful for last-minute information about weather, beach closings, parking fees, museum hours, and Sunday closings (*see* Important Addresses and Numbers in the county chapters).

New Jersey Division of Travel and Tourism (CN 826, Trenton, NJ 08625, tel. 609/292–2470). The state's blanket tourism department can supply general brochures but is spotty on local details.

Atlantic City Visitors Bureau (Dept. of Public Relations, 2311 Pacific Ave., Atlantic City, NJ 08401, tel. 609/348–7044).

Cape May Convention and Visitors Bureau (Box 403, Cape May, NJ 08204, tel. 609/898–0280).

Cape May County Chamber of Commerce (Box 74, Cape May Court House, NJ 08210, tel. 609/465–7181).

Long Beach Island—Southern Ocean County Chamber of Commerce (265 W. 9th St., Ship Bottom, NJ 08753, tel. 609/494–7211).

Monmouth County Dept. of Public Information/Tourism (27 E. Main St., Toms River, NJ 07728, tel. 800/365–6933).

Ocean County Tourism Advisory Council CN 2191, Administration Bldg., Toms River, NJ 08753, tel. 908/929–2163).

Tour Groups

For details on excursions from Boston, Pittsburgh, and Washington, DC, to Atlantic City casinos, *see* Chapter 5, Atlantic City.

Package Deals for Independent Travelers

All Atlantic City casino hotels, many of the larger noncasino hotels, and an increasing number of bed-and-breakfast establishments offer discounted packages for Sunday–Thursday, typically during the slower off-season spring and fall months. Call the sales and marketing staff of the casino of your choice, or consult your travel agent. **Fabulous Tours** (8523 18th Ave., Brooklyn, NY 11214, tel. 718/259–2532 or 800/828–3344) offers casino packages of varying lengths. Some are land only; others include round-trip air transportation via USAir. **Domenico Tours** (751 Broadway, Bayonne, NJ 07002, tel. 201/823–8687 or 800/554–TOUR) has two- and three-night hotel packages for Atlantic City.

Tips for British Visitors

Visitor Information Contact the **U.S. Travel and Tourism Administration** (22 Saville St., London W1X 2EA, tel. 071/439–7433) for information and brochures.

Passports and Visas You will need a valid 10-year passport to enter the United States (cost: £15 for a standard 32-page passport, £30 for a 94-page passport). Application forms are available from most travel agents and major post offices, or contact the **Passport Office** (Clive House, 70 Petty France, London SW1H 9HD, tel. 071/279–3434 for recorded message, or 279–4000). A visa is not necessary if you are visiting either on business or for pleasure; are staying for less than 90 days; have a return ticket; are flying with a major airline (in effect, all airlines that fly to the United States); or if you complete visa waiver Form I791 (supplied either at the airport of departure or on the plane and to be handed in on arrival). If you fail to comply with any one of these requirements or are entering the United States by land, you will need a visa. Apply to a travel agent or by post from the **United States Embassy** (Visa and Immigration Dept., 5 Upper Grosvenor St., London W1A 2JB, tel. 071/499–3443 for recorded message, or 499–7010). Visa applications made to the U.S. Embassy must be made by mail, not in person. A visa can only be given to holders of 10-year passports. Visas in expired passports are still valid.

Customs
Entering the United States Visitors age 21 or over can take in 200 cigarettes, 50 cigars, or three pounds of tobacco; one U.S. quart of alcohol; and duty-free gifts to a value of $100. Be careful not to try to take in meat or meat products, seeds, plants, or fruits. Avoid illegal drugs of any kind.

Returning to the United Kingdom From the United States you may import duty free: (1) 200 cigarettes, 100 cigarillos, 50 cigars, or 250 grams of tobacco (if you live outside Europe these allowances are doubled); (2) 1 liter of alcoholic drink over 22% volume or 2 liters of alcoholic drink under 22% volume or of fortified or sparkling wine; (3) 2 liters of still table wine; (4) 60 milliliters of perfume and 250 milliliters of toilet water; (5) other goods to the value of £32.

Though it is not classified as an alcoholic drink by EC countries for customs' purposes and is thus part of the "other goods" allowance, you may not import more than 50 liters of beer.

For further information, contact **HM Customs and Excise** (Dorset House, Stamford St., London SE1 9PS, tel. 071/928–0533).

Insurance We recommend that you insure yourself against health and motoring mishaps, theft, flight cancellation, and loss of luggage. Most major tour operators offer holiday insurance, and details are given in brochures. For general advice on all aspects of holiday insurance, contact the **Association of British Insurers** (Aldermary House, Queen St., London EC4N 1TT, tel. 071/248–4477). A proven leader in the holiday insurance field is **Europ Assistance** (252 High St., Croydon, Surrey CRO 1NF, tel. 081/680–1234).

Tour Operators No British tour companies offer packages to the New Jersey Shore. Similarly, there are no companies with houses or apartments in the region for rent. The best bet is a fly/drive package, which includes use of a car or motor home as well as discounted flights and hotel vouchers (reservations can be made in advance—advisable in high season—or en route). Help in planning itineraries is also available. Days Inn, Ramada, Hilton, Howard Johnson, Econolodge, and Best Western are among the participating hotels.

Leading companies offering fly/drive packages include **American Express Holidays** (Portland House, Stag Pl., London SW1 5BZ, tel. 071/834–9744); **Pan Am Fly Drive** (14 Old Park La., London W1Y 3LH, tel. 071/409–3377); **Premier Holidays** (Westbrook, Milton Rd., Cambridge CB4 1YQ, tel. 022/335–5977); and **Poundstretcher** (Atlantic House, Hazelwick Ave., Three Bridges, Crawley, West Sussex RH10 1NP, tel. 029/354–8241).

Airports and Airlines **Philadelphia International** is the closest airport to the New Jersey Shore, though with only one direct flight a day from Britain—a British Airways flight from London Heathrow Airport—it is not necessarily the most convenient airport. New Jersey's **Newark** and New York's **JFK** airports have up to 14 flights a day from Britain. Newark Airport has the most convenient transportation links with the New Jersey Shore.

Six airlines fly to New York from Heathrow: **Air India** (tel. 071/491–7979), **British Airways** (tel. 071/897–4000), **El Al** (tel. 071/437–9255), **Kuwait Airways** (tel. 071/935–8795), **Pan Am** (tel. 071/409–0688), and **TWA** (tel. 071/439–0707). British Airways has the most flights, with up to six a day (two on the Concorde). British Airways, **Continental Airlines** (tel. 029/356–7955), and **Virgin Atlantic Airways** (tel. 029/356–7711) have up to four flights to New York from London Gatwick every day. British Airways also has one flight a day to New York from Manchester. Flying time from all airports is approximately 6½ hours on most flights; the Concorde takes about 4 hours.

Fares vary enormously with the type of ticket you buy and the time of year you fly. All the airlines offer a range of round-trip tourist tickets, with peak-season prices starting at £360. Off-season tickets are much lower, with mid-January to mid-March the cheapest months, when fares can sometimes start at £150 round-trip, though £250 is an average figure. Most airlines advertise specials in the national papers. Ticket agencies such as **Trail Finders** (tel. 071/937–5400), **STA** (tel. 071/937–9962), and **Travel Cuts** (tel. 071/637–3161) often offer good deals. Full-fare prices start from £700 round-trip for economy (coach class), £1,760 round-trip for business class, and £3,270 for first class. The Concorde costs £2,125 one way, but it flies only into New York airports. Fares on scheduled flights to New York and Philadelphia are the same.

Electricity 110 volts. Take along an adapter because American razor and hair-dryer sockets require flat, two-prong plugs.

When to Go

Stretching from Memorial Day (usually the last Monday in May) to Labor Day (the first Monday in September), the summer season packs the Jersey Shore's stretch of beaches and resort towns with day-trippers, summer residents, and young people out for a thrill. You get the best, and worst, of the New Jersey Shore in these three short months, with July being just about the best month of all. By the second week in July, the ocean temperature is perfect for swimming.

The warm weather brings a few pests and unsightly natural phenomena. Stinging jellyfish wash onto beaches around the first week in August. Another August oddity is a green tide, when algae and other microscopic marine organisms multiply to such an extent that the water is predominantly a bright, foamy green.

Two airborne Shore pests that become increasingly annoying in August are the mosquito and the greenhead fly. The greenhead, so called for its dingy green front, is common to Shore communities near open marshland. Its stinging bites raise a welt that itches for several days.

Hotels charge their highest rates in the summer and typically require advance bookings and stays of at least three to four nights. Also during the summer season, nearly all communities charge a daily beach admission, ranging from $3 to as much as $9, whether there's any room left or not.

In September the only crowds are in Cape May, where birdwatchers flock to see the annual migration of more than 700 species of waterfowl, and in Atlantic City, which braces for its annual Miss America Pageant and Parade. The sun begins to set a little earlier, and the Jersey Shore is wonderfully atmospheric. No one charges you to use the beach, and the ocean is usually still warm enough for swimming.

After September, most restaurants and diversions catering to visitors close during weekdays. Farmers' markets along the back roads overflow with the bounties of the harvest. The late-October foliage is not as spectacular at the New Jersey Shore as it is in other parts of the state, but it is beautiful enough for a trip. A few die-hard surfers in wet suits ride the choppy waves.

In December, with the exception of Christmas festivals in Spring Lake and Cape May, and Atlantic City's high-rolling New Year's Eve, the entire Shore slips into hibernation.

Some hotels and bed-and-breakfasts stay open during the cold winter, offering a quiet, inexpensive, get-away-from-it-all escape or an overnight stay to early birds who have come to the Shore to reserve rental apartments and homes for the summer. Sea gulls soar over snow-clad beaches. This is Atlantic City's slowest time, so luxury casino hotel suites are easy to get, and reservations at the expensive restaurants and even a free parking space are a cinch.

By Easter some hotels and restaurants are open and fixing themselves up, looking forward to the summer season with new optimism. Bicycles appear again on the roads and streets; runners trot on the boardwalks or along the beach tide lines. Sailboats skip across the back bays. Toddlers march in Easter parades while adults talk of new amusements, new development, and great shows to see in Atlantic City. In spring, from mid-April to the end of May, the air is balmy, bright, and dazzlingly fresh, and restaurants open for weekend business.

Climate The following are average daily maximum and minimum temperatures for Atlantic City.

Jan.	45F	7C	May	70F	22C	Sept.	76F	24C
	29	−2		52	11		58	14
Feb.	45F	7C	June	79F	26C	Oct.	67F	19C
	29	−2		61	16		49	9
Mar.	50F	10C	July	85F	29C	Nov.	56F	13C
	34	1		67	19		38	3
Apr.	61F	16C	Aug.	83F	28C	Dec.	47F	8C
	43	6		65	18		31	−1

WeatherTrak provides information on 750 cities around the world—450 of them in the United States. To hear a recent, recorded Atlantic City weather report, call WeatherTrak (900/370–8728) on a touch-tone telephone, and then dial 609, the area code for Atlantic City. The service costs 75¢ for the first minute and 50¢ per minute thereafter. For a list of all cities served and their access codes, send a self-addressed, stamped envelope to Cities, Box 7000, Dallas, TX 75209, or call 800/247–3282.

Festivals and Seasonal Events

Jan.: "Cape May Cooks . . . Does It Ever," Cape May. Restaurant and cuisine clinics are held in a handful of restaurants and bed-and-breakfasts. *Tel. 609/884–4710.*

Feb.: Cape May's Shakespeare Festival features performances of at least one play, lectures, and themed restaurant menus. *Tel. 609/884–5404.*

Mar.: Martin Z. Mollusk Day in Ocean City is a fun, silly boardwalk event that spoofs Groundhog Day. You can be sure that Martin Z. Mollusk, Ocean City's costumed mascot, will romp on the beach and see his shadow, and thus assure plenty of sunshine for the season ahead. *Tel. 609/399–6111, ext. 222.*

Mar. 31: Atlantic City's **Easter Parade** is the oldest on the Jersey Shore. It was started to encourage people to visit the city earlier in the year. It's not quite as classy as it used to be when Irving Berlin wrote the song, but it still draws a crowd. Prizes are awarded for the best-dressed paraders, the best hat, and so on. *Tel. 609/348–7044.*

Apr.: Doo-Dah Parade in Ocean City, dedicated to nonsense and fun, is intended to help taxpayers release tension after the April 15 filing deadline. *Tel. 609/399–6111, ext. 222.*

Apr.: The **Tulip Festival** in Cape May celebrates the annual explosion of spring flowers with special house and garden tours. *Tel. 609/884–5404.*

May: Memorial Day parades kick off the summer season in some Shore towns. Banks and offices are closed.

June: The **National Bocce Tournament** is one of the few remaining seasonal events held inside Asbury Park's flamboyant Convention Hall. *Bocce* is the Italian version of the popular European bowling game. *Tel. 908/775–7676.*

July: Fourth of July fireworks light up the night sky in many Shore towns. Banks and government offices are closed.

July: The **New Jersey Off-Shore Power Boat Race** in Point Pleasant is the state's largest, and loudest, powerboat race. Hundreds of thousands of spectators watch from the boardwalks, beaches, and beachfront hotels. *Tel. 908/899–2424.*

July: The high point of Ocean City's beloved **Night in Venice Parade** is a festive, occasionally raucous, boat parade through the city's lagoons. *Tel. 609/399–6111, ext. 222.*

Aug.: The **Lifeguard Tournament** on Brant Beach, Long Beach Island, gives guards from several municipalities the opportunity to demonstrate both their strength and their life-saving skills. The guys and gals with the whistles take this very, very seriously. *Tel. 609/494–7211.*

Aug.: Ocean City stages a series of wacky events in August that appeal to both children and adults. Among them are the **Hermit Crab Race and Miss Crustacean Pageant** (which satirizes the Miss America Pageant), the **Artistic Pie-Eating Contest,** and the **Miscellaneous Sun Tan Tournament.** *Tel. 609/399–6111, ext. 222.*

Sept.: The **Clam Shell Pitching Tournament** in Cape May is a hilarious annual event involving the lowly, common quahog shell and compulsive types who spend hours of their time hurling them about on the beach. Some contestants practice all year to win. *Tel. 609/884–9565.*

Sept.: The **Miss America Scholarship Pageant and Parade,** held in Atlantic City, is the Jersey Shore's most famous yearly event as well as America's most celebrated beauty pageant. *Tel. 609/344–7571.*

Sept.: For one weekend in September, Stone Harbor celebrates seashore culture, folklore, and environmental awareness with the **Wings of Water Festival.** Scheduled events include lectures, nature tours, crafts shows, and theatrical performances. *Tel. 609/368–1211.*

Oct.: Victorian Week in Cape May is actually a 10-day festival in early October filled with colorful events that range from special house tours and serious lectures on restoration and antiques to sing-alongs, costumed banquets, and dramatic performances. *Tel. 609/884–5404.*

Nov.: Cape May's **Sherlock Holmes Festival** features dramatic readings, costume balls, and a murder mystery to solve. *Tel. 609/884–5404.*

Dec.: Spring Lake's **Christmas Tours** include visits to historic houses and themed restaurant meals. *Tel. 908/449–0577.*

Dec.: Cape May celebrates Christmas the entire month of December with candlelight walks, strolling carolers, tours of decorated houses, and a citywide Christmas lights competition. The high point for many is the **Dickens Christmas Extravaganza,** which offers the added attractions of dramatic readings and a costume banquet. *Tel. 609/884–5404.*

What to Pack

As a general rule, pack light because porters and luggage trolleys can be hard to find at New York and Philadelphia airports. Also include an extra pair of sunglasses, contact lenses, or prescription sunglasses. Remember to bring any prescription medicines you use regularly as well as any allergy medication you may need.

In the summer you'll need mostly comfortable, casual clothing that permits you to adapt to the heat as well as the arctic air-conditioning you'll find whenever you go indoors. For women this can include pairs of light-colored cotton long and short pants, and perhaps a skirt. Also add a few casual cotton pullovers, polos or T-shirts, a light sweater or windbreaker for cool nights, and comfortable shoes that you can slip off and shake out if they are filled with sand. Sweatpants and sweatshirts are also acceptable and quite common in residential areas.

People like to pretend that it never rains at the Jersey Shore; it does, though unpredictably, so pack a small folding umbrella. For the sun, pack a hat and sunscreen. Include some kind of foot protection—open-toe sandals are best—because beach sand reflects heat, and you can burn the soles of your feet before you reach the water.

For evening a long-sleeve shirt or blouse, a lightweight dress jacket for men, and a dressy sweater for women are appropriate in almost all restaurants; ties are optional. Women should think twice before wearing high-, narrow-, or spiked-heel shoes when venturing out on a boardwalk. The cracks between the boards are usually wide enough to trap a heel and tear it off.

On the topic of bathing suits: The New Jersey Shore does not possess the progressive morals of the Riviera, Rio de Janiero, or even Southern California (though there are two nude beaches on the Shore). Topless bathing for women is not permitted anywhere, and people who wear too little will find themselves subject to ridicule or even arrest.

Now that the legal drinking age is 21, most nightclubs have adopted some kind of dress code, usually excluding blue jeans, T-shirts and shirts without a collar, sandals, and sneakers—no matter how expensive or stylish they are. For the night out, pack light, smart sport clothing.

If you plan to conduct business at the New Jersey Shore, the typical urban business uniform applies. For men, the darker and more conservative the suit, the more respect and attention you'll get, no matter what the season. For women, a suit is also preferred, though some lighter colors are acceptable.

Carry-on Luggage   Passengers on U.S. airlines are limited to two carry-on bags. For a bag you wish to store under the seat, the maximum dimensions are $9'' \times 14'' \times 22''$. For bags that can be hung in a cabin closet or on a luggage rack, the maximum dimensions are $4'' \times 23'' \times 45''$. For bags you wish to store in an overhead bin, the maximum dimensions are $10'' \times 14'' \times 36''$. Any item that exceeds the specified dimensions can be rejected as a carryon and handled as checked baggage. An airline can adapt these rules to the circumstances, so on a crowded flight you may be allowed only one carry-on bag. In addition to carryons, you may bring aboard a handbag (pocketbook or purse); an overcoat or wrap; an umbrella; a camera; a reasonable amount of reading material; an infant bag; crutches, a cane, braces or other prosthetic device; and an infant/child safety seat.

Checked Luggage   Luggage allowances vary slightly from airline to airline. Many carriers allow three checked pieces, but some allow only two, so check before you go. In all cases, check-in luggage cannot weigh more than 70 pounds per piece or be larger than 62 inches in total dimensions (length + width + height).

Cash Machines

Most New Jersey Shore savings banks and all Atlantic City hotel casinos have automated teller machines (ATMs) in their lobbies or located near their entrances. The machines accept plastic cards and dispense cash 24 hours a day. Eight major networks operate in the United States, the largest of which are Cirrus (owned by MasterCard) and the Plus System (affiliated with Visa). American Express also has cash machines in some casino hotels. Each network has a toll-free telephone number for specific locations of ATMs in a given city. The Cirrus number is 800/4–CIRRUS; the Plus number is 900/THE–PLUS. Along the southern New Jersey Shore, you'll also find the MAC system. Visa and MasterCard may also be used in automated teller machines, but these companies treat the service as a short-term loan and charge interest on the amount advanced even if you pay your monthly bills on time. If your bank offers automated teller cards, request them. Check with your bank for information on fees and the amount of cash you can withdraw on any given day.

Because of an increase in fraudulent checks and a preponderance of stolen credit cards in and around Atlantic City, banks are increasingly reluctant to cash personal checks. Most require checks be deposited in an account and then held for several days until the funds are transferred. An automated teller machine is the easiest way to get cash fast.

Traveling with Film

If your camera is new, shoot and develop a few rolls of film before leaving home. Pack some lens tissue and an extra battery for your built-in light meter. Invest about $10 in a skylight filter and screw it onto the front of your lens: it will protect the lens and also reduce haze. Check your camera's operating manual about such factors as humidity, exposure to salt water, and sand. Consult your camera shop about other filters for bright sunlight and polarized lenses.

Film doesn't like hot weather or the rapid temperature changes that you'll find at the New Jersey Shore. Avoid storing film in dark leather or plastic cases, the automobile glove compartment, the shelf under the rear window, or any location where heat from sunlight can raise temperatures. As a general rule put film in a light-colored bag behind the front seat of your car on the floor on the side opposite the exhaust pipe.

On a plane trip never pack unprocessed film in check-in luggage; if your bags are X-rayed, your pictures may be destroyed. Always hand-carry undeveloped film through security and ask to have it inspected by hand. If you put all of your film in a clear plastic bag, the inspection will go faster. Inspectors at U.S. airports are required to honor requests for hand inspection.

Newer X-ray machines at U.S. airport security checks will not affect film on the first few scans. With repeated scanning, however, your film may get fogged. It's best to ask for a hand inspection to reduce the chances of damaging your film. If your film is fogged and you want an explanation, send it to the **National Association of Photographic Manufacturers** (550 Mamaroneck Ave., Harrison, NY 10528). The staff will attempt to determine what went wrong. This service is free.

Traveling with Children

A week or two at the Jersey Shore is an excellent family vacation, though some towns are better at catering to the whims of small children than others. Atlantic City, for example, offers no activities for preschoolers, though casinos can arrange for baby-sitters. Nearby Ocean City overflows with activities and events for children from preschool age through the midteens.

Children's activities range from supervised story hours at local libraries to guided nature walks, sand-castle contests, athletic competitions, and sailing and water-sports instruction. Events such as Ocean City's Hermit Crab Race or Wildwood's National Marble Shooting Tournament are great fun. Amusement rides, parades, theme parks, sightseeing cruises, and other family-oriented activities round out the list. You'll also find lower-priced, children's menus at many Shore restaurants. Children age 6 years and younger are usually admitted free to museums and most beaches. Children age 12 and under get a reduced rate.

Publications *Family Travel Times* is a newsletter published 10 times a year by TWYCH (Travel With Your Children, 80 8th Ave., New York, NY 10011, tel. 212/206–0688). A one-year subscription costs $35 and includes access to back issues and twice-weekly opportunities to call in for specific advice.

Great Vacations With Your Kids, by Dorothy Jordan and Marjorie Cohen, offers complete advice on planning a trip with children (from toddlers to teens) and is available for $12.95 from E. P. Dutton (375 Hudson St., New York, NY 10014, tel. 212/366–2000).

Kids and Teens in Flight is a U.S. Department of Transportation brochure about children flying alone. To order a free copy, call 202/366–2220.

Getting There On domestic flights, children under age 2 not occupying a seat travel free. Various discounts apply to children age 2–12. If possible, reserve a seat behind the bulkhead of the plane; these offer more legroom and usually enough space to fit a bassinet (supplied by the airlines). At the same time inquire about special children's meals or snacks, which most airlines offer. (*See* "TWYCH's Airline Guide" in the February 1990 issue of *Family Travel Times* for a rundown on children's services offered by 46 airlines; an update is planned for the February 1992 issue.) Ask the airline in advance if you can bring aboard your child's car seat. For the booklet "Child/Infant Safety Seats Acceptable for Use in Aircraft," contact the Community and Consumer Liaison Division (APA-400 Federal Aviation Administration, Washington, DC 20591, tel. 202/267–3479).

Hints for Disabled Travelers

Casino hotels, newer hotels, most motels, public libraries, and government buildings offer handicapped access ramps and at least one rest room on the ground floor. Most public parking lots and garages provide a few spaces for disabled drivers. Atlantic City, Long Branch, and Island Beach State Park have handicapped access ramps for beach use.

The **Governor's Committee on the Disabled** (Labor and Industry Building, Room 200, Trenton, NJ 08625, tel. 609/633–6959) can provide information on travel for the disabled in New Jersey. County offices for the disabled are listed below:

Atlantic County Office for the Aging and Disabled (1333 Atlantic Ave., Atlantic City, NJ 08401, tel. 609/345–6700, ext. 2831).

Monmouth County Office of the Handicapped (29 Main St., Freehold, NJ 07728, tel. 908/431–7399).

Ocean County Office for the Disabled (34 Hadley Ave., CN 2191, Toms River, NJ 08754, tel. 908/244–6804).

New Jersey Transit (tel. 800/582–5946, 6 AM–10 PM), the state transportation company, can put a bus with a wheelchair lift on the route you plan to take, provided you give them 24-hour notice. New Jersey Transit trains are also accessible to the handicapped.

Mobility International USA (Box 3551, Eugene, OR 97403, tel. 503/343–1284) is an internationally affiliated organization with 500 members. For a $20 annual fee, it coordinates exchange programs for disabled people in the United States and around the world and also offers information on accommodations, organized study, and other activities around the world.

The **Information Center for Individuals with Disabilities** (Fort Point Pl., 1st floor, 27-43 Wormwood St., Boston, MA 02210, tel. 617/727–5540) offers useful problem-solving assistance, including lists of travel agents who specialize in tours for the disabled.

Moss Rehabilitation Hospital Travel Information Service (12th St. and Tabor Rd., Philadelphia, PA 19141, tel. 215/329–5715) provides information for a small fee on tourist sights, transportation, and accommodations in destinations around the world.

The Society for the Advancement of Travel for the Handicapped (26 Court St., Penthouse Suite, Brooklyn, NY 11242, tel. 718/858–5483) offers access information. Annual membership costs $40, $25 for senior citizens and students. For information, send $1 and a stamped, self-addressed envelope.

Travel Industry and Disabled Exchange (TIDE, 5435 Donna Ave., Tarzana, CA 91356, tel. 818/343–6339) publishes a quarterly newsletter and a directory of travel agencies that specialize in service to the disabled. Annual membership is $15 per person.

Greyhound will carry a disabled person and companion for the price of a single fare. The company no longer operates a toll-free number; consult your local phone directory.

Amtrak (tel. 800/USA–RAIL) advises that you request redcap service, special seats, or wheelchair assistance and inquire if your station is equipped to provide these services when you make reservations. All handicapped passengers are entitled to a 25% discount on regular, discounted coach fares. A special children's handicapped fare is also available, offering qualified children age 2–12 a 50% discount on already-discounted children's fares. Check with Amtrak to be sure that discounts are in effect when you plan to travel. For a free copy of Amtrak's "Travel Planner," which outlines all its services for the elderly and handicapped, contact Amtrak, National Railroad Corporation (400 N. Capitol St. NW, Washington, DC 20001, tel. 800/872–7245).

Publications   **Twin Peaks Press** publishes a number of useful resources: *Travel for the Disabled* ($9.95), *Directory of Travel Agencies for the Disabled* ($12.95), and *Wheelchair Vagabond* ($9.95). Order through your local bookstore or directly from Twin Peaks Press (Box 129, Vancouver, WA 98666, tel. 206/694–2462). Add $2 per book for postage; $1 for each additional book.

Access to the World: A Travel Guide for the Handicapped, by Louise Weiss, offers tips on travel and accessibility around the world. It is available from Henry Holt & Co. (tel. 800/247–3912) for $12.95; use order number 0805001417.

"Fly Rights," a free U.S. Department of Transportation brochure, offers airline access information for the handicapped. To order, call 202/366–2220.

The Itinerary (Box 1084, Bayonne, NJ 07002, tel. 201/858–3400) is a bimonthly travel magazine for the disabled.

Hints for Older Travelers

There is no standard policy for discounts for senior citizens at the New Jersey Shore. There is also no consistent age limit to determine who can take advantage of the few policies that exist. For example, some communities provide discounts on beach admissions to people age 62 and older, while others make it available only for those 65 and older. Some shopping districts, such as those in Atlantic City, have experimented with discounts for senior citizens. And a few communities offer free or discounted transportation for senior citizens.

Contact the following offices for more information:

Atlantic County Office of the Aging (1133 Atlantic Ave., Atlantic City, NJ 08401, tel. 609/345–6700).
Monmouth County Office on Aging (Hall of Records Annex, Freehold, NJ 07728, tel. 908/431–7450).
Ocean County Office of Aging (101 Hooper Ave., Toms River, NJ 08753, tel. 908/929–2091).
Cape May County Department of Aging (Box 222, Social Services Bldg., Rio Grande, NJ 08242, tel. 609/886–2785).
The **American Association of Retired Persons** (AARP, 1909 K St. NW, Washington, DC 20049, tel. 202/662–4850) has two programs for independent travelers: (1) The **Purchase Privilege Program** offers discounts on hotels, airfare, car rentals, recreational vehicle rentals, and sightseeing; and (2) the **AARP Motoring Plan,** which gives emergency aid (road service) and trip-routing information for an annual fee of $33.95 per couple. (Both programs include the member and his or her spouse, or the member and another person who shares the household.) The AARP also arranges group tours through **American Express** (Box 5014, Atlanta, GA 30302, tel. 800/241–1700, or, in GA, 800/637–6200). AARP members must be 50 years or older. Annual dues are $5 per couple. When using an AARP or other identification card, ask for a reduced hotel rate when you make your reservation or when you check in—not when you check out. Because restaurant discounts may be limited to set menus, days, or hours, present your card before being seated. When renting a car, remember that promotional rates on economy cars may be less than cars available with your discount ID card.
Elderhostel (80 Boylston St., Suite 400, Boston, MA 02116, tel. 617/426–7788) is an innovative program for people age 60 and older. Participants live in dormitories on some 1,200 college campuses around the world. Mornings are devoted to lectures and seminars, afternoons to sightseeing and field trips. Fees for two- to three-week trips, including room, board, tuition, and round-trip transportation, range from $1,700 to $3,200.

The catalogue is free for the first year (and if you participate in a program); after that it costs $10.

National Council of Senior Citizens (925 15th St. NW, Washington, DC 20005, tel. 202/347–8800) is a nonprofit advocacy group with more than 4,000 local clubs across the country. Annual membership is $10 per person or $14 per couple. Members receive a monthly newspaper with travel information and an ID card for reduced-rate hotels and car rentals.

Saga International Holidays (120 Boylston St., Boston, MA 02116, tel. 800/343–0273) operates tours for Elderhostel and specializes in group travel for people over age 60. A selection of variously priced tours allows you to choose the package that meets your needs.

Mature Outlook (Box 1205, Glenview, IL 60025, tel. 800/336–6330), a subsidiary of Sears, Roebuck and Co., is a travel club for people over age 50, with hotel and motel discounts and a bimonthly newsletter. Annual membership is $9.95. Instant membership is available at participating Holiday Inns.

Golden Age Passport is a free lifetime pass to all parks, monuments, and recreation areas run by the federal government. People over age 62 can pick it up at any national park that charges admission. The passport also provides a 50% discount on camping, boat launching, and parking (lodging is not included). A driver's license or other proof of age is required.

September Days Club is run by the moderately priced Days Inns of America (tel. 800/241–5050). The $12 annual membership fee entitles individuals or couples over age 50 to reduced rates on car rentals and discounts of 15%–50% at most of the chain's 350 motels.

Greyhound offers special fares for senior citizens subject to date and destination restrictions.

Amtrak (tel. 800/USA–RAIL). Elderly passengers are entitled to a 25% discount on regular, nondiscounted coach fares. Check with Amtrak about possible exceptions to these discounts. (For more information, *see* Hints for Disabled Travelers, above.)

Publications   "Travel Tips for Senior Citizens" (U.S. Dept. of State Publication 8970) is available for $1 from the Superintendent of Documents (U.S. Government Printing Office, Washington, DC 20402).

The International Health Guide for Senior Citizen Travelers, by W. Robert Lange, MD, and *The Senior Citizens Guide to Budget Travel in the United States and Canada,* by Paige Palmer, are available for $4.95 plus $1 shipping each from Pilot Books (103 Cooper St., Babylon, NY 11702, tel. 516/422–2225).

The Discount Guide for Travelers Over 55, by Caroline and Walter Weintz, lists helpful addresses, package tours, reduced-rate car rentals, and other pertinent information concerning the United States and abroad. To order send $7.95, plus $1.50 shipping, to Penguin USA/NAL (120 Woodbine St., Bergenfield, NJ 07621, tel. 800/526–0275). Include order number ISBN 0-525-483-58-6.

"Fly Rights," a free brochure published by the U.S. Department of Transportation, offers information on airline services available to elderly passengers. Call 202/366–2220.

Further Reading

History, Biography, and Folklore

In the early '30s, Henry Carlton Beck, a newspaper columnist and editor for the *Camden Courier Post* and later for the *Newark Star Ledger*, began to wander southern New Jersey's back roads and ghost towns, searching for trivia, folklore, and the oral history of this rapidly changing area. His books, collections of his anecdotal newspaper columns, are classics: *Forgotten Towns of Southern New Jersey*, *More Forgotten Towns of Southern New Jersey*, *The Roads of Home*, and *Jersey Genesis: The Story of the Mullica River* provide wonderful bits and pieces of New Jersey Shore folklore. Beck also wrote *The Jersey Midlands*, which contains some Shore history, though its focus is midstate, from Trenton to New Brunswick. All are published by the Rutgers University Press.

So Young, So Gay, by *Atlantic City Press* columnist William McMahon, is a warm, whimsical history of Atlantic City. *South Jersey Towns* has reliable, lively accounts of nearly every town and hamlet south of Ocean and Burlington counties. McMahon's *Pine Barrens: Lore, Legends and Lies* is an entertaining companion to John McPhee's *The Pine Barrens*.

For general Shore history, see also *The Story of the Jersey Shore*, by Harold F. Wilson; *The New Jersey Shore*, by John T. Cunningham; and, if you can find it, the 1971 facsimile reprint by Baltimore's Gateway Press of Gustav Kobbe's *Jersey Coast and Pines*, a Shore guidebook originally published in 1889 with priceless accounts of famous and infamous resort towns way back then.

Born to Run: The Bruce Springsteen Story, by Dave Marsh, is a drooling fan biography of Asbury Park's most famous rock-and-roll star. The Shore scenes place the Boss in his element.

Atlantic City

Atlantic City: 125 Years of Ocean Madness, by photo historian Vickie Gold Levy and *Esquire* magazine editor Lee Eisenberg, tells the town's colorful history through its casino era in a series of unforgettable pictures. Most enjoyable are the photos of Ronald Reagan and Marilyn Monroe in the Miss America Parade, Jimmy Durante lounging in a rolling chair, and a young, doe-eyed Ali MacGraw as the winner of a Prettiest Waitress contest.

By far the wittiest account of the city is Charles E. Funnell's *By the Beautiful Sea*. Focusing on the city from 1890 to 1910, Funnell punctures the myth of Atlantic City as a "classy" resort, revealing it as a fantasyland where the emerging working and middle classes could pretend they were kings of the world.

Ovid Demaris's *Boardwalk Jungle* is a cynical history of the postcasino era in which the author of *The Green Felt Jungle* (an exposé of Las Vegas) tries to say something bad about every casino company.

Cape May

Shipwrecks and Legends 'Round Cape May, by David J. Seibold and Charles J. Adams III, has tales of pirates, smuggling, sunken ships, and salvage operations in and around the lower Cape May coast.

Fiction

Atlantic City Proof, by Christopher Cook Gilmore, is a nostalgic spoof of rum-running in Atlantic City's Prohibition days. Gilmore also wrote *The Bad Room*, a grisly story of madness inside a Pine Barrens insane asylum. *The Pines*, another Pine

Barrens account by Robert Dunbar, mines the Jersey devil myth. *Red Whiskey Blues,* by Denise Gess, is a wry story of emotional loss and healing in a fictitious Jersey Shore town. Jack Engelhard's bitter morality tale, *Indecent Proposal,* involves a debauched but powerful Arab sheik who meets our brooding, down-on-his-luck hero in an Atlantic City casino and offers him $1 million if he'll let him spend a night with his wife. *Under the Boardwalk,* a novel by Bill Kent, provides a tour of Atlantic City's meaner streets through the eyes of a naive but dedicated vice-squad cop who wants to clean up the town.

Arriving and Departing

By Plane

Airports and Airlines The major airports in Philadelphia, Newark, and New York City are closest to Atlantic City and the New Jersey Shore. From each, you can rent a car to drive to Atlantic City or other Shore points. The drive varies from 1⅛ hours (Philadelphia to Atlantic City) to slightly more than 3 hours (Newark to Cape May).

The southern Shore has its own airport, **Atlantic City International,** located approximately 22 miles west of the city in Pomona, NJ. A number of expansion and development programs have been planned to expand the terminal, add parking (currently unused space on a nearby field), and provide another landing strip. **USAir** (tel. 800/331–3131) is currently the only airline with scheduled flights to Atlantic City International, though other airlines are considering service. A round-trip ticket from Philadelphia International is $112, $56 one way. A taxi from the airport to the Boardwalk costs about $30.

Bader Field, the nation's first airport, is located within the Atlantic City limits. It only accommodates small-engine aircraft. **Continental Express** (tel. 800/525–0280) offers the only scheduled service to this airport. A taxi from Bader Field to Bally's Grand, the nearest hotel casino, is $3.

Smaller county and municipal airports accommodate charters and private planes, but transportation isn't always easy to obtain.

Smoking Recent federal laws have banned smoking of any kind on domestic flights within the 48 contiguous United States as well as within the states of Hawaii and Alaska, to and from the U.S. Virgin Islands and Puerto Rico, and on flights of under six hours to and from Hawaii and Alaska. This rule applies to both domestic and foreign carriers.

On a flight where smoking is permitted, you can request a nonsmoking seat during check-in or when you book your ticket. If the airline tells you there are no seats available in the nonsmoking section, insist on one: Department of Transportation regulations require carriers to find seats for all nonsmokers, if they meet check-in time restrictions. These regulations apply to all international flights on domestic carriers; however, the Department of Transportation does not have jurisdiction over foreign carriers traveling out of, or into, the United States.

Lost Luggage Attach tags to your luggage with your name and address written legibly. This aids airline staff in locating your luggage if it is misplaced or damaged in transit.

Airlines are responsible for lost or damaged property only up to $1,250 per passenger on domestic flights. If you're traveling with valuables, either carry them with you on the airplane or purchase additional insurance for lost luggage. A few airlines sell additional luggage insurance when you check in. Insurance for lost, damaged, or stolen luggage also is available through travel agents and from various insurance companies. Two companies that issue luggage insurance are **Tele-Trip** (Box 31685, 3201 Farnam St., Omaha, NE 68131, tel. 800/228–9792), a subsidiary of Mutual of Omaha, and the **Travelers Insurance Co.** (Ticket and Travel Dept., 1 Tower Sq., Hartford, CT 06183, tel. 203/277–0111 or 800/243–3174). Tele-Trip operates sales booths at airports and also issues insurance through travel agents. Tele-Trip insures checked luggage for up to 180 days and for a $500 to $3,000 valuation. For one to three days, the rate for a $500 valuation is $8.25; for 180 days, $100. The Travelers Insurance Co. will insure checked or hand luggage for $500 to $2,000 valuation per person for a maximum of 180 days. Rates for one to five days for $500 valuation are $10; for 180 days, $85. Other companies with comprehensive policies include **Access America Inc.,** a subsidiary of Blue Cross–Blue Shield (Box 807, New York, NY 10163, tel. 212/490–5345 or 800/284–8300) and **Near Services** (450 Prairie Ave., Suite 101, Calumet City, IL 60409, tel. 708/868–6700 or 800/654–6700).

Before you go, make a list of the contents of each bag and carry this list with your travel documents. Use this list if you must file an insurance claim. If your luggage is lost and later recovered, the airline must deliver the luggage to your home free of charge.

By Helicopter

Trump Air (tel. 800/448–4000) helicopter service has daily flights from New York's West 34th Street Heliport to Atlantic City's Steel Pier (opposite Taj Mahal Casino Resort on the boardwalk) and Trump Castle Casino Resort in Atlantic City's marina section. The fare ranges from $125 to $145 each way.

By Car

Increased development over the past 50 years has filled the New Jersey Shore's once sleepy back roads with traffic. Also Atlantic City's casinos, some of which get as many as 120 busloads of gamblers each day during the summer season, have brought additional millions of visitors.

During the peak beach season—late May to mid-September —the Shore experiences weekend rush hours similar to the midweek commuter clogs that afflict major cities. Arriving rush hours tend to be Friday from 6 to 8 PM and Saturday noon to 3 PM. Departing rush hours are on Sunday, from noon to late evening.

The majority of Atlantic City's 43,000 casino employees commute to work by automobile, and the city has its own minirush. Add their numbers to those of the casino buses, and you get a lot of people going nowhere fast. Driving conditions are slowest weekdays from 8 to 10 AM and daily from 5 to 7 PM.

Most roadwork is done in the late spring and early fall. Lane-widening projects on the Garden State Parkway and the Atlantic City Expressway may also cause delays.

From New York The main road serving the New Jersey Shore is the **Garden State Parkway,** a north–south toll road that ends in Cape May. Southbound travelers from New York City should go into New Jersey at I–80, continuing to the **New Jersey Turnpike** (also a toll road), and cross over to the Garden State Parkway at Turnpike Exit 11. Travel time from New York City to Atlantic City is approximately 2½ hours.

From Philadelphia The **Atlantic City Expressway,** a toll road, connects Philadelphia and the southern New Jersey suburbs to the **Garden State Parkway** and Atlantic City. Travel time from Philadelphia to Atlantic City is approximately 1¼ hours.

From the South Northbound traffic originating south of New Jersey can enter the state at the **Delaware Memorial Bridge,** then either continue north on the **New Jersey Turnpike** to **Route 168 South** (the Black Horse Pike) to **Route 42** (the north–south freeway) to the **Atlantic City Expressway;** or take slow, rural **Route 40** south, to faster, wider **Route 55** south to **Route 47** for Cape May County, or continue to the **Atlantic City Expressway.** Travel time from Washington, DC, to Atlantic City is approximately 4½ hours.

Car Rentals Major auto-rental companies have offices at the Philadelphia, Newark, New York airports, or you can arrange transportation to car pickup sites. Some have offices at Atlantic City International Airport in Pomona. All maintain offices within the New York and Philadelphia city limits and in some New Jersey suburbs. Rates vary, so call several companies to compare prices.

The following companies service the Jersey Shore: **Alamo** (tel. 800/327–9633), **American International** (tel. 800/527–0202), **Avis** (tel. 800/331–1212), **Budget** (tel. 800/527–0700), **Dollar** (tel. 800/421–6868), **Enterprise** (tel. 800/634–3476), **Hertz** (tel. 800/654–3131), **Holiday Payless** (tel. 800/237–2804), **National** (tel. 800/227–7368), **Sears** (tel. 800/527–0770), **Snappy** (tel. 800/669–4800), and **Thrifty** (tel. 800/367–2277). **Ugly Duckling** (tel. 800/843–3825) rents older automobiles at lower costs. Most New Jersey Shore automobile new-car dealerships also provide rental cars.

By Ferry

The **Cape May–Lewes Ferry** joins the somewhat out-of-the-way town of Lewes (pronounced **LOO**-is), Delaware, to Cape May at the southernmost point of the state; from there take the Garden State Parkway north. During the summer season ferries leave Lewes 15 times a day, beginning at 8:40 AM. The last boat leaves at midnight. There are four departures in winter, beginning at 9:30 AM, with the last boat leaving at 10:30 PM. The one-way voyage is approximately 70 minutes. For fees, exact departure times, and cancellations due to inclement weather, call either the Cape May terminal (tel. 609/886–2718) or the Lewes terminal (tel. 302/645–6313).

By Limousine

Shore points can also be reached by limousine service from Philadelphia International Airport, Newark Airport, and Kennedy Airport in New York. The costs vary considerably and return trip service is not always available.

By Train

In May 1989, **Amtrak** (tel. 800/USA–RAIL) introduced direct rail service to Atlantic City from Philadelphia International Airport, Philadelphia's 30th Street Station, and points along the northeast rail corridor. Round-trip rates start at $15 for the Philadelphia to Atlantic City part of the trip. Train passengers who visit specified casinos can take advantage of coin refunds and casino discounts.

New Jersey Transit offers two commuter rail services to the New Jersey Shore. One train links the Monmouth and Ocean County towns of Red Bank, Long Branch, Asbury Park, Ocean Grove, Point Pleasant, and Seaside Heights with New York's Pennsylvania Station at 7th Avenue and 33rd Street. Another commuter train connects Atlantic City to the PATCO Hi-Speed line in Lindenwold, New Jersey. For schedule information and fares, call 800/722–2222 in northern New Jersey, 800/582–5946 in southern New Jersey, 201/762–5100 from New York, and 215/569–3752 in Philadelphia. The hearing-impaired can call the TTD/TTY phone service (tel. 800/772–2287) from 6 AM to midnight.

By Bus

New Jersey Transit (same telephone numbers as above) serves most New Jersey Shore towns, though service cutbacks have reduced the number of trips and left some areas, such as Long Beach Island, without bus service.

Academy Bus Line (tel. 212/964–6600) serves the bay shore, Sandy Hook, and other Monmouth County towns to Long Branch from the New York Port Authority Terminal at 41st Street and 8th Avenue. The **Asbury Park–New York Transit Company** (tel. 908/774–2727) links New York with Asbury Park, Long Branch, and Point Pleasant.

Greyhound offers service to Atlantic City from the New York Port Authority Terminal (tel. 212/971–6363) and from Philadelphia's bus terminal at 10th and Filbert streets (tel. 201/642–8205). Round-trip passengers going directly to specific casino hotels can get coin and discount coupon bonuses.

For details on line buses that offer daily trips to Atlantic City's casino hotels, *see* Chapter 5, Atlantic City.

Staying at the New Jersey Shore

Getting Around

By Car In addition to traffic congestion (*see* Arriving and Departing by Car, above), parking is a problem at the Shore. Many communi-

ties, especially those with many year-round residents, ticket
and tow illegally parked cars with an almost manic zeal. Atlantic City issues more than 90,000 parking tickets every year.
Towing fees, added to parking violation fines, can easily reach
$75, and the fee must be paid in cash. So make sure that you are
legally parked at all times, especially near beaches and commercial areas.

The more expensive restaurants provide valet parking free
with dinner, though you will be expected to tip the parking at-
tendant ($1 is sufficient). Casinos have free parking garages,
though some require that you have your ticket stamped or validated in the casino area.

By Bus and Trolley **New Jersey Transit,** the state-owned transportation company,
has bus routes that link the Shore communities (tel. 800/722–
2222 in northern NJ, 800/582–5946 in southern NJ, 201/762–
5100 from NY, 215/569–3752 in Philadelphia). Trolleys, jitneys, and other small transportation companies also offer
scheduled rides from residential sections to shopping, beach,
boardwalk, and amusement areas.

By Taxi Taxis aren't difficult to find in Atlantic City. Elsewhere, cab
companies tend to be small and slow to respond to calls, especially during the busy summer season. If you think you'll need a
cab, call a day ahead to determine availability.

Shopping

Beyond the dubious pleasures of buying schlocky boardwalk
souvenirs, the Jersey Shore is not known for its shopping. Suburban malls, shopping strips, and department stores, usually
located a short drive west of the beach areas, offer few surprises or bargains in the high season. Bargain hunting at the
Jersey Shore begins in August, especially for summer clothes
and swim wear. Prices for seasonal goods drop with the temperature, reaching rock bottom in October, after which many
shops close for the winter.

Serious shoppers should seek out regional crafts, outlet shops,
antiques, and flea markets. Of the regional crafts, by far the
most interesting are the antique wooden duck decoys. Within
the past 30 years what were once throwaways carved by East
Coast Shore inhabitants during the cold winters have become
prized collectibles, and New Jersey's are among the most val-
ued. As is the case with most antique collectibles, fakes out-
number originals, and even crudely made, modern decoys can
carry high price tags. If you intend to purchase a duck decoy,
spend time examining them in shops and speaking with knowl-
edgeable dealers. An easy way to learn about them is to attend
crafts shows and speak with the carvers directly. Antiques
shops and dealers are scattered up and down the Shore.

The most famous outlet shop is **Lenox China** (tel. 609/641–3700)
on Tilton Road in Pomona, a 30-minute drive from Atlantic
City. Some spectacular china can also be found here, but at regular retail prices. Once a year, usually in October, the shop has
a sale.

A word on T-shirts: Printed T-shirts, the most popular Jersey
Shore souvenir, can be found hanging in the schlockiest boardwalk junk shop and in some of the Shore's toniest clothing
stores. Be wary of boardwalk shops that advertise T-shirts for

99¢. These usually fit infants only and are so cheaply made that the act of pulling the shirt over your toddler's head will cause the seams to break. Good-quality souvenir T-shirts cost at least $5, with sweatshirts starting at $10 and up. Some of these garments with the names of the Shore communities stamped on them are churned out in bulk in faraway factories, without regard for the character of the region. The way to distinguish between a regional shirt and a shameless, mass-produced garment is to look for palm trees in the shirt's design. No one has bothered to tell the manufacturers that palm trees don't grow at the Jersey Shore. Some examples of printed slogan T-shirts that do evoke the character of the region: "Good girls go to heaven, bad girls go to Wildwood," "Cape May: Reality stops here," and "I lost my shirt in Atlantic City."

Participant Sports and Outdoor Activities

Beaches   The most popular outdoor activity at the Jersey Shore is finding a beach, sprawling on a blanket or towel, lathering on tanning lotion, and doing absolutely nothing.

This and the joy of people-watching, wading or swimming in the surf, building sand castles, and collecting seashells make beaches the New Jersey Shore's primary attraction. The sand is made of ground silicates that have washed down over centuries from the Hudson Bay and New York Harbor areas. If you travel the length of the Shore, you'll notice that the sand changes, from the gray, coarse grit of Sandy Hook to the white, finely powdered sand of Wildwood, to the yellow, finely polished pebbles off Cape May Point.

By state law there are no private beaches on the Jersey Shore, though access to some beaches is difficult. Most beaches are owned by municipalities, though a few, such as Sandy Hook and Cape May Point, are protected parks. The only free municipal beaches on the New Jersey Shore are Atlantic City's, Wildwood's, and North Wildwood's, which is wider than a quarter mile in places. The beach at Cape May Point State Park is free, but swimming is not recommended because of the strong ocean currents.

At all other beaches, anyone age 12 or older must pay a fee to use municipal beaches from Memorial Day (or on June 15 in some towns) through Labor Day. You pay by purchasing a daily, weekly, or seasonal beach badge—a plastic tag with a pin affixed to the back that you can attach to your bathing suit. Badges are sold by mail, at city or borough hall offices, or by inspectors who prowl the beaches to make sure everybody has a tag (some hotels and inns provide beach badges free to their guests—ask when you book your room). If you're on the beach and you don't have a beach badge, you will be asked to buy one. If you don't buy one, you'll be asked to leave. If you don't leave, you can be arrested by local police. Daily badges average $3; weekly badges cost $5–$10. Seasonal badges range from $8 to $25, depending on the community. Prices tend to be lowest on Long Beach Island and in Atlantic County.

Fees from badge sales pay for lifeguards, beach maintenance, and local recreation services. Most municipalities offer badges at a discount if you purchase them before the season begins (Memorial Day or June 15, depending on the town). Discounted badges are also available for senior citizens.

The consumption of alcoholic beverages, picnicking, and lighting fires is prohibited on most New Jersey beaches, although some municipalities permit picnics and small, enclosed fires (for cooking food) on July 4 and Labor Day. Check with lifeguards and municipal officials.

Recently the Shore's summer season has been marred by occasional beach closings because of pollution problems. State and local governments have taken steps to improve local waste-disposal facilities and prosecute illegal ocean dumping. Adverse weather conditions, changes in ocean currents, new construction, and other factors, however, can cause beach closings. The New Jersey Department of Environmental Protection operates two toll-free hotlines covering beach conditions and water quality along the entire Shore. In addition, individual counties and municipalities offer local information through their health departments and police stations (*see* Important Addresses and Numbers in individual county chapters). The hotlines listed below operate during the normal swimming seasons, from late spring to early autumn.

New Jersey Department of Environmental Protection Beach Conditions (all beaches on the Shore): tel. 800/648–SAND.

New Jersey Department of Environmental Protection Coastal Watch Hotline (ocean conditions covering the entire shore): tel. 800/451–0252 in NJ, 800/458–1966 elsewhere.

Bicycling After water sports, bicycling is the Shore's most popular outdoor recreation. Shops that rent bicycles are plentiful, and boardwalks permit bicycling daily until 10 AM. Be sure to lock your bicycle to a secure post or railing if you leave it.

Boating Boating is the Jersey Shore name for piloting something that floats, doesn't make you wet all the time, and doesn't have a sail. You can rent rowboats and small-engine powerboats for fishing or waterskiing at docks and marinas. Jet-skis, which are aquatic motorcycles, can also be rented. A deposit is usually required.

Canoeing This relaxing form of boating is especially popular along the creeks and streams of the Pine Barrens. This 3½-million-acre nature reserve features pristine freshwater streams and such bizarre wildlife as miniature tree frogs and sea-level dwarf-pine forests. Several companies rent boats and paddles, and some will even transport you upriver and pick you up at the end of the day. Remember to bring insect repellent! (*See* Chapter 4, Ocean County, for details on rental companies.)

Fishing Fishing is easy and comes in three varieties at the New Jersey Shore. The easiest is the do-it-yourself, off-the-dock or -pier kind. Bait-and-tackle shops are within driving distance. Some communities have fishing piers. We'll list those that can be used by visitors.

Fishing and crabbing are not permitted off bridges because it can be dangerous for motorists and fishermen alike, though people tend to do it anyway. In some areas where new bridges have been erected, the old bridge piers have been left for fishing. Local bait-and-tackle shops can point you toward the best fishing areas.

Party-boat fishing is also easy, especially if you have never fished before. For $10 to $20, which sometimes includes a rod and reel, you board a boat and set off for the ocean or a back bay, returning in four to six hours, hopefully with a pail full of fish. Party boats are listed in local telephone directories under Fishing Charters.

Charter-boat fishing requires some planning. You basically rent a boat and a captain, for a minimum of $600, for a one- to two-day (with an overnight on the water), deep-sea fishing trip. The most popular offshore location is the Hudson Canyon, about 120 miles east of the New Jersey Shore.

It's best to go on a charter before arranging one yourself. Experienced anglers know that a good captain is more important to an enjoyable fishing charter than the age, comfort, or speed of the boat. The captain should not only know where to catch fish, but also be familiar with the boat and be able to make whatever special accommodations you require. Reputation is the best way to find a good captain. Boats available for charter and their captains are listed in local phone directories, at bait-and-tackle shops, at marinas, and at boat-supply shops.

The New Jersey Department of Environmental Protection's Division of Fish, Game, and Wildlife prepares an annual list of party and charter boats and their captains. For a copy of the list, and information on seasonal catches and fishing licenses, contact the Division of Fish, Game, and Wildlife (CN-400, Trenton, NJ 08625, tel. 609/292–2965).

Golf The Shore has many golf courses, but most are private clubs. Some hotels and one Atlantic City casino, the Sands, provide golfing privileges to guests. Miniature golf, a surrealistic amusement typically found on or near boardwalks, is great for adults and children.

Horseback Riding Due to rising insurance costs, only a few stables offer horseback trail rides to walk-in customers. A list of stables and riding services in the state can be obtained from the New Jersey Department of Agriculture (Horse Program, CN 330, Trenton, NJ 08625, tel. 609/292–2888).

Jogging Running or jogging at the beach is wonderful, especially along the tide line. Some towns have races on the beaches or boardwalks. Check with the beach patrol or local recreation directors.

Nature Walks and Bird-watching Nature walks, a good way to appreciate the diversity of living creatures that share the Shore's habitat, are led regularly, usually free of charge in county and state parks. Another popular activity is birding, also called bird-watching, as an excuse to wander away from the beach. Favorite birding sites are Sandy Hook (tel. 908/872–0115), Forsyth Wildlife Refuge (tel. 609/652–1665), and the Cape May Point Bird Observatory (tel. 609/884–2736).

Sailing Yacht clubs offer sailing instruction to members, and sailing shops can arrange private lessons and then rent you a boat when you are qualified. Yacht clubs, boat clubs, and community groups sponsor various regattas at the Jersey Shore.

Scuba Diving There are hundreds of wrecks (including aircraft and a few German U-boats) lurking within a few miles of the New Jersey beaches, and you don't need to buy or bring your scuba equipment with you to explore them. Dive shops will rent equipment to certified divers.

Surfing Favored by youngsters and teenagers, surfing isn't as much of a "scene" on the Jersey Shore as it is in California. Because ocean waders can be injured by stray boards rushing in, lifeguards may request that surfers stay in a specific area. Surfing next to ocean piers is dangerous. Waves average 4–6 feet high. Surf conditions vary with season and tides.

Tennis Municipal courts are plentiful but available on a first-come, first-served basis. Larger resorts and casino hotels have courts for their guests and even provide racquet rentals.

Windsurfing Also called board sailing, this California blend of surfing and sailing is quite at home on the Jersey Shore, especially in the calm waters of the open bays. Many surf-and-sailing shops offer lessons for prospective windsurfers on tethered boards, and they will then rent boards and sails.

Spectator Sports

Before Atlantic City started sponsoring attention-getting boxing matches, horse racing was the shore's most popular spectator sport. **Monmouth Park** is the county's best-known horse-racing track. *Monmouth Park Highway, Oceanport, tel. 908/222–5100. Open June–Sept., Mon.–Sat.*

You can watch harness racing fall and winter at **Freehold Raceway.** *Route 33, Freehold, tel. 908/462–3800. Open mid-Aug.– May, Mon.–Sat.*

In Atlantic County, **Atlantic City Race Course** has Thoroughbred racing in summer, simulcast betting in winter season. *Rte. 40, McKee City, tel. 609/641–2190. Mailing address: Box 719, Atlantic City, NJ 08404. Racing June–Sept., Mon. and Wed.–Sun.; Oct.–May, simulcast betting Mon.–Sat. Restaurant on premises.*

National and State Parks

National Parks **Sandy Hook** (tel. 908/872–0115), part of **Gateway National Recreation Area,** is the northern reach of the Jersey Shore. Sandy Hook has some nature reserves, a Coast Guard base and military museum, the oldest operating lighthouse on the Jersey Shore, and a "secret" nude beach at the entrance to New York Harbor. The **Edwin B. Forsythe National Wildlife Refuge** (tel. 609/652–1665) is in Oceanville, near Atlantic City. The Forsythe boasts an 8.1-mile car trail over fresh- and saltwater marshes, with platforms for observing birds at play.

State Parks New Jersey has 22 state parks. Those adjacent to or a short car trip from the New Jersey Shore are listed below, from north to south, and are described in the individual county chapters.

Allaire State Park (Rte. 524 between Farmingdale and Lakewood, Box 220, Farmingdale, NJ 07727, tel. 908/938–2371).
Island Beach State Park (at the end of Central Ave., Box 37, Seaside Park, NJ 08752, tel. 908/793–0506).
Barnegat Lighthouse State Park (Barnegat Light, at the end of Broadway, Box 167, Barnegat Light, Long Beach Island, NJ 08006, tel. 609/494–9086).
Lebanon State Forest (watch for signs off of Rte. 70 or Rte. 72, Box 215, New Lisbon, NJ 08064, tel. 609/726–1191).
Wharton State Forest (Rte. 542, Batsvot RD #4, Hammonton, NJ 08037, tel. 609/561–3262).

Bass River Forest (Stage Rd., 2 mi off of Rte. 9, Box 118, New Gretna, NJ 08224, tel. 609/296–1114).

Penn Forest (off of Rte. 563, Jenkins Neck, Box 118, New Gretna, NJ 08224, tel. 609/296–1114).

Belleplain Forest (County Rte. 550, Exit 17 off of Garden State Pkwy. south, Box 450, Woodbine, NJ 08270, tel. 609/861–2404).

Corson's Inlet Park (Exit 25 off of Garden State Pkwy. south, southernmost end of Ocean City, Box 450, Woodbine, NJ 08270, tel. 609/861–2404).

Cape May Point State Park (Lighthouse Ave., Box 107, Cape May Point, NJ 08212, tel. 609/884–2159).

Admission fees vary with each park. Most parks have a visitor center with a small museum, rest rooms, and picnic areas. Special permits are required for camping and hunting. Educational nature programs, nature walks, and other activities are scheduled throughout the year. For general information, contact the **Department of Environmental Protection Office of State Parks and Forests** (CN 402, Trenton, NJ 08625, tel. 609/292–2797).

If you plan to make frequent visits to a state park, consider purchasing a **State Park Pass,** which provides unlimited admission to all state parks for one year. It costs $35 per person and is available at the entrance to most state-park service offices or from the Department of Environmental Protection (501 E. State St., Trenton, NJ 08625). Requests must be made in writing.

Dining

Restaurants By Memorial Day, nearly all Jersey Shore restaurants are up and running, many sporting fresh coats of paint, new decor, and new menus. Every large town has at least one surf-and-turf house, named for the dish that features both seafood and beef. Many such places are family-owned, have been operating for several generations, and cater to an older, affluent crowd.

The second-most common restaurant is the family place, usually Italian-American, with a moderate to inexpensive menu of steaks and hamburgers, broiled and fried seafood, spaghetti, and baked chicken dishes; a separate children's menu; all-you-can-eat nights; and early-bird specials for diners seated before 6 PM.

Another popular Shore restaurant might be dubbed a "meetery," a tavern for young people who have just turned 21 (or appear as if they have) and are paying more attention to each other than to the food. Expect loud music from a local pop band performing near a tiny dance floor that no one uses. The menu will have more appetizers than entrées, hamburgers, and Mexican, Italian, and Chinese dishes. And there will be a little card on the table listing drinks from the bar.

The neighborhood place, a restaurant that caters to locals but tends to be jammed with sunburned out-of-towners, is becoming scarce. The food tends to be deceptively plain, ordinary items such as steaks and chops with a seafood special, but typically they are very good.

The trendy café is an outgrowth of a restaurant renaissance that began in Philadelphia, spread to Cape May, and is slowly working its way up the Shore. These are moderate to expensive places featuring peculiar, quirky chalkboard menus of pasta salads, Oriental soups and appetizers, and grilled seafood served in small portions made larger with sauces.

This is not to say you won't find variations on these themes as well as a trend toward more interesting, international, or ethnic fare beyond the typical Chinese and tomato-sauce Italian. Sushi bars, Mexican, Cajun, Middle Eastern, kosher-style, delicatessen, and vegetarian restaurants have popped up. More and more restaurants are adding low-salt, low-fat entrées to their menus for those seeking healthier cuisines.

Category	Cost*
Very Expensive	over $35
Expensive	$25–$35
Moderate	$15–$25
Inexpensive	under $15

per person, excluding drinks, service, and 7% sales tax

Seafood Though the cuisine is varied and the prices range from cheap snack fare to pretentious haute cuisine, seafood is the Jersey Shore's biggest deal. It's on virtually every menu, sometimes with the word "Jersey" appended to give the dish a local touch.

Long before the hamburger, hot dog, and a slice of pizza invaded the New Jersey Shore, fast food consisted of a walk to the local raw bar. Raw bars, also called clam bars and oyster bars, were the rage in the late 19th century, primarily among men. They crowded around a drab little shack—usually located near the fishing docks or on the inland bays and causeways—for a quick feast on raw clams and oysters served on the half-shell with spicy tomato sauce, a wedge of lemon, and a hard, round oyster cracker.

A round ball of toasted flour about the size of a quarter, the oyster cracker is still served in most New Jersey Shore seafood restaurants. It's delicious when munched with horseradish sauce, shrimp cocktail sauce, or crumbled into soup. If you look at it carefully, you'll see the letters OTC—for Original Trenton Cracker—stamped on the side. Like saltwater taffy, a candy attributed to the Shore but invented elsewhere, the original Trenton cracker is not from the Shore or Trenton. It is a variation of the ship biscuit, a hard, baked cracker that doesn't become stale on long ocean voyages. During the late 19th century several bakeries in Trenton made these. Now all OTCs are made by the Original Trenton Cracker Company, which has relocated its bakery to Lambertville, about 15 miles north of Trenton. You can buy them in boxes in Jersey Shore grocery stores and in specialty stores.

The OTC used to be a staple of raw bars. Only a few of these raw bars remain, chased out by rising real-estate prices and changes in the eating habits of Shore visitors. Today's raw bars also serve steamed shellfish (including shrimp, most of which comes frozen from the Gulf of Mexico), oyster stew (oysters sautéed in butter and served in hot milk with a dash of salt and pepper), and various seafood chowders.

You might think that your proximity to the ocean and bays might make seafood a fresher, somewhat less expensive treat than in a major city. But today even seafood that is caught a few miles off the New Jersey Shore travels many miles on land before it reaches your plate.

A few restaurants either have their own fishing boats or are located so close to the docks that they can buy fish as it is unloaded from the boats. The bulk of seafood served at the New Jersey Shore, however, is not native to the region. Virtually all shrimp comes frozen from the Gulf of Mexico and because of decreasing harvests, more imported oysters are served at the New Jersey Shore than are caught locally. No chef, no matter how resourceful, can maintain a diverse restaurant menu without relying on imported seafood.

This is not to say you can't find luscious, wonderfully fresh, locally caught seafood. Every Shore community is within driving distance of a commercial fishing dock. Cape May has the Shore's largest commercial seaport (the third largest on the East Coast, behind Gloucester and New Bedford, Massachusetts), with other fishing enterprises scattered up and down the Shore.

What do they catch? Flounder is available nearly year-round. Clams, scallops, some oysters, and a variety of lobster somewhat scrawnier than the famed New England rock are also available locally. If you're visiting in the summer, make sure you try fresh tuna, mako shark, swordfish, weakfish (sea trout), monkfish (called the poor man's lobster because of its slight resemblance to lobster tail), and bluefish, available toward the end of the summer. Porgies, mackerel, and squid are also abundant but are not widely served.

Anglers and party-boat captains sometimes make their catches available to locals, but most chefs do not buy from them, simply because they have no way of knowing if the fish was caught or handled in a safe, professional manner.

Snack Foods Inexpensive snack and fast-food eateries are ubiquitous at the Shore, especially on the boardwalks. In addition to the typical hot dogs, hamburgers, and pizza (now available with a profusion of toppings, including shrimp, pineapple, and fresh garlic cloves), you'll see hoagies and cheesesteaks on many menus. Both sandwiches hail from Philadelphia and are served on long, Italian rolls.

The classic cheesesteak consists of frozen sirloin steak sliced into extremely thin slivers. After thawing, the meat is fried in olive oil on a griddle, and a slice of provolone cheese is melted on top. This steaming, meaty, cheesy mess is then shoveled, with chopped fried onions, into a sliced Italian roll. In addition to mushrooms, sliced raw onions, hot peppers, sweet peppers, and green peppers, cheesesteaks are sometimes served with red pizza sauce or catsup.

The basic hoagie (believed to be named for a sandwich popular among workers at Philadelphia's Hog Island shipyard) is an antipasto in bread: various sliced Italian deli meats, provolone cheese, lettuce, tomato, sliced raw onions, a splash of oil and vinegar, a dash of oregano, salt, and pepper. Other permutations include sliced turkey, roast beef, tuna salad, chicken salad, and sometimes pickles. At the Jersey Shore this is also called a "sub," because of the roll's submarine shape.

Take-out food emporia have also hit the Shore, especially in some of the more affluent residential communities. These shops are perfect for the romantic picnic lunch or the lazy meal.

Lodging

Accommodations along the New Jersey Shore vary from the sumptuous, penthouse high-roller suites in casino hotels—where even the whirlpool bath has a view—to a simple room in a guest house. Many visitors staying a week or more take advantage of rental housing, with either apartments or complete houses available. Rental properties during the prime months of July and August are usually leased as far in advance as January.

Many smaller hotels, motels, and bed-and-breakfasts insist on two- to three-night stays, especially on weekends. Always ask about packages and discounts when booking. Staying midweek instead of over a weekend can mean substantial savings, even in the high season.

There are two prime locations, beachfront or bayfront. The most desired is beachfront, which means the accommodation is *right on the beach*, facing east, though sometimes you'll have to cross a street or go over a boardwalk or an embankment to reach the sand. All rooms may not have an "ocean view," and what passes for a view might be a slice of blue glimpsed between rooftop exhaust fans. Breezes can be expected, but not promised. *Beach block* means that the accommodation is on a city block that adjoins the beach or the boardwalk. Street noises can be a factor here, so always ask for a room as far above the street as possible. *Near ocean* can mean an accommodation several blocks, or miles, away.

Bayfront accommodations are located on waterways that separate islands from the New Jersey mainland. Those on the mainland face east; those on islands face west, ideally over sweeping, open meadows where you'll see spectacular sunsets. Bayfront accommodations tend to be less expensive than beachfront and are more convenient for anglers who want to be near marinas and water-sports facilities. They get less street noise, but more of the noise and fumes of overpowered marine engines.

Rooms in casino hotels on the New Jersey Shore are the most popular accommodations, the most expensive, and the most difficult to get, especially in the summer season. Expect prices to start at $140 a night for the smallest casino hotel room ($220 for suites), though less-expensive packages can be arranged. Not all casino hotel rooms can be booked by paying guests—the more luxurious are held for high-rolling gamblers and entertainers. Because casino hotels do a heavy weekend business, even in the colder months, they require considerable advance booking.

A few of the grand old stone hotels remain, and some are slowly being restored. Asbury Park's completely restored Berkeley-Cartaret hotel has become the centerpiece of renovation activity there. While the Berkeley-Cartaret completely changed the interior of its rooms, not all restorations have been as sensitive to modern tastes. Rooms in older hotels tend to be small, with high ceilings and eccentric plumbing. Motels, still an econom-

ical alternative, are well-suited for families. Within recent
years, the New Jersey Shore hotel stock has been enhanced by
the condo hotel, basically condominiums that rent rooms by the
night.

The Shore is also enjoying a slow but steady increase in small
inns, guest houses, and B&Bs. Fueled by success stories in
Cape May and Spring Lake, more guest houses are being renovated for travelers who want a different experience from standardized hotel or motel rooms. What was once a low-cost,
intimate vacation alternative can now be just as expensive and,
in many cases, more expensive than the motels and hotels that
crowd the beach blocks. Room sizes, amenities, and features
vary widely. These facilities do *not* take pets, many do not accept credit cards, and most prefer to accept children no younger than 12 years old. Smoking is generally limited to porches
and public areas.

B&Bs are recommended to those who want to sample more of
the character and personality of the New Jersey Shore. Innkeepers tend to be friendly and more sensitive to their guests'
needs, and they are reliable sources of advice about restaurants, attractions, and local lore. B&B accommodations, however, are not for everyone: Rooms tend to be smaller, sound
travels, and sharing a bathroom can tax one's patience. Guests
must also understand that, in many situations, they are sharing
a private house and must be considerate of others.

Bed & Breakfast of New Jersey, Inc. (103 Godwin Ave., Suite
132, Midland Park, NJ 07432, tel. 201/444–7409) is a reservation service offering rooms in 100 inns and private homes, many
of which are at the Jersey Shore. The service costs $15 per
booking in addition to the cost of the room, or you can purchase
a $25 membership for unlimited bookings throughout the year.
The service can also answer questions about specific properties. Some package tours and discounts are also offered.

Category	Cost*
Very Expensive	over $120
Expensive	$90–$120
Moderate	$50–$90
Inexpensive	under $50

*All prices are for a standard double room, excluding 7% state
sales tax. Hotels in Atlantic City charge an additional 6% luxury tax.*

Rentals   Rentals are a cost-saving alternative for small groups or families who want to visit the New Jersey Shore. The property
might be a house, a condominium, or an apartment that you
take for a week, two weeks, a month, or the season (usually
June, July, and August). The savings are obvious: Shared a-
mong four people, daily room rates are lower than most motels.
If a kitchen is included, you can prepare some of your meals,
cutting down on food expenses. You may be able to bring pets,
which most hotels don't allow. Rentals are handled by individual landlords or local real-estate agents. Some rentals are available in the spring and fall, but many are simply locked up to
await the summer months. The best time to select rental

properties for the summer is January through March. *See* the Appendix: Vacation Rentals, for additional advice on selecting a property and a list of rental agencies on the shore.

Time-Sharing A few time-sharing facilities have set themselves up in former motels and apartment complexes. The premise behind time-sharing is that for a one-time payment you purchase the use of a specific room in a complex for a specific period of time each year.

Home Exchange Exchanging homes is a surprisingly low-cost way to enjoy a vacation in another part of the country. **Vacation Exchange Club Inc.** (12006 111th Ave., Unit 12, Youngstown, AZ 85363, tel. 602/972–2186) specializes in domestic home exchanges. The club publishes one directory in February and a supplement in April. Membership is $24.70 per year, for which you receive one listing. Photos cost another $9; listing a second home costs $6.

Camping The Jersey Shore has two kinds of campgrounds: state campgrounds, which charge small fees for camping use, and commercial campgrounds, some of which offer recreational vehicle hookups, swimming, tennis, video arcades, and general stores. Commercial campgrounds tend to operate on a first-come, first-served basis, though a few take reservations.

Credit Cards

The following credit card abbreviations are used in this guide: AE, American Express; D, Discover; DC, Diners Club; MC, MasterCard; V, Visa.

2 Portraits of the Jersey Shore

Atlantic City:
The City of Numbers

It is impossible not to be somewhat amazed, bedazzled, and overwhelmed by the casinos of Atlantic City. To call them garish is almost complimentary. Though they are nowhere near as extravagant as their cousins in Las Vegas, Atlantic City's 12 casino hotels are islands of ostentatious glitz and glamour. Everywhere—in the lobbies, gaming areas, restaurants, showrooms, shopping arcades, health clubs, and even in some of the parking garages—it's obvious that enormous amounts of money have been spent to impress and insulate you from the outside world. Once through the doors, you get a desire to explore this overindulgent interior world; you want to see and be seen, to move around, see a show, eat a fancy dinner, tap your feet to the up-tempo music from the lounge band, and join the crowd on the casino floor.

This expansive feeling recalls what the city's visitors must have felt around the turn of the century when they strolled the Boardwalk. Then as now, architecture, music, gambling, entertainment, and other diversions offered people a chance to escape, to dream, to indulge. It's as if the casinos had taken the essence of the Atlantic City Boardwalk and pulled it inside.

Though legalized casino gambling is well into its second decade in Atlantic City, it's impossible to visit the once and future seaside Queen of Resorts without getting a bit of a shock. No matter how you arrive—by boat, helicopter, bus, or car—there is no avoiding the dingy streets, burned-out houses, forbidding slums, and struggling shops, all sad and sorry remnants of the city's post-'50s decline.

That decline has been blamed on almost everything, from the competition of new Shore resorts to the advent of jet travel, which dramatically improved access to Europe and other distant locales. As the automobile replaced the railroad as the most popular mode of transportation, motor hotels, or motels, drew family vacationers from the old grand-hotel haunts. The new, mobile generation quickly moved on to Long Beach Island, or to Ocean City, Stone Harbor, or Wildwood, where renting a house on or near the beach cost less than a room in an Atlantic City hotel.

Convention business, an essential component of the city's tourist trade, began to trail off as other cities (most significantly now jet-accessible Miami and Las Vegas) built larger convention centers and more elaborate hotels. Atlantic City, with its flamboyant, beaux arts, and Greek Revival Boardwalk hotels, was increasingly seen as old-fashioned and dowdy. And the fact that some of the hotel owners did little to maintain their properties in the '50s and '60s didn't help.

Stages that hosted just about every great name in show business went dark as the number of visitors dwindled. Restaurants closed or changed their menus to follow a trend for standardized fast food. The fine jewelry, clothing, and collectibles that once filled elegant shop windows on the Boardwalk were replaced by auction houses known as jam joints, and schlocky souvenir shops. To make matters worse, the city was rocked by several highly publicized investigations into government corruption.

Other diversions—prostitution, gambling, and, as the '60s continued, illicit drugs—thrived. Though long a part of the city's mystique, the sleazier side of Atlantic City and its image as a place for fast hustles and inside deals finally overwhelmed the wholesome, family-oriented image that had been fostered so carefully since the 1850s. What the city's power brokers forgot was that it was the balance of wholesomeness and looseness—of innocent fun in the sun and wild nights on Kentucky Avenue—that had made the city a successful resort.

Still it's a mistake to think that the decline was pervasive. While grand hotels fell into disrepair and restaurant quality suffered, the sea continued to provide clammers and fishermen with a decent living. The city's beaches never stopped offering clean, easy swimming during the summer. The large state-owned marina kept attracting pleasure boaters and anglers. The Miss America Pageant—a 1921 scheme to extend the summer season—was still going strong, bringing in families from all over the country. The Boardwalk remained the only one in the world with the right to be spelled with a capital *B*.

By the early 1970s, nearly everyone in Atlantic City and the rest of New Jersey admitted that something had to be done to bring tourists back. Legalized gambling was proposed, as were nude beaches. Both were defeated. On the third try, New Jersey's voters were asked if they would permit an experiment that would use legal casino gaming (the word "gambling" was considered to have too many negative connotations) in Atlantic City as a "unique tool for urban development."

On November 2, 1978, most of New Jersey's voters said yes, and Atlantic City immediately sought to recapture its heritage. Would-be casino developers looked back to vintage Atlantic City and saw a showplace. The legendary Steel Pier once offered big-name entertainers and attractions such as the Diving Horse, whose punctual plunges into a pool of water would shake the pier's frame. Developers wanted to revive nightclubs like the 500 Club, where struggling singer Dean Martin teamed up with a madcap comic waiter, Jerry Lewis, to form Martin & Lewis, one of the 1950s' most popular comedy duos. At Club Harlem the 4 AM breakfast shows featured nearly every major black entertainer in the country.

Of course, upstairs at the 500 Club and around the back of Club Harlem were gambling tables whose profits fueled the high-living excitement out front. Gambling, whether out in the open on the Boardwalk or out of sight in fashionable clubs, had been part of Atlantic City since the first excursion trains brought in tourists more than 100 years ago.

Indeed the city had two faces from the beginning: a bright and sunny smile that boasted of the healthy benefits of seafood, family amusements, theater, salt breezes, and ocean bathing; and a party-town snicker that hinted at gambling, smuggled whiskey during Prohibition, and prostitution in "flower houses" along Chalfonte Alley and elsewhere. So it is not without a sense of historical irony that gambling was touted as the savior of Atlantic City.

Of course, the casino industry would rather see itself as a purveyor of a very specific kind of adult escapism and entertainment than as operators of enticing gambling machines. From the opulent spa at Bally's Park Place to the eye-jangling Arabesque casino floor of the Taj Mahal, the casinos offer a fantasy landscape that can be appreciated without gambling a cent, though the temptation to gamble is never far away.

In modern Atlantic City, 10 casinos are arrayed along a 3-mile stretch of the Boardwalk or within a block of it. Two additional hotel casinos, Harrah's Marina and Trump Castle, stand beside the Absecon Inlet in the city's marina district. Thanks to these casinos Atlantic City receives more than 32 million visits each year. This number does not account for repeat visitors, but it still makes Atlantic City one of the most successful tourist destinations in the world.

The casinos have provided 65,000 new jobs (43,000 in the industry itself, 20,000 more in service and support businesses), new housing, and a new future for many New Jersey citizens. A $7 million joint effort by two casino hotels, the Claridge and the Sands, converted Brighton Park into a festive plaza suitable for strolling and outdoor entertainment. Taxes from gambling revenues pay for senior citizens' relief programs and are used to fund urban redevelopment, including low- and moderate-income housing in the city's Inlet section. Plans have been drawn up for a new $400 million convention center that will connect itself to the Amtrak railroad terminal at Arkansas and Kirkman avenues.

These and other statistics have made Atlantic City a "city of numbers." It looks good on paper but has yet to look good in person. The city still has no large museum and no movie theater. Covering only 40 city blocks, Atlantic City is a small town strapped with standard big-city problems: crime, poverty, traffic, and urban blight. It's a city with a racy, edgy, fast-living atmosphere. Comedian David Brenner once described Atlantic City's character as "that of an 80-year-old man who was sick and dying and woke up and discovered he was 21 again. Put yourself in his shoes. If you were 21 again, with all your memories and knowledge intact, would you go out and sweep the front yard? Or would you find some hot-looking girl and have a night on the town?"

While the casino industry has suffered setbacks (the Atlantis Casino Hotel went bankrupt in 1989 and is now the Trump Regency Hotel), it has accomplished two very important goals: It has brought back visitors and created a new excitement in the area. Thanks largely, but not completely, to efforts by the Trump organization, the city has hosted a series of lavish, world-class boxing matches that put it on a par with Las Vegas as an international boxing capital. During the summer season, Atlantic City's casino showrooms host more headliners than any other city in the world.

The question is, Why hasn't the city around the casinos benefited from the boom? Atlantic City's Boardwalk today is not nearly as exciting as Wildwood's, or as comforting for families as Ocean City's, or as restfully beautiful as Spring Lake's. Outside a few upscale shops and one chic shopping compound (Gordon's Alley), Atlantic City's main street, Atlantic Avenue, still suffers from a lack of business.

Though there are several good shops, restaurants, and nightclubs beyond the casinos, they are not frequented by gamblers, who prefer the bright, glitzy interior world of the casinos to the forbidding streetscape of the city that depends on them for survival. Likewise, most of the 65,000 people who work for the casinos or their support industries reside in suburban communities within a 40-minute drive of Atlantic City. These towns have quiet, tree-lined streets, new public schools, shopping malls, multiscreen movie theaters, and trendy nightclubs. Somers Point has a legitimate playhouse, the South Jersey Regional Theater.

Casino owners, government officials, unions, and organized crime figures have all been blamed at one time or another for the city's frustratingly slow recovery. Some critics believe that Atlantic City would be well on its way if the state had specified *how* the casinos would rebuild the town. It took eight years for the state to create the Casino Reinvestment Development Authority and another year to figure out where the money would go.

Under the current arrangement, most of an estimated $1.4 billion derived from the casinos will be spent in Atlantic City, with a gradually increasing portion going to other

New Jersey cities to finance urban growth in disadvantaged areas. In the past 10 years some casino-sponsored low-income housing has been built, and more than 1,000 additional housing units are on the way. There are plans for a supermarket and a new high school.

A trend—call it an attitude—is emerging as casino-industry leaders, government power brokers, and private developers are joining forces to make the city more diversified and attractive to people other than gamblers. This enthusiasm is not the result of civic idealism. Gambling revenues have not been increasing as rapidly as the industry wants, and some casinos may face financial ruin if the city doesn't broaden its appeal beyond its gambling clientele. It may be possible that enlightened self-interest can accomplish what altruism and good intentions have not.

Few would benefit more from an Atlantic City renaissance than New York real-estate developer Donald Trump, who appeared to be the only person to emerge from the city of numbers with most of those numbers in his pocket—until the economy caught up with him last year.

If Trump's luck runs out, as does the luck of most gamblers here, he will join notable company: Hugh Hefner lost heavily when the New Jersey Casino Control Commission refused to license him to oversee his Playboy Casino Hotel for reasons pertaining to his "moral character," dealing a mortal blow to his gambling empire. The commission also dealt Barron Hilton of Hilton Hotels a bad hand when it refused to grant him a casino-operating license—Hilton was forced to sell his $330 million casino hotel (to none other than Donald Trump).

While the licensing board has been called capricious, the Casino Control Commission and the Division of Gaming Enforcement must be praised for keeping organized crime out of the casino industry. Though isolated incidents of criminal activity have occurred, Atlantic City has been spared the gratuitous abuses of power, justice, and financial responsibility that marred Las Vegas's early years. If you gamble in Atlantic City, you can be assured that the games are honest and the casinos are owned by corporations that use lawyers to collect their debts, not enormous men with names like Big Louie.

Today Atlantic City survives as a dazzling interior world, a city of numbers for gamblers, businesspeople, entertainers, and visitors. It has also become a city of prayer.

"Whenever anybody tells me anything bad about casino gambling, I tell them that I used to design churches before I started designing casinos," says architect Joel Bergman, designer of the Bally Grand Hotel Casino in Las Vegas and Atlantic City. "And I hear more people praying in my casinos than in my churches."

The Life of a Redshirt

From the days the first Jersey Shore police departments were given shorts and a whistle, in the mid-1850s, New Jersey's choice party animals have been lifeguards. One of the most famous, if not the top, party of every year is on the sleepy little island of Brigantine, just north of Atlantic City.

It takes place on the night of the Brigantine Beach Patrol lifeguard competitions, usually held in late July. At around 8 PM, when teams from various cities along the Shore have rowed, run, swum, and rescued their way to victory or defeat, the lifeguards—men and women from 15 to 60 years of age—will turn their backs to the sea and make a two-block trek to the house of the most famous lifeguard in the history of the Jersey Shore.

Oh, there might be some lifeguards—kids up around Sandy Hook and Point Pleasant—who, if you said you were going down to Brigantine to drop in on Richard Blair, would give you that seen-it-all look that a lifeguard gets after long hours of sitting in the stand and staring at the beach, with sunscreen on his nose, his finger on the whistle, and his voice hoarse from screaming at the idiots who are standing too far out in the surf.

The guys who know Richard Blair—and the girls, for since the mid-'70s about one out of every five lifeguards on the Jersey Shore is a woman—are those you see on the beach at 7 in the morning, doing push-ups, running the morning mile, and then shoving a rescue boat into the surf and pulling back on those oars like career criminals busting out of Alcatraz. These guards are on the beach early because when the beach officially opens, they must be in the stands watching. During beach hours lifeguards up and down the Jersey Shore are forbidden to practice what is considered the one activity that cuts the men from the boys, the sport that has replaced beer chugging, sex, and pizza-eating as the essence of lifeguard macho and beachy brawn—rowing!

And the man who made it macho was Richard Blair. But nobody calls him Richard Blair. They call him by the nickname he got back in 1949, when he weighed 250 pounds, stood 6 feet, 5 inches tall, and played tackle and place-kicker for a succession of farm teams, starting with the Newark Bears and going on to the Jersey City Giants and the Bethlehem Bulldogs. Blair had a special way of kicking a football and tackling people. People whom he tackled swore that a sound could be heard when Blair pounced on them.

They called him Boomer Blair.

Today Boomer is nearing retirement age. As a union carpenter, he's done work in some Atlantic City casino hotels. He also makes displays for several conventions meeting in that city. He hasn't guarded a beach for more than a decade, when he was a chief of the Avalon Beach Patrol. But in his day, he elevated lifeguarding to a profession. During his last summer on the Avalon beach, for example, in August 1977, he mortally embarrassed the Sea Isle City Beach Patrol.

A television news team drove its van over the tranquil Avalon dunes, and an indignant reporter wanted to know why Avalon's beaches were open when Sea Isle's beaches, located just north of Townsends Inlet, were closed after the guards saw sharks churning the waters a few yards off.

"Guy comes up to me and says there are sharks in Sea Isle," Blair recalls. "I said, 'There may be sharks in Sea Isle, but there are no sharks here.' I took the guy up on the fishing pier. It was in August and it was the mating season of the manta rays. And when the rays go crazy in the water, they have their fins up and they look like sharks. I pointed them out to the reporter and he wondered why the guys in Sea Isle didn't know that these were rays and not sharks. He had his camera man take pictures of the rays and then he went back to Sea Isle. I hear Sea Isle was upset. They had a bunch of young guys on their beach. I had 34 years on the beach, and in 34 years you get to learn a lot about the ocean."

On a moonless summer night during the following summer, somebody chain-sawed one of the Avalon rescue boats in half. An act of retaliation? Blair doesn't know who did it and didn't investigate because, with Atlantic City's casinos under construction, Boomer's winter skill, carpentry, was so much in demand that he decided, for the first time since he served in the Navy during World War II, to be "off beach" for a summer. But if the casinos hadn't opened, if Boomer Blair hadn't hung up his whistle, he would have investigated the infamous Avalon boat slicing of '78. Boats are the lifeguard's chariot, especially along the South Jersey Shore, where the majority of rescues are performed with boats.

This was a wood boat. And though lifeguards are justifiably proud of the modern, sturdy, fiberglass rescue boats built by John Van Duyne in Linwood, a wood boat was something special to Boomer Blair. For 16 incredible years, from 1946 to 1962, Boomer Blair was the most powerful rower on the Jersey Shore. He won 16 rowing tournaments—more than any other lifeguard.

"I would've won more, but the chief we had around then said I was hogging it away from the other guys. So if I won one race in competition, I was beached after that."

Boomer's fame extended to crew teams in New York, Pennsylvania, and Annapolis whose members would become summer lifeguards at the Jersey Shore just so they could compete against Boomer Blair and beat him. Few did. No one won enough competitions to challenge his record, and those who finished second and third behind him suffered deeper envy when they learned that Boomer was the rarest of all athletes: a 100% natural, a man who never worked out and never exercised, who learned how to row by trying it in the Jersey surf, and who would rather spend his mornings sleeping and his nights drinking beer than doing anything as onerous as practicing.

Boomer Blair put Atlantic City's Beach Patrol on the map. He rowed wood boats because that's the kind of boats lifeguards used in those days. For Boomer Blair, slicing a wood boat in half was like taking a sledgehammer to a vintage Packard.

If he had stayed on the Avalon Beach Patrol, Boomer Blair would have found out who cut that boat in half, and that culprit would have learned how a guy who got his nickname in the '40s managed to hold on to it all those years. The culprit would have heard the Boom.

Getting the right nickname as a lifeguard is a kind of apotheosis. The mob may have its Little Nickys and Fat Tonys. Lifeguards have their Love men and Monster men and Woo Woo dudes. Many of these nicknames are attributed to adventures that begin in bars after the sun has gone down. Most of these adventures are highly exaggerated. Boomer's are not. He was a lifeguard at 16. He was married when he was 33. He met his wife, Gloria, on the Atlantic City beach. There had been others before her.

"I always say it's better to look 'em over than to overlook 'em," Boomer booms. "I would see most of the girls on the beach in the daytime and make appointments to see 'em at night in the Senator bar, which was in the old Senator Hotel on South Carolina Avenue. You had to catch 'em in a bar because you couldn't just lollygag on the beach or you'd lose somebody."

He adds, "My wife does a lot of work for the Miss America Pageant. I tell her she should make me a pageant judge. I've seen my share."

Boomer was the party animal that helped end the party. In 1955 Boomer Blair did something so outrageous—something that combined lunacy, dumb luck, and brute strength—that it changed the lifestyle of lifeguards forever. The change would not be felt until the mid-'70s, but Boomer's incredible feat established rowing and not partying as the Jersey Shore lifeguard's sport of sports once and for all. It is now the measure of all that is high and mighty in a guard.

His feat has never been equaled. In 1955, a man bet Boomer Blair that he couldn't row a rescue boat 1,000 feet to the end of Steel Pier into the tail of a hurricane, and row the boat back.

"The first time I pitchpoled and went over. Second time I filled up with water and went back to the beach. Third time I went out and got to the end of Steel Pier with the boat about half full of water. I got to looking for the bucket to bail. I found the bucket tied to the boat. But there was no bottom in the bucket."

A 15-foot wave hit him and threw him out of the boat. Blair righted the boat, rode with it, and as he drifted north toward the Absecon Channel, he eventually got back into the boat and rowed it, completely submerged, back to shore.

When he returned he found thousands of people lined up on the Boardwalk staring at him. He thought he was going to be fired from the beach patrol. Two photographers from competing newspapers took his picture. The photographers wanted their pictures printed, but ultimately the papers would not print pictures of a macho lunatic who had irresponsibly risked his life and a beach-patrol boat for a $10 bet.

"So they made up a story that I was testing the boat in heavy seas," Blair said. "They made me a hero and everybody went along with it."

Blair wasn't fired. For a few weeks he was the toast of the city, the brave rower, the man who beat a hurricane, a guard with the right stuff. His only difficulty was in collecting the bet.

"I had to threaten the guy to get the money," Boomer remembers. "I told him that if he didn't pay me, I'd take him out with me next time."

Along the 127-mile Jersey Shore, every municipality and private beach, as well as three state-park beaches, has slightly different qualifications and pay scales for kids seeking to enter the lifeguard life. You can start as a "mascot" at age 10 or 11. A mascot is a glorified gofer for guards on the stand and is usually given a whistle and tank top for his summer labors.

At age 16 (15 in some municipalities) any boy or girl can take the local beach-patrol qualifying exams, given anywhere from March to mid-May. Generally these exams include a 1-mile run and a 1-mile (sometimes shorter) ocean swim. Contestants must also demonstrate proficiency with rescue boards or torps—large, torpedolike polyurethane floats that guards push toward panicking swimmers—and rowing. Kids usually pick up these skills as mascots.

There might be a written test as well as a personal interview. Those who pass are trained in accordance with guidelines set up by the United States Lifesaving Association, a national certifying organization. Training includes first aid, cardiopulmonary resuscitation, and lore and wisdom about the stretch of beach they will guard.

They will be told how to rescue people, which most lifeguards will say with complete seriousness is more an art than a skill. The methods vary with the kind of shore. In Monmouth and Ocean counties, the majority of ocean and bay rescues are performed using a flotation device to which a rope is frequently tied. The guard swims out toward the bather in distress, pushing the device ahead of him. The device can be a torp or a rescue board similar to a surfboard. When the guard reaches the swimmer, he tells the swimmer to grab the board. The guard then tows the swimmer back to shore. Sometimes the swimmer is hauled by rope.

Because of the broader, flatter beaches along the South Jersey Shore, the majority of rescues there are performed by boat. Usually a team of guards will put the boat in the surf, row out to the swimmer, and have the swimmer hold on to the boat as they row back. If the swimmer is ill, injured, or too tired to hold on, the guards will pull him or her into the boat.

Deciding how to effect a rescue is the art of the guard, and the guards rescue more people than you might think. Bob Cresbough, captain of Lavalette's Beach Patrol, says there have been days when he has fished more than 50 people out of the water. Bob Levy, chief of the 190-guard Atlantic City Beach Patrol (the state's largest), has rescued more than 100 people a day at the States Avenue beach (opposite the Showboat Hotel & Casino), which is notorious for its high waves and quick currents.

Drownings are rare during the hours when New Jersey beaches are open. This isn't to say that people are not injured or killed while in the ocean during the summer. Each year the ocean takes its toll. But the majority of these incidents occur after 6 PM or before 10 AM, when most Jersey Shore beaches are officially closed.

In addition to actually rescuing people, guards uphold law and order on the beach. In some municipalities, such as Atlantic City, they are deputized as special police and have the power to arrest people who disturb the peace or refuse to do as they are told.

Beginning pay is slightly higher than minimum wage, and there is no age limit, though the older guards (Atlantic City has three that are hovering around their sixties) tend to be involved in more administrative duties.

But what about the stories? The wild parties? The long nights in local bars ending in love under the Boardwalk? On the beach, lifeguards are like bartenders in a singles bar, approachable, easy to talk to, but, ultimately, stuck with a job to do. About the only official acknowledgment that male lifeguards have a social life can be found in the few surviving "Miss Beach Patrol" pageants and dances held during the last week of August. With the exception of Atlantic City's Miss America Pageant, which was inspired to a degree by the roving eyes of that city's beach patrolmen (the first "constable of the surf" walked his sandy beat in 1855), these local pageants have suffered the slings and arrows of fashion and feminism. When women began to take and pass lifeguard entrance exams in the early '70s, these events began to lose favor. Besides, lifeguards had their own unsanctioned ways of picking favorites.

"When I first started in the early '60s, things were different," Lavalette's Jim Cresbaugh laments. "I had a lot of girlfriends. From about 1972 to 1974 we had some great times. We had a smaller crew, the guys were closer, we went out at night, and everybody drank together. We were a wilder bunch, and there was much more partying than goes on today. The kids we get now are more athletic, more into sports. They're very serious about what they do. There's some beer-drinking, but nothing else. These kids work out, and they want to stay in shape. They go to bed early."

Cresbaugh says his biggest problem is not disciplining his crew—it's hard finding enough bodies to take the job. "There's a shortage up and down the Shore," he says. "And it's getting worse each year."

You don't have to hunt too far for the causes. Pay is one of them. Though lifeguards make an adequate wage by summer standards, the overall cost of living at the Shore has turned a carefree lifestyle into a hustle. It is no longer possible to rent a back-bay house for the summer and make enough money as a guard to pay the rent, the beer bill, and maybe save some money for college.

Add to this New Jersey's raising the drinking age to 21 and the threat of enormous liability lawsuits against taverns, liquor stores, and hosts who serve underage drinkers—that puts a real damper on hard drinking. Sexual conquests are overshadowed by the chilling threat of sexually transmitted diseases. Also there is the newly acknowledged health threat: the sun itself. A few years ago, Arthur R. Brown, chief of the Atlantic City Beach Patrol for 13 years, died of skin cancer due to many years of prolonged exposure to sunlight. He was 58.

Lifeguards are currently being recruited at job fairs around the country, even around the world where a Beach Boys lifestyle of sun, surf, and Jersey girls is being pitched to the Irish, the British, and the Australians eager for a subsidized summer in America.

What they find when they arrive is that the lifeguard life has changed. Though wild times persist, the party's mostly over in what were once the traditional party towns of Point Pleasant, Asbury Park, Seaside Heights, Beach Haven, Margate, and Wildwood. "I miss some of the old times," Jim Cresbaugh says. "But I like it better this way."

For some people, having a job is just something to do when you're not being a lifeguard. It's called having sand in your shoes. For these people, once that sand gets in your shoe—once you've had time under the sun, with the whistle around your tank-suit strap (never around your neck because a swimmer could grab it while you're attempting a rescue and inadvertently strangle you) —you keep coming back for more.

Bob Levy was 14 years old when he became a redshirt—Atlantic City slang for a lifeguard because of the red tank tops the guards wear. He's in his forties now, and the beach-patrol chief. Being a chief is a full-time job with a pension.

"The hardest part of the job is that you have to be down there in that stand eight hours a day. You have to respect the redshirts for that. They put in a long day. The wind, the sun, it's blowing in your face. There are a million and one distractions, but you have to be constantly looking. It's the time you let your guard down, that's when something happens. I call it defensive lifeguarding—you keep the people in a situation in which as little as possible can happen to them."

Levy considers lifeguards to be "the ambassadors of the beach," so he can't divulge the most outrageous thing he ever did as a redshirt. But he can tell the second most outrageous thing he ever did. It happened before he worked his way up through the ranks of guard, lieutenant, and captain. From 1966 to 1984 Levy was a member of the Army's elite Special Forces Green Berets.

You can get tired of Rambo-ing your way on secret missions deep in the Vietnam jungle. Levy didn't get tired. He just missed the beach. In 1969 he was holed up in Tay Nyn, an outpost along the Cambodian border. He got a 15-day leave, flew back to Atlantic City, put on his red shirt, and guarded the States Avenue beach until it was time to get on a jet and go back to Vietnam.

He did this a few times, using every opportunity to zoom back to the beach, sit in the stand, and yell at the swimmers who had gone too far out.

Of course, this was when States Avenue was *the* beach in Atlantic City. Located directly in front of the Showboat Hotel & Casino, the States Avenue beach used to be jammed with vacationers who, two decades ago, would rent rooms in the many guest houses in the South Inlet. The guest houses and the nearby bars made States Avenue the place to be.

The majority of these guest houses have been torn down now, but the beach is known for getting the largest waves on Absecon Island and attracts a moderate surfing crowd. It is still Bob Levy's favorite. Kentucky Avenue is the favorite of another guard who has sand in her shoes: Elaine Blair, daughter of Boomer Blair.

When she was a child she would go down to the beach with her father and hear stories of his glory days. She's a college graduate now, but she doesn't know if she could live without the beach. Elaine started out playing on the Brigantine dunes. Then she became a beach inspector—checking to see who had tags and who didn't. At 5 feet, 10 inches tall, Elaine, who is the youngest of Boomer's three kids, could be reasonably persuasive.

When her older brother, Richard Jr., became an Atlantic City lifeguard, she decided to try it, too.

"Everybody treats me equal," she says. "I like the Kentucky Avenue beach because that's where my father was a captain for 10 years."

She was nervous when she did her first rescue. The senior guard nodded at her, and she pushed a torp—called a can in Atlantic City—out to two elementary-school kids who had drifted out too far. The feeling of having potentially saved a life was, she says, "something you don't forget."

Her favorite time is from 10 AM to noon, when the beach is relatively free of people and she can feel alone and at peace with the ocean. Then the beach starts to fill up and people begin to ask her what time it is, if jellyfish bite, and if she happened to see a set of keys lying around anywhere.

She says the stories about socializing are a myth, at least for her. "There's a lot more girls tramping up and down the beach than guys." The girls on the sand get more attention than the girls in the lifeguard stand. "Guys don't usually prance in front of us."

There is only one aspect of lifeguarding in which women have yet to gain the respect of men, and that's rowing. All women lifeguards learn how to do it, but few work at it long enough to place significantly in the lifeguard competitions.

Elaine Blair fears she'll have to stop lifeguarding and "grow up" one day, maybe entering a career in medicine. Until then, though, she has not discounted the possibility that history will be made again in Atlantic City. Last year she competed in a can rescue. She says she did it for the fun of it. And her father is teaching her how to row.

3 Monmouth County

Introduction

While Sandy Hook gets a strong summertime day-tripping crowd, most visitors to Monmouth County flock to the resort towns from Deal through Manasquan and Brielle. Primarily residential in character, and somewhat exclusive, the majority of the towns view themselves as enclaves for year-round residents and discourage commercial developments that would increase tourism. Few rental houses are available in this area. The pace is slow, genteel, and a bit snooty—a few of the resort towns have tried to limit seasonal visitors by imposing parking bans and unusually high fees for beach tags, although recent efforts by the New Jersey Public Advocate have resulted in reduced beach fees.

Monmouth County's boardwalks are not as large or elaborate as those farther south. They range from the deliberate minimalism of Spring Lake, whose boardwalk has absolutely no commercial development, to the busy boardwalk bars of Belmar and Manasquan. Long Branch and Belmar have a few amusement rides, though the best in the region are in Seaside Heights (*see* Chapter 4, Ocean County). Asbury Park's boardwalk is perhaps the most poignant. It provides visitors with a hint of what the town once was and inspires hope that it can return to its former glory.

Consider a drive through the rocky, scenic, historic areas around Freehold, where Colonial houses cling to steep narrow streets that plunge dramatically toward the sea.

Every so often a few hale and proud citizens of Long Branch state that their town is New Jersey's oldest Shore town, knocking the claim of Cape May—at the very end of the Shore—as the state's first year-round settlement. Like Cape May, the upper reaches of the Monmouth County shore were first mapped by the Dutch in the early 1600s. Unlike Cape May, which became a lone whaling and fishing settlement at the mouth of the Delaware Bay, Monmouth County was a strategic outpost that controlled access to the Raritan Bay and New York Harbor. One could stand on the rock scarp of the Navesink Highlands and view all shipping activities for 25 miles. For this reason the British established one of their most important garrisons at Sandy Hook. The officers who manned this garrison settled in nearby Middletown, Shrewsberry, and Red Bank, establishing the northeastern corner of Monmouth County as a Tory stronghold that remained loyal to the British Crown during the Revolutionary War and through the War of 1812.

Easy access made Monmouth an ideal vacation spot for New York's working and middle classes. The first hotels sprouted near Sandy Hook in the late 17th century. By the mid-1800s, Long Branch, named for a tributary of the Shrewsberry River, had established itself as a racy, summertime "sin city" for those who took the ferry from New York to Sandy Hook and then endured a dusty stagecoach ride south. The stagecoach has been replaced by a train, bringing ever more people to what was then New Jersey's most famous resort city, with its racetrack and gambling dens.

More wholesome summer fun was offered in the small community of Ocean Grove, founded in 1869 as a Methodist retreat. Gambling, the consumption of alcoholic beverages, making

Monmouth County

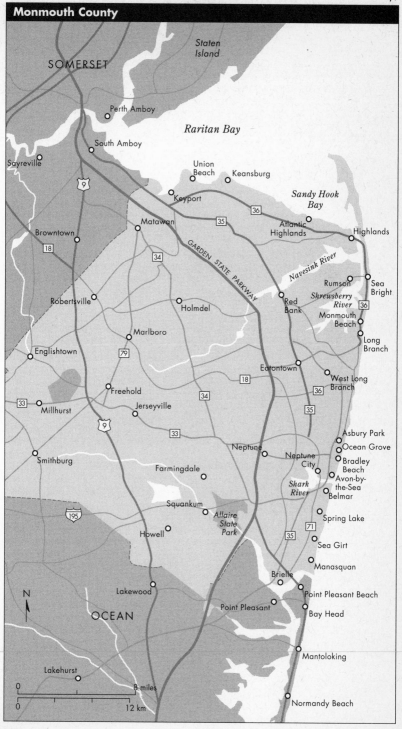

Staten Island

SOMERSET

Perth Amboy

Raritan Bay

South Amboy

Sayreville

Union Beach

Keansburg

Keyport

Sandy Hook Bay

[9]

Browntown

Matawan

[35]

[36]

Atlantic Highlands

Highlands

[18]

[34]

GARDEN STATE PARKWAY

Navesink River

Robertsville

Holmdel

Red Bank

Rumson

Sea Bright

Shrewsberry River

[36]

Marlboro

Monmouth Beach

Englishtown

[79]

Long Branch

Eatontown

[18]

West Long Branch

Freehold

[34]

[36]

[33]

Millhurst

Jerseyville

[35]

[9]

[33]

Asbury Park

Ocean Grove

Smithburg

Neptune

Neptune City

Bradley Beach

Avon-by-the-Sea

Farmingdale

Shark River

Belmar

[195]

Squankum

Allaire State Park

Spring Lake

[71]

Howell

[35]

Sea Girt

Manasquan

Brielle

Lakewood

Point Pleasant Beach

N

Point Pleasant

Bay Head

OCEAN

Mantoloking

Lakehurst

0   8 miles

0   12 km

Normandy Beach

loud noises or nonreligiously inspired music, and "obscene bathing costumes" were all taboo in Ocean Grove. Ocean bathing was, at first, banned altogether, then permitted only very early in the morning. Men and women could not share the same beach together, and no one was permitted in the water on Sunday, when the town's gates were locked and everyone gathered for services in the huge Great Auditorium. Constructed entirely of wood in 1869, the auditorium was supposed to resemble Solomon's Temple as described in the Bible, and it is still used for concerts and religious services.

Under its initial charter, all land in Ocean Grove was owned by the Methodist camp-meeting organization. The community became so popular among family visitors that forward-thinking investors purchased land just north of the community, named it after Methodist leader Francis Asbury, and made a killing selling subdivided lots in what was ironically to become Monmouth County's second sin city, Asbury Park. After the railroad was extended farther south, Asbury Park quickly eclipsed Long Branch as *the* summer place on the Shore.

Until just 20 years ago, it was illegal to drive a car, cut grass, hang laundry, or play sports in Ocean Grove on Sunday. With the relaxation of these laws, Ocean Grove has blossomed into a prim, pleasant Victorian resort community, with a delightful, colorful Main Street reminiscent of Cape May's Washington Mall and San Francisco's Union Street. Alcohol is still banned, and Sundays are still blessedly peaceful. Self-guided walking tours are available at the Camp Meeting Association headquarters across from the Great Auditorium.

With Long Branch, Asbury Park, and Ocean Grove representing the extremes of Monmouth County Shore life, other towns sprouted along the marshy coast, each one appealing to various ethnic groups. Spring Lake drew a strong, upper-middle-class Irish population. Deal, Bradley Beach, and, later, Asbury Park, attracted a Jewish clientele. Italians flocked to Long Branch, Avon, and Point Pleasant. After World War II, marinas were constructed in the county's natural harbors. Today, the county is the capital of the Jersey Shore's sportfishing fanatics.

In the past 30 years, Long Branch and Asbury Park have withered, though recent efforts to restore and enhance those cities' hotel stock may turn the tide. The smaller, affluent suburban resort towns of Avon, Belmar, and Spring Lake never suffered declines. Each year more of the area's grand hotels are renovated. More and more stately residences are blossoming as bed-and-breakfast inns, offering a kind of genteel hospitality that, in Monmouth County, never went out of style.

Essential Information

Important Addresses and Numbers

Tourist Information Monmouth County Department of Public Information/Tourism (27 E. Main St., Freehold 07728, tel. 908/431–7476).

Greater Asbury Park Chamber of Commerce (Lake and Ocean Aves., Box 649, Asbury Park 07712, tel. 908/775–7676).

Belmar Chamber of Commerce (Box 297, Belmar 07719, tel. 908/681–2900).

Long Branch Chamber of Commerce (494 Broadway, Long Branch 07740, tel. 908/222–0400).

Manasquan Chamber of Commerce (108 Main St., Manasquan 08736, tel. 908/739–4883).

Matawan-Aberdeen Chamber of Commerce (2 Woodland Rd., Holmdel 07733, tel. 908/739–4883).

Middletown Chamber of Commerce (24 Leonardville Rd., Middletown 07748, tel. 908/671–3360).

Ocean Grove Chamber of Commerce (Box 415, Ocean Grove 07756, tel. 908/774–1391).

Red Bank Area Chamber of Commerce (5 Broad St., Red Bank 07701, tel. 908/741–0055).

Sea Bright Chamber of Commerce (Box 13, Sea Bright 07760, tel. 908/842–4390).

Spring Lake Chamber of Commerce (Box 694, Spring Lake 07762, tel. 908/449–0577).

Wall Chamber of Commerce (2100 Hwy. 35, Sea Girt 08750, tel. 908/223–9255).

Emergencies
Medical

Freehold: Freehold Area Hospital (W. Main St., tel. 908/431–2000).

Holmdel: Bayshore Community Hospital (727 North Beers, tel. 908/739–5900).

Long Branch: Monmouth Medical Center (300 Second Ave., tel. 908/870–5014).

Neptune and Southern Monmouth County: Jersey Shore Medical Center (1945 Rte. 33, Neptune, tel. 908/776–4555).

Northeastern Monmouth County: Riverview Medical Center (1 Riverview Plaza, Red Bank, tel. 908/741–2700).

Publications

The *Asbury Park Press,* Monmouth County's daily newspaper, does a very good job of covering regional entertainment as well as supplying visitor-oriented information. Smaller newspapers include the *Courier,* the *Wall Herald,* and the *Register.* The *Ocean Grove Times* and the *Neptune Times* list events in those communities. *Coast Magazine,* published in Point Pleasant, has articles about history and restaurant information.

Arriving and Departing

By Car

Monmouth County's Shore resort towns are easily accessible from north and south by the **Garden State Parkway,** a toll road. From the east take **I–195,** which also connects with the **New Jersey Turnpike** (I–95), the state's major toll road. **Route 35** skirts the northeastern corner of the county into Red Bank, and then parallels the shore, offering direct access to Asbury Park and Shore resort towns as far south as Brielle.

By Bus and Train

In addition to **New Jersey Transit** (tel. 800/722–2222 in northern NJ) and **Greyhound** (tel. 908/642–8205 or 212/971–6363), the Monmouth County Shore resort towns are linked to the New York Port Authority Terminal (41st St. and 8th Ave.) by the

Academy Bus Line (tel. 212/964–6600), the **Asbury Park–New York Transit Company** (tel. 908/774–2727), and the **New York–Keansburg–Long Branch Bus Company** (tel. 908/291–1300). New Jersey Transit also provides regular daily commuter railroad service from all major Shore resort towns to New York City's Pennsylvania Station (7th Ave. and 33rd St.).

By Ferry High-speed commuter ferry service on the **T-N-T Hydroline** (tel. 800/BOAT–RIDE) links the towns of Atlantic Highlands, Highlands, and Keyport to Manhattan's Pier 11 (Wall and South Sts.) and Brooklyn's Pier 69. Boats depart Pier 6 at the Atlantic Highlands Municipal Harbor Marina (Connor's Hotel, 326 Shore Drive, Highlands) and the Municipal Fishing Pier in Keyport.

Getting Around

By Car Major north–south arteries are **Route 35,** which curves along the "shoulder" of northeastern Monmouth County, and **Route 71,** which connects the beach resorts of Long Branch to Manasquan and Brielle. **Route 36** runs east and west, paralleling the Raritan Bayshore from Keyport to Highlands, then becomes **Ocean Avenue** as it turns south at Sandy Hook to Long Branch. Ocean Avenue becomes **Route 57** through Long Branch, Deal, Allenhurst, and Asbury Park. You must return to Route 71 as you bypass Ocean Grove. At Bradley Beach, Ocean Avenue becomes Route 18 through Avon, Belmar, Spring Lake, and Sea Girt, rejoining Route 71 north of Manasquan. The drive is a scenic, slow, but enjoyable path through the resort towns.

By Taxi Cabs are plentiful in every town, and many stake out train and bus stations. Consult local phone directories. **Oak Glen Limousine** (tel. 908/367–4536 or 800/322–4536) has stretch limousines and vans. **Citi Cab** (tel. 908/776–5700 or 908/988–8850), in Asbury Park, also provides these services.

By Bus and Trolley Bus transportation is rather good in Monmouth County, with a variety of lines serving many routes. For schedule and fares, call **New Jersey Transit** (tel. 800/772–2222) or the **Monmouth County Transportation Information Center** (tel. 908/780–1121). The town of Spring Lake operates a seasonal trolley Memorial Day–Labor Day, daily 10–6. Fare is 50¢. For information call 908/449–1415. Monmouth SCAT (tel. 908/431–6480) provides transportation for the elderly and handicapped.

Guided Tours

Special-Interest *Music* Asbury Park's nonprofit Society of Associated Performers (of which B. B. King and Clarence Clemons are members) sponsors Asbury Park Musical Heritage Walking Tours to groups of 20 and more. The tours, which last about 1½ hours and take in the sites, locations, and landmarks important to the development of Asbury Park's music scene, are led by people who were there when it happened and know Springsteen, Lyons, Clemons, and other Asbury Park musicians personally. Proceeds go to a fund for a museum and performance space for local musicians.

"We're doing the tours to make people aware of Asbury Park's musical importance, past, present, and future," says Margaret

Potter, who gave Bruce Springsteen his first job in Asbury Park when she ran the Upstage Club. "We want to make the Jersey Shore a focal point for music again." (For more information write to the Society of Associated Performers, Box 355, Asbury Park 07712.)

Exploring Monmouth County

A Rock-and-Roll Walk Through Asbury Park

Numbers in the margin correspond with points of interest on the Asbury Park map.

A century ago Asbury Park outclassed Atlantic City as the Shore's toniest resort. While evidence of this past glory remains, this favorite beach town is nowadays a bit down at the heels. The causes of Asbury Park's current problems are complex, and current efforts to turn the tide have, unfortunately, not been entirely successful. The superb 1985 renovation of the 1925 grande dame, the Berkeley-Carteret Hotel, has experienced financial difficulties. The ambitious 300 Ocean Mile condo project, the first phase of the planned $1 billion commercial and residential beachfront redevelopment, must sell more units before redevelopment can proceed. What brings a small but steady trickle of visitors from Europe, Japan, and even the Middle East and Australia to Asbury's boardwalk and beach is the music of Bruce Springsteen, Southside Johnny Lyon, and a host of lesser-known rock musicians who, despite the fact that they no longer live in or even frequent the town, have brought a poignant, nostalgic image of the Jersey Shore to a world that is still hungry for self-made heroes.

This tour, which was created by Margaret Potter and members of the Society of Associated Performers, confines itself to Asbury Park and places frequented by Bruce Springsteen, who was nicknamed "the Boss" by members of the E Street Band (named after a street in Belmar). Born in nearby Freehold, Springsteen frequented Asbury Park as a teenager in the mid-1960s, and lived in Bradley Beach while performing in Asbury Park nightclubs in the early 1970s. He currently owns a home in Rumson and is rarely seen in Asbury Park. The 3-mile tour takes a leisurely two hours on foot, 45 minutes by car, passing through some of Asbury Park's less appealing neighborhoods.

❶ The **metal gate at 702 Cookman Avenue**, near the corner of Cookman Avenue and Bond Street, used to lead to the **Upstage Club,** a second-floor nightclub that did not serve alcohol, and so could accommodate teenagers. The Upstage was a rendezvous for many young musicians, including a young guitarist named Bruce Springsteen, who played with his band Earth at the Upstage in 1968. The band became Steel Mill in 1969. While at the Upstage, Springsteen met Garry Tallant, Miami Steve Van Zandt, Danny Federici, Vini Lopez, and David Sancious, many of the musicians who would become the E Street Band and play on Springsteen's first three record albums.

"We didn't see Bruce until the summer of 1968," says Margaret Potter. "He was 19 and had been playing with a small band called Earth, doing the teeny bopper scene. In those days As-

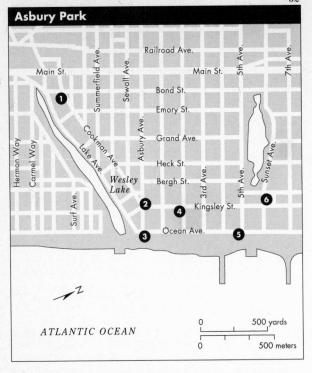

Asbury Park

bury Park had a big teeny bopper scene. Kids would come from all over and try to talk their way into the clubs and some would let them in and some didn't. A lot of kids just hung out on the street listening to the music being played inside. That was why we founded the Upstage Club."

Follow Cookman Avenue east toward the beach. Cookman ends at the intersection of Kingsley Street and Asbury Avenue, where, past the X-rated movie theater, the abandoned **Palace Amusements** is one of the last remaining amusement arcades that hasn't been demolished to make way for Asbury Park's redevelopment. The Palace, as it was called in the 1960s, contained many amusement rides, including a carousel, Ferris wheel, rocket plane, fun house, and tunnel of love. Springsteen frequented the Palace Amusements as a youngster. The tunnel of love later became the inspiration for one of his more ironic love songs.

Continue on Asbury Avenue to the boardwalk **Casino** and carousel. Park in nearby spaces and walk on to the boardwalk.

"After the Upstage closed at 5 AM, Bruce and his friends would come down here and hang out and play guitar," Potter says. "The cops would sometimes chase him away and he'd go down to the end of the jetty." According to Potter, Springsteen slept on the beach or under the boardwalk, in this general location, on many nights in the late 1960s.

The casino, the carousel enclosure, and the Convention Hall—the large, square building on the left—were built in the late 1920s in a beaux arts "eclectic style." The carousel was built by the Philadelphia Toboggan Company, enclosed in a beautifully ornate art nouveau pavilion highlighted by intricately cut glass. *Tel. 908/988–8585. The carousel is open on summer weekends; one ride costs $1.50.*

The large structures to the right of the carousel contained an indoor amusement park and auditorium for roller skating and ice skating. Woody Allen used this and other Asbury Park boardwalk locations in his film *Stardust Memories.* In Springsteen's day, rock concerts were also staged here. Storm damage forced the closing of the arena in the 1980s, though some arcade games remained. In 1987, the structure had deteriorated so badly it had to be boarded up. The monolithic tower beyond the arena is a heating plant that heated both the casino and Convention Hall. It is no longer in use, though Springsteen used the heating plant interior as a setting for the video of his "Tunnel of Love" song.

Walk north on the boardwalk. Near Fourth Street is **Madam Marie's,** the small fortune-telling booth Springsteen mentioned in his song "Fourth of July, Asbury Park."

Walk south on the boardwalk to 2nd Street. Turn right onto the ❹ 2nd Street beach block and continue to **The Stone Pony** nightclub, which opened in 1974 as an adjunct to Mrs. Jay's beer garden. (Frank Sinatra, who performed in Asbury Park's Convention Hall, was known to favor the hot dogs sold at this beer garden.) In the mid-1970s, The Stone Pony was one of several music clubs featuring rock, rhythm-and-blues, and a blend of rock and soul, with rhythm-and-blues horn sections. This became the "Jersey Shore sound" of Springsteen, Southside Johnny Lyon, and other musicians. Springsteen frequently performed here in 1974. He had already released his first two records and was working on "Born to Run," which made him world famous when it was released a year later. For the next five years Springsteen would make surprise appearances at The Stone Pony. In the mid-1980s, he opened his "Born in the USA" tour here. The rambling cedar-paneled bar near The Stone Pony was the Empire Bar, another club that Springsteen frequented.

The Stone Pony still functions as a nightclub, though its future is uncertain. Redevelopment plans for this largely barren section of Asbury Park's beachfront do not include The Stone Pony.

Go west to the intersection of 2nd and Kingsley streets. Several clubs used to stand at this dismal corner, now taken over by go-go bars. At one of them, the **Sunshine Inn,** Springsteen opened for Chuck Berry in the early 1970s. At another, the **Student Prince,** Springsteen first met saxophone player Clarence Clemons.

❺ Turn right onto 5th Street to **Convention Hall.** On your right, as you face the ocean, is the 300 Ocean Mile condo project. Look briefly west, at Sunset Lake. Fifth Street runs on the south side of the lake. The beach block portion of 5th Street specialized in rhythm-and-blues nightclubs—all of them torn down—where Ray Charles, Ella Fitzgerald, Della Reese, and B. B. King performed. Clarence Clemons frequented this area, as did Johnny Lyon, whose nickname "Southside" came from his love of the rhythm-and-blues performers who played these clubs.

Convention Hall, in front of you on the boardwalk, is one of the most flamboyant structures remaining on the Jersey Shore. Covered with bright purple, green, and terra-cotta figures, it resembles a boxy brick birthday cake. Refurbished briefly for the premiere of Asbury Park native Danny Devito's film *Throw Mama from the Train,* the hall still holds trade shows, cultural events, and concerts. From the 1930s to the late 1950s, the hall was a regular stop on the Jersey Shore concert circuit for Jimmy Durante, Sophie Tucker, Tommy Dorsey, Harry James, Benny Goodman, and dozens of other entertainers.

Go into the hall's arcade area. "There were a lot of pinball machines and skeeball games here," Potter remembers. "After spending a whole night playing music, Bruce would play those games and would eat hot pretzels and Pepsi for breakfast."

❻ Follow Ocean Avenue north, turning left onto Sunset Avenue. The **Berkeley-Carteret Hotel** is a remarkably good restoration, one that was supposed to lead Asbury Park's renaissance. Country singer Johnny Cash has a suite of apartments in one wing of the hotel. Inside is the **National Broadcasters Hall of Fame Museum,** a collection of memorabilia and old tube-type radios from the era in which radio became the heart and soul of America.

Time Out The **Adriatic Restaurant and Lounge** (tel. 908/774–7834), past Sunset on Kingsley, has inexpensive burgers and beers. "Bruce has eaten there," Potter says. "We all have." The spicy goulash is recommended.

Continue north on Kingsley. Turn right onto 8th Avenue and stop at the corner of 8th and Webb. The white house at 303 8th Avenue, on the north side of the street, was **Southside Johnny's house** (now a private residence) until he moved to California in the late 1970s.

Turn right onto Webb and stop at **1703 Webb,** a low, humble yellow house with a broad, flat first-floor roof. During the early 1970s, Daniel "Big Danny" Gallagher, an ironworker, let Bruce Springsteen use this house as a "crash pad." Southside Johnny and Springsteen would jam together on the roof of the house. Gallagher, who later became a roadie in Springsteen's band, remembers hearing his neighbors yelling at him. "I remember one old guy looking up at Bruce and Southside and saying, 'Those guys are going nowhere,'" laughs Gallagher, who no longer tours with Springsteen. He has since moved elsewhere.

Turn left onto Deal Lake Drive and admire the tranquil lakeside scenery. Turn left onto Main Street and continue six blocks to Asbury Avenue. Turn right and pass the Asbury Park **YMCA.** Springsteen spent some nights here in the early 1970s when he couldn't stay with Big Danny and others. Nearly 15 years later he quietly donated an estimated $40,000 to the YMCA to pay for new exercise equipment and general renovations. "Bruce keeps very quiet about what he does for people," Potter says. "But he never forgets the people who helped him out along the way."

Historic Sites and Attractions

U.S. Army Communications and Electronics Museum. Exhibits
tell the history of the "wireless" radio and other military-
inspired communications developments. *Fort Monmouth, Rte.
35, Eatontown, tel. 908/532–2445. Admission free. Open Mon.–
Thurs. noon–4.*

Long Branch Historical Museum (Church of the Presidents).
Once a church, this museum now contains books, photos, and
memorabilia from the area's past. Presidents Grant, Garfield,
Arthur, McKinley, Hayes, Harrison, and Wilson worshiped
here during Shore visits. *1260 Ocean Ave., Long Branch, tel.
908/229–0600 or 908/222–9879. Admission free, by appointment.*

Spy House Museum. This notorious tavern was neutral ground
for spies during the Revolutionary War. It now houses a small
maritime museum and a collection of crafts and local folklore.
*119 Port Monmouth Rd., Port Monmouth, tel. 908/291–0559 or
908/787–1807. Open weekends by appointment.*

What to See and Do with Children

Asbury Park has the single most wonderful **carousel** on the Jersey Shore. Built by the Philadelphia Toboggan Company, the
carousel is enclosed in a charming art nouveau structure located at Ocean Avenue between Convention Hall and the Casino Pier. *Tel. 908/988–8585. Admission: $1.50. Open summer
weekends.*

Monmouth County **libraries** provide free preschool and school-
age story-telling hours and other educational activities. **Asbury
Park** (500 1st Ave., tel. 908/774–4221); **Atlantic Highlands** (100
1st Ave., tel. 908/291–1956); **Avon** (Garfield Ave. and 5th St.,
tel. 908/775–6998); **Belmar** (10th Ave., tel. 908/681–0775);
Bradley Beach (511 4th Ave., tel. 908/775–2175); **Brielle** (601
Union La., tel. 908/528–9381); **Holmdel** (Crawfords Corner
Rd., tel. 908/946–4118); **Little Silver** (484 Prospect Ave., tel.
908/747–9649); **Long Branch** (3288 Broadway, tel. 908/222–
3900); **Manasquan** (55 Broad St., tel. 908/223–1503); **Matawan-
Aberdeen** (165 Main, tel. 908/583–9100); **Monmouth Beach** (18
Willow Ave., tel. 908/229–1187); **Navesink** (Monmouth Ave.,
tel. 908/291–1120); **Neptune City** (106 W. Sylvania Ave., tel.
908/988–8866); **Neptune Township** (25 Springdale Ave., tel.
908/775–8241); **Red Bank** (84 W. Front St., tel. 908/842–0690);
Sea Girt (Ocean Ave. and Beacon Blvd., tel. 908/449–9493);
Spring Lake (1501 3rd Ave., tel. 908/449–6654); **Tinton Falls**
(664 Tinton Ave., tel. 908/542–3110); **Wall** (Old Mill Plaza, 2100
Rte. 35, tel. 908/449–8877); **West Long Branch** (95 Poplar Ave.,
tel. 908/222–5993).

Off the Beaten Track

The historic town of Freehold, near Monmouth Battlefield
Park, is a good base for exploring a region that, with some obvious exceptions, remains close enough to Colonial days to transport you into the past. The **Monmouth County Historical
Association** offers tours, lectures, and programs highlighting
the region's complex interplay between Tory holdouts and revolutionary forces. *Historical Museum, 70 Court St., tel. 908/*

*462–1466. Nominal admission charge. Open Tues.–Sat. 10–4,
Sun. 1–4.*

Shopping

Malls and shopping strips line Routes 35 and 71. Recommended
shopping districts for boutiques, fashion clothing, and gift
items include Norwood Avenue in Deal, Main Street in Ocean
Grove, and 3rd Avenue in Spring Lake.

Several farmers' markets beckon along the highways and back
roads. **Delicious Orchards** has become a traditional stop for
those whose mouths water at the thought of ripe, juicy Jersey
beefsteak tomatoes, sweet Silverqueen corn, and fresh-
pressed apple cider. *Rte. 34, Colts Neck, tel. 908/542–0204.
Open Tues.–Sun. 10–6.*

You may also consider stopping at pick-your-own farms, where
you can go into fields and pluck the freshest berries, beans,
peaches, and other produce, for prices far below roadside farm
markets and commercial supermarkets. Call ahead to find out
what is in season. **Battleview Orchards** (RD 1, Wemrock Rd.,
Freehold, tel. 908/462–0756); **The Berry Farm** (Rte. 34, behind
Delicious Orchards, Colts Neck, tel. 908/583–0707); **Boyce Berry Farm** (Rte. 537, Clarksburg, tel. 609/259–9198); **Casola
Farms** (Rte. 34, Colts Neck, tel. 908/946–8885 or 908/946–
4286); **Crest Fruit Farm** (4 Thompsons Grove Rd., Freehold,
tel. 908/462–5669); **Eastmont Orchards** (Rte. 537, 1 mi north of
Rte. 34, Colts Neck, tel. 908/542–5404); **Laurino Farms** (773
Sycamore Ave., Tinton Falls, tel. 908/842–3470 or 908/842–
3125); **Lone Cedar Farm** (Jackson-Mills Rd., Freehold, tel. 908/
462–3072); **Menzel Bros.** (Rte. 34, Holmdel, tel. 908/946–3060
or 908/946–4135); **Shwahla Farm** (Fort Plains Rd., Howell, tel.
908/462–7587); **Slope Brook Farm** (¼ mi east of Rte. 34 on Rte.
537, Colts Neck, tel. 908/462–4285); **Stattels' Brookrest Farm**
(Rte. 520, Marlboro, tel. 908/946–9666); **Westhaven Farm** (Rte.
524, Allentown Clarksburg Rd., Allentown [Exit 11 on I–195],
tel. 609/259–2186).

Auctions and   Auctions can be great rainy-day shopping fun—you don't *have*
Flea Markets   to buy anything, and listening to the patter of the auctioneer is
a blast.

Collingwood Auction & Flea Market. *Rtes. 33 and 34, Howell,
tel. 908/938–7941. Open Fri. noon–10, Sat. 10–10, Sun. 10:30–
10.*

The Englishtown Auction, established in 1929, is one of the oldest in the state. *90 Wilson Ave., Englishtown, tel. 908/446–
9644. Open Sat. 7–5, Sun. 9–5.*

Howell Antique Village and Flea Market. *Rte. 9, Howell Township, tel. 908/367–1105. Open Fri. 11–10, weekends 9–6.*

Peddler's Village. *Rte. 35, Manasquan Circle, Wall Township,
tel. 908/223–2300. Open Fri. 10–10, Sat. 10–10, Sun. 11–7.*

Sports and Outdoor Activities

Participant Sports

Beaches Storms and tides have eroded some of Monmouth County's beaches. In the Highlands area, from Sandy Hook to just north of Long Branch, a strong seawall is all that stands between Shore homes and the sea. Elsewhere, beaches are in reasonably good condition. You must purchase a badge to use all beaches in Monmouth County except for Sandy Hook, which charges admission every day except Tuesday from Memorial Day to Labor Day. Monmouth County has the highest beach-use fees on the Jersey Shore.

Beach Information The **Monmouth County Beach Quality Hotline** (tel. 908/431–7456) supplies information about water quality and beach conditions in Monmouth County.

Asbury Park (tel. 908/775–0900).
Avon (tel. 908/774–0871).
Belmar (tel. 908/681–1176).
Bradley Beach (tel. 908/776–2999).
Deal (tel. 908/531–1454).
Highlands (tel. 908/872–1515).
Long Branch (tel. 908/222–0400).
Manasquan (tel. 908/223–0544).
Ocean Grove (tel. 908/775–0035).
Sandy Hook (tel. 908/872–0115).
Sea Bright (tel. 908/842–0215).
Sea Girt (tel. 908/449–9433).
Spring Lake (tel. 908/449–0800).

Bicycling Inexpensive rentals are available at the **Brielle Cyclery** (205 Union Ave. [Rte. 71], Brielle, tel. 908/528–9121) and at **DJ's Cycles** (15th and Main Sts., Belmar, tel. 908/681–8228). Regional cycling clubs: **Atlantic Bicycle Club** (c/o M. P. Whitfile, Box 94, Holmdel, tel. 908/671–6810 or tel. 908/528–7198), **Jersey Shore Touring Society** (Box 8581, Red Bank, tel. 908/747–8206).

Boating and Canoeing Monmouth County doesn't have as many opportunities for boating and canoeing as Ocean County, but the activity still is highly recommended. Canoeing and rowing instruction for the **disabled and handicapped** is available, by appointment, from the **Monmouth County Park System** (Newman Springs Rd., Lincroft, tel. 908/842–4000).

Boat Rentals **Skippers Landing** (52 Shrewsbury Ave., Highlands, tel. 908/291–1115), **Fisherman's Den** (Rte. 35, Belmar, tel. 908/681–6677), **Oceanic Marina** (8 Washington Ave., Rumson, tel. 908/842–1194).

Canoeing **Mohawk Canoe Livery & Recreation** (Squankum-Yellowbrook Rd., Farmingdale, tel. 908/938–7755); on Deal Lake, in Asbury Park, rent canoes in summer at **Sunset Landing Restaurant** (1215 Sunset Ave., tel. 908/776–9732).

Schools **New Horizons Sailing School** (1 1st St., Rumson, tel. 908/530–3237), **Red Witch Sailing Yachts Inc.** (Rte. 35, Lawrence Harbor, tel. 908/566–7733).

Waterskiing   **Shore Ski School** (1154 17th Ave., Belmar, tel. 908/681–2838).

Fishing   Monmouth County has more charter and party boats than any other area along the Shore. Most boat-rental companies are clustered in Brielle (site of the county's largest marina, the Brielle Marine Basin, tel. 908/528–6200), along Belmar's Shark River, Oceanport's Shrewsbury River, the Navesink around Monmouth Beach, and along the Raritan Bay shore from Highlands to Keyport.

Golf   The following courses are open to the public:

Allenwood   **Bel-Aire Golf Club** (Allaire Rd. and Rte. 34, tel. 908/449–6024).

Colts Neck   **Hominy Hill Golf Course** (Mercer Rd., tel. 908/462–9222).

Farmingdale   **Howell Park Golf Course** (Squankum-Yellowbrook Rd., tel. 908/938–4771), **Spring Meadow Golf Course** (R.R. 1, Box 396, tel. 908/449–0806).

Neptune   **Jumping Brook Golf Club** (Jumping Brook Rd., tel. 908/922–8200), **Shark River Golf Course** (Old Corlies Ave., tel. 908/922–4141).

Wannamassa   **Colonial Terrace Golf Club** (Wickapecko Dr., tel. 908/775–3636).

Health Clubs   **Ocean Fitness Center** (1602 Rte. 35S, Ocean Township, tel. 908/531–0058) offers admission to its facilities on a day-by-day basis.

Horseback Riding   Monmouth County is the Shore's equestrian capital, with several riding stables nestled among the rolling inland hills. In addition to trail rides arranged by those listed below, the **Monmouth County Parks System** (tel. 908/842–4000) sponsors occasional rides through Allaire State Park and other protected wildlife areas. For the handicapped and disabled: **Handicapped High Riders** (Box 2760, Rte. 526, Allentown, tel. 609/259–3884) and **Circle A Riding Stable** (667 Herbertsville Rd., Howell, tel. 908/938–2004).

Duchess Pines Ranch (Bowman Rd., Jackson, tel. 908/928–3131).

Muddy Creek Farm (568-A Ramtown-Greenville Rd., Howell, tel. 908/840–8977).

New Horses Around (Belmar Blvd., Farmingdale, tel. 908/938–4480).

Ouiet Season Stables (Vanderveer Rd., Howell, tel. 908/780–2675).

Tall Oaks Farm (Oak Glen Rd., Howell, tel. 908/938–5445).

Windward Farm (Baileys Corner Rd., Wall, tel. 908/449–6441).

Scuba Diving   **Diver's Cove** (Rte. 35, Lawrence Harbor, tel. 908/583–2717). **Diver's Two, Inc.** (1 Main St., Avon, tel. 908/776–7755). **Dosil's Sports Center** (261 Rte. 36, E. Keansburg, tel. 908/787–0508). **Professional Divers, Inc.** (70 Rte. 35, Neptune, tel. 908/775–8292).

Tennis   Memberships may be required at private racquet clubs.

Allaire Racquet Club (Rte. 38, Wall Township, tel. 908/681–3366).

Deal Casino Tennis Courts (Ocean Ave., Deal, tel. 908/531–0234).

Madison Indoor Tennis Club (Rte. 34, Matawan, tel. 908/583–1010).

Matawan Indoor Tennis Club (Line Rd., Aberdeen, tel. 908/566–5200).

Spectator Sports

Horse Racing **Monmouth Park** is the county's best-known horse-racing track. *Monmouth Park Hwy., Oceanport, tel. 908/222–5100. Open June–Sept. Mon.–Sat.*

Harness racing fall and winter at **Freehold Raceway** (Rte. 33, Freehold, tel. 908/462–3800).

Auto Racing Hot rods and bicycle motocross competitions at **Raceway Park** (Rte. 527, Englishtown, tel. 908/681–6370).

Auto racing at **Wall Stadium,** the county's oldest continuously operating asphalt track. *Rte. 34, Wall Township, tel. 908/681–6400. Open Apr.–Nov., Sat. nights.*

State and County Parks

Allaire Village State Park. A pleasant, 3,000-acre natural area built around a 17th-century ironworks village. Restored buildings and a small museum, nature trails, picnicking, camping, and a children's playground area are also available. *Rte. 524, between Farmingdale and Lakewood, tel. 908/938–2371. Parking fee charged in season, fee for camping. Free admission Tues.*

Monmouth Battlefield State Park. Molly Pitcher earned her place in American history books here. There's a small playground, too. The Craig House has historic displays and exhibits. *Rte. 33, Freehold, tel. 908/462–9616. Admission free.*

Sandy Hook. Part of the Gateway National Recreation Area, Sandy Hook includes America's oldest operating lighthouse (built in 1764), public beaches, gun emplacements, an old weapons range and military encampment, a nature center, changing rooms and showers, and a fabulous view of New York Harbor, only 6 miles away. The mix of history, wildlife, and military and historical architecture makes it well worth a visit, especially in the off-season, when admission is free. Free nature tours and programs are offered (reservations required). The nude beach overlooks New York Harbor. During the busy summer season, gates open at 7 AM; the park closes to vehicles after 10 AM or when parking areas fill up. *Off Rte. 36, Sandy Hook, tel. 908/872–0092. Admission: Memorial Day–Labor Day $4 per car weekdays, $5 holidays and weekends. Free admission Tues.*

Seven Presidents Oceanfront Park. This is a small landscaped beach area near Church of the Presidents. *Ocean Ave., Long Branch, tel. 908/842–4000. Admission free.*

Shark River Park (School House Rd., Neptune, tel. 908/922–3868). This is a small park with fishing pond, hiking/fitness trail, ball fields, picnic area.

Dining

Our list of Monmouth County restaurants was compiled with the assistance of Brooke Tarabour, restaurant columnist of the Asbury Park Press, *and J. M. Lang, food critic for* New Jersey Monthly.

Monmouth County has its share of good restaurants but suffers from a shortage of moderately priced family eateries and innovative Cape May–style bistros. For prices, consult the price chart in the Dining section of Chapter 1, Essential Information. Highly recommended restaurants are indicated with a star ★.

Expensive–Very Expensive

Brielle Yacht Club. Perfect for the blue blazer, white pants, and deck shoes set, this is the largest restaurant with a marina view in Monmouth County. The yacht club represents the elder elite of the county's sportfishing set, and the menu is solid surf-and-turf. *1 Ocean Ave., Brielle, tel. 908/528–7000. Reservations recommended. Dress: casual, but no shorts. Open daily for lunch and dinner. Entertainment Thurs.–Sun. evenings. AE, D, DC, MC, V.*

★ **Fromagerie.** This superb French restaurant with a thoroughly unpretentious approach to good food and wine is Monmouth County's best Continental restaurant. Though many of the entrées involve cheese, the menu is well-rounded, with seafood, meat, duck, and chicken amply represented. *26 Ridge Rd., Rumson, tel. 908/842–8008. Reservations recommended. Jacket required. AE, D, DC, MC, V. Open for dinner nightly, lunch on weekdays.*

Expensive

★ **Doris and Ed's.** This is a traditional, old-guard surf-and-turf house that does as good a job at seafood as anyone, anywhere. Fried dishes compete with traditional steamed and trendy grilled fare. The atmosphere is family casual. *36 Shore Dr., Highlands, tel. 908/872–1565. Reservations advised. Dress: neat but casual. Open Feb.–Dec., Tues.–Sat. dinner only. AE, MC, V.*

★ **Farmingdale House.** Genuine northern Italian cuisine that tastes as if Mama made it is served here in an elegant setting. The attention to detail and a tangible sense of perfectionism make this Monmouth County's best Italian restaurant, in a region overrun with them. *105 Academy St., Farmingdale, tel. 908/938–7951. Reservations advised. Jacket required. Handicapped access. AE, MC, V. Open Tues.–Sun. for dinner.*

The Little Kraut. Spicy sauerbraten, wiener schnitzel, bratwurst, roast goose, and potato pancakes are served at this zesty German restaurant. *115 Oakland St., Red Bank, tel. 908/ 842–4830. Reservations advised. Dress: casual. AE, D, DC, MC, V. Open daily for dinner, lunch on weekdays.*

Periwinkle's. A warm, busy, above-average bistro-style surf-and-turf house. *1070 Ocean Ave., Sea Bright, tel. 908/741–0041. Reservations advised. Dress: casual. AE, MC, V. Open Wed.–Mon. for dinner, Mon. and Wed.–Fri. for lunch. Closed Tues.*

Yankee Clipper. The ocean is just across the street, crashing just beyond the Sea Girt boardwalk. The upstairs restaurant offers surf-and-turf and Continental entrées. Downstairs is more moderately priced "California" fare: salads, burgers, seafood, and steaks. *Chicago Blvd. and Ocean Ave., Sea Girt, tel.*

908/449–7200. Reservations suggested for dinner and brunch. Dress: casual. AE, D, DC, MC, V. Open Tues.–Sat. for lunch and dinner. Sun. brunch.

Moderate–Expensive

Bahr's. A classic surf-and-turf house, this place is crammed with nautical knickknacks and offers a great view of Sandy Hook and the Shrewsberry River. Live entertainment is featured on Friday and Saturday night. *2 Bay Ave., Highlands, tel. 908/872–1245. Reservations suggested for dinner and brunch. Dress: casual. Handicapped access. AE, DC, MC, V. Lunch and dinner Mon.–Sat. and Sun. brunch.*

Moderate

Christie's. An Italian-American family restaurant, overlooking a golf course, with entertainment and valet parking. *1 English La., Wanamassa, tel. 908/776–8558. Reservations advised. Dress: casual. AE, DC, MC, V.*

Koh's Shanghai Wok. This is probably Monmouth County's best Chinese restaurant, and it serves Szechuan, Cantonese, and Hunan styles. *Rte. 35 and Deal Rd., Middlebrook Shopping Center, Ocean Township, tel. 908/493–8118. Reservations not necessary. Dress: casual. MC, V.*

Memphis Pig-Out. Luscious barbecued and grilled meat, fish, and chicken, in a variety of sauces, are offered at differing levels of spiciness. *67 1st Ave., Atlantic Highlands, tel. 908/431–7594. Reservations not necessary. Dress: casual. AE. Open Wed.–Sun. for dinner.*

★ **Taxco Village.** This is a genuine family-run Mexican restaurant that manages to serve food with a true south-of-the-border taste. The menu includes superb fajitas, mole, and cactus salad, as well as margaritas and traditional Tex-Mex fare. *4th and Kingsley Sts., Asbury Park, tel. 908/776–8100. Reservations not necessary. Dress: casual. Street parking. AE, MC, V. Open daily for lunch and dinner.*

Inexpensive

Casa Comida. Simple spicy Tex-Mex cuisine, with tacos, burritos, chili dishes, and mesquite grilled seafood. *336 Branchport Ave., Long Branch, tel. 908/229–7774. Reservations not necessary. Dress: casual. Handicapped access. AE. Open Tues.–Sun. for lunch and dinner.*

Cravings. This lusciously decadent dessert shop and bakery also serves tea, coffee, and juices. *310 Main St., Allenhurst, tel. 908/531–7122. Reservations not necessary. Dress: casual. Open Tues.–Sat. 7–5, Sun. 7:30–2. Closed Mon. No credit cards.*

Everybody's Cafe. A good place to hit when shopping, Everybody's is also worth a trip because of the diversity of the menu. The restaurant offers *global* cuisine, and the menu includes a changing array of Polish, Greek, Middle Eastern, African, Indian, French, Chinese, and Japanese dishes. *Sea Girt Mall, Rte. 35, Sea Girt, tel. 908/223–0235. Reservations not necessary. Dress: casual. Handicapped access. AE. Open daily for lunch and dinner.*

★ **Harrigan's Pub.** A warm tavern that serves enormous portions of freshly prepared steaks, chops, chicken, and seafood at prices so low you'll want to keep the place a secret. The steak sandwich is superb. Harrigan's gets a lively, sports-oriented crowd, a good mix of natives and characters. *Rte. 71, Sea Girt, tel. 908/449–8228. Reservations not necessary. Dress: casual. AE, MC, V. Free parking. Open daily for lunch and dinner.*

The Inn Place. A modest but hearty restaurant serving traditional American fare, with some seafood and Continental items. *68 Main St., Ocean Grove, tel. 908/774–0013. Reservations advised. Dress: casual. AE, MC, V. Open daily for breakfast, lunch, and dinner.*

Raspberry Cafe. A bright, cheery cafe designed for grandparents with grandchildren who want something sweet. Smoothies, fresh waffles, fresh juices, sandwiches, salads, and light entrées are served. *60 Main St., Ocean Grove, tel. 908/988–0833. Reservations not necessary. Dress: casual. No credit cards. Open daily for breakfast, lunch, and dinner.*

Lodging

Lovers of old, creaky hotels and bed-and-breakfast properties will be surprised to find that Monmouth County offers a range of these accommodations at rates much lower than Victorian Cape May's. Room rates used to rank accommodations are for the peak summer season, June through August. The prices below are for a standard double room. Rates for suites and rooms with ocean views can increase the rate. Rates drop significantly in the cooler "shoulder" seasons of spring and autumn and are lowest of all in winter. Ask for weekend and midweek package rates, which also offer savings.

All rooms in hotels and motels have a private bath, unless noted. Many small hotels, guest houses, and bed-and-breakfasts have shared baths. Children can stay with an adult at the single room rate where indicated. There are few acceptable accommodations in the inexpensive category during the summer season.

For prices, consult the price chart in the Lodging section of Chapter 1, Essential Information. Highly recommended properties are indicated with a star ★.

Asbury Park

Expensive–Very Expensive ★ **Berkeley-Carteret.** This excellent restoration of Asbury Park's grandest hotel, one of the few remaining stone and brick hotels from the Shore's 1920s' building period, is intended to revitalize the city. The hotel overlooks the boardwalk and is also the site of American Radio Museum, which displays memorabilia, photographs, and recordings from the Golden Age of radio to the present. Country singer Johnny Cash maintains an apartment in one of the wings. *1401 Sunset Ave., Asbury Park 07712, tel. 908/776–6700, 800/524–1423 (outside NJ), or 800/445–0126 (inside NJ); fax 908/776–9546. 254 rooms, 25 suites. Facilities: restaurant, bar, cable TV, heated pool, convention facilities, free crib, concierge, barber and beauty shop, shopping arcade, tennis and golf privileges, game room, valet parking. Weekly, monthly rates. Children under 12 free. Free transportation from local bus and railroad station. AE, D, DC, MC, V.*

Moderate   **Deal Lake Motel.** This is a 1950s-style motel in the nicest part of Asbury Park, north of the downtown area across from Deal Lake, one block from the boardwalk. All rooms have efficiency kitchens and balconies. *Kingsley St. and 8th Ave., Asbury Park 07712, tel. 908/775–7070. 37 rooms. Facilities: air-conditioning, restaurant, snack bar, outdoor pool. AE, MC, V.*

Inexpensive   **Hermitage Guest House.** Asbury Park's only bed-and-breakfast is a simple, functional affair. Nothing's fancy, but nothing's pretentious, either. Two blocks from the beach, the Hermitage caters to families on a budget. Innkeepers Philip and Sylvia Poprocki accept children of all ages and provide cribs and toys for youngsters to enjoy. *309 1st Ave., Asbury Park 07712, tel. 908/776–6665. 8 rooms, with 2 shared baths; apartment has private bath and full kitchen. Street parking. Continental breakfast. Beach tags provided. Two-night minimum stay. Open May 15–Oct. 21. No credit cards.*

Avon-by-the-Sea

Moderate–Expensive ★   **Cashelmara Inn.** This deceptively small gabled house with a proud, Greek Revival porch faces Sylvan Lake on the Ocean Avenue beach block. Stuffed with antiques, Oriental rugs, and period furnishings, it's considered to be Avon's best B&B. A hot breakfast is served on the veranda when the weather permits. *22 Lakeside Ave., Avon-by-the-Sea 07717, tel. 908/776–8727. 14 rooms, all with private baths. Facilities: air-conditioning. Afternoon tea. AE, MC, V.*

Belmar

Moderate   **The Seaflower.** Belmar's only B&B—situated about a half block from the beach and boardwalk—is a Dutch Colonial with mixed antiques, seashore bric-a-brac, and a superb hot breakfast of breads, quiches, omelets, and fruit. One room has an ocean view; all rooms have fans. *110 9th Ave., Belmar 07719, tel. 908/681–6006. 7 rooms, 5 with private baths. No smoking. Full breakfast. Facilities: off-street parking; beach badges available.*

Moderate–Expensive ★   **Hollycroft.** Extraordinary for its unique "craftsman" architecture, Hollycroft's heavy log beams and brooding fieldstone fireplace suggest the mood of a rustic Adirondack ski chalet. Set back on a bluff above Lake Como, which separates Belmar from Spring Lake, the inn has a breezy, informal "mountain" atmosphere, though private houses lurk a little too close. Rooms are furnished with English country antiques. The inn's one suite has a large sitting room; four of the rooms are air-conditioned. Innkeepers Linda and Mark Fessler stage mystery weekends and a Christmas festival in the off-season. *506 North Blvd., South Belmar 07719, tel. 908/681–2254. 6 rooms with private bath. Continental breakfast. Facilities: off-street parking, beach towels provided. 2-night minimum stay summer weekends, 3 nights holiday weekends. No smoking in guest rooms. AE.*

Long Branch

Very Expensive ★   **Ocean Place Hilton Resort and Spa.** Opened in August 1990, this Hilton on Long Branch's boardwalk is the Shore's newest resort hotel. Local developers are hoping that this complex—both a conference center and legitimate health spa—will help revitalize the town. Rooms, which are decorated in modern pastels, have balconies, twin telephones, data ports, and ocean views. Free transportation from Long Branch train station is provided to guests. *1 Ocean Blvd., Long Branch 07740, tel. 908/ 571–4000 or 800/HILTONS; fax 908/571–3314. 255 rooms, 5 suites. Facilities: gourmet restaurant, seafood restaurant, coffee shop, poolside lounge, piano bar, disco; nonsmoking floors; health spa including exercise machines, indoor pool, whirlpool, steam room, saunas, therapy rooms, wrap room; separate spa menu and spa package plan; 33,000 sq. ft. of meeting and convention space; garage parking; free use of beach tags, towels, and chairs. 3-night minimum stay on summer weekends. AE, D, DC, MC, V.*

Moderate   **Fountains Motel.** This used to be Long Branch's only beachfront motel. It's still a reasonable alternative for those who don't want a facility as expensive or as elaborate as the Ocean Place Hilton. The upstairs rooms have the best ocean views. *160 Ocean Ave., Long Branch 07740, tel. 908/222–7200. 116 rooms. Facilities: cable TV, pool. AE, MC, V.*

Ocean Grove

Very Expensive   **Shawmont Hotel.** A quaint, rambling Victorian with porches, terraces, and beach views in straight-laced Ocean Grove. All rooms have private baths; many have private terraces and balconies. *17 Ocean Ave., Ocean Grove 07756, tel. 908/776–6985. Closed Nov.–Apr. AE, MC, V.*

Moderate   **Keswick Inn.** This bed-and-breakfast offers simple, plain furnishings at affordable rates. Guest rooms have ceiling fans. *32 Embury Ave., Ocean Grove 07756, tel. 908/775–7506. 21 rooms, with 5 shared baths. Continental breakfast. Facilities: bicycle rental on premises, beach badges available at reduced rate. AE, MC.*
Sampler Inn. In the heart of Ocean Grove, right on Main Avenue, this inn is plain but convenient. The dining room serves wholesome American fare. *28 Main Ave., Ocean Grove 07756, tel. 908/775–1905. 34 rooms. Facilities: dining room. No credit cards. Closed Oct.–Apr.*

Neptune

Moderate   **Howard Johnson.** *Rte. 35 at Asbury Park Circle, Neptune 07753, tel. 908/776–9000. 60 rooms. Facilities: pool, bar, free crib, cable TV with in-room movies. Children under 18 free. AE, DC, MC, V.*

Red Bank

Very Expensive   **Oyster Point Hotel.** One of the best first-class small hotels on
★   the Shore, the Oyster Point overlooks the Navesink River and is a short drive from the beach resort areas. The many nice touches include a TV in the bathroom and free in-room movies. *146 Bodman Pl., Red Bank 07701, tel. 908/530–8200 or 800/ 345–4584. 60 rooms. Facilities: air-conditioning, restaurant, coffee shop, lounge, spa with whirlpool and exercise machines. AE, DC, MC, V.*

Moderate **Molly Pitcher Inn.** Some rooms in this 1928 Greek Revival downtown hotel overlook the Navesink River. *88 Riverside Ave., Red Bank 07701, tel. 908/747–2500 or 800/441–0156. 106 rooms, 5 suites. Facilities: 2 restaurants, lounge, pool, air-conditioning, child-care assistance available; facilities for the handicapped. AE, DC, MC, V.*

Spring Lake

Very Expensive **The Chateau.** Very convenient to the Spring Lake railroad station, the Chateau's rambling complex of rooms is four blocks from the beach, across from the municipal park with tennis courts and a children's playground. The hotel is perfect for families. Rooms are named after some of the hotel's more famous guests—Buster Keaton, Basil Rathbone, Arthur Treacher. Furnishings are reproductions and wicker. Some suites have large tubs, private balconies, kitchens, VCRs, wet bars, and parlors. *5th and Warren Aves., Spring Lake 07762, tel. 908/974–2000; fax ext. 137. 40 rooms, 6 suites, all with private baths. Facilities: air-conditioning, cable TV, in-room movies, on- and off-site parking, bicycle rental on premises. Free beach tags, tennis passes, and trolley fares for guests. 3-night minimum stay in summer season. Afternoon tea. AE, MC, V.*

Hewitt-Wellington. Located across from the lake for which Spring Lake is named, the Hewitt-Wellington is a business-oriented condo hotel with solid furnishings and marble bathrooms. The complimentary Continental breakfast is served in the adjacent restaurant, but the atmosphere is more that of an urban luxury hotel than a private house. *20 Monmouth Ave., Spring Lake 07762, tel. 908/449–8220. 29 rooms, some with private porches; 17 suites. Facilities: restaurant, heated outdoor pool open in summer season, free beach tags and towels for guests. AE, MC, V.*

Expensive **Ashling Cottage.** This wonderfully relaxed cottage is adjacent to the Colonial Hotel, one block from the beach. The atmosphere is immediately easygoing, and innkeepers Goodi and Jack Stewart are experts at down-to-earth informality. Rooms are furnished in mixed antiques; one room has a private porch. Games are available to help guests while away the evening hours. *106 Sussex Ave., Spring Lake 07762, tel. 908/449–3553. 10 rooms, 8 with private bath; 1 room with private porch. Continental breakfast. AE, MC, V. Closed Jan.–Mar. 3-night minimum stay July and Aug. weekends, 2-night minimum on other weekends.*

The Breakers. One of Spring Lake's old beachfront hotels has gone the luxury route, recapturing a little of the breezy, front-porch rocking-chair atmosphere. This is a popular place for weddings. *1507 Ocean Ave., Spring Lake 07762, tel. 908/449–7700. 65 rooms with private bath. Facilities: restaurant, cable TV, whirlpool, air-conditioning. AE, DC, MC, V.*

★ **Normandy Inn.** A huge, eclectic inn with bizarre Queen Anne touches, the Normandy provides a textbook study in period High Victorian furnishings. Originally a private house, it became an inn in 1910; it still has beautiful heavy wood bedroom sets, an airy parlor, and a spacious dining room. Innkeepers Susan and Michael Ingino have taken the greatest care to ensure that all furnishings and ornamentation are true to period style. Guests who stay in the turret room use a tiny chamber bathroom with a bright cupola one flight down (bathrobes are provided). *21 Tuttle Ave., Spring Lake 07762, tel. 908/449–7172. 17 rooms and a 2-bedroom carriage house, all with private bath. Full hot breakfast. Facilities: on- and off-site parking, use of bicycles, air-conditioning. 2- to 4-night minimum stay. AE, MC, V.*

★ **Sea Crest by the Sea.** This whimsical, cheery Queen Anne–style B&B seeks to be just a little different from the pack. Innkeepers John and Carol Kirby have furnished the rooms along colorful, fantasy themes, reflecting characters and motifs from fairy tales, history, literature, and such exotic realms as Casablanca and New Orleans. Some of the rooms have ocean views. Chocolates at bedtime, turndown service, afternoon player piano recitals, and other amenities make this a first-class inn. *19 Tuttle Ave., Spring Lake 07762, tel. 908/469–9031. 12 rooms, all with private baths. Continental breakfast, afternoon tea. Facilities: off-street parking, air-conditioning, use of bicycles, beach tags, and towels. 2-night minimum stay, 3-night minimum holiday weekends. Smoking on porch only. MC, V.*

Warren Hotel. This gabled Queen Anne hotel on the Spring Lake beach block has an air of old-fashioned resort formality. *901 Ocean Ave., Spring Lake 07762, tel. 908/449–8800 or 908/449–8730. 200 rooms, some with shared bath. Facilities: restaurant, lounge, pool, tennis court, putting green, free parking. Babysitters available. Closed Dec.–mid-May. AE, D, DC, MC, V.*

Moderate– Expensive

Stone Post Inn. A gracious rooming house surrounded by lush trees and gardens, the Stone Post is a block from the beach. The rooms are clean and bright; all are decorated with mixed antiques, wicker, and reproductions. Guests can use the upstairs TV lounge, guest kitchen, and refrigerator. *115 Washington Ave., Spring Lake 07762, tel. 908/449–1212. 20 rooms, 8 with private bath. Continental breakfast. Facilities: piano, use of beach tags and towels for guests staying at least one week, off-street parking. 2-night minimum stay weekends, 3 nights holiday weekends. AE, MC, V.*

Victoria House. This cozy little house is situated on a quiet residential street 2½ blocks from the beach. The stained-glass windows are original to the house. Furnishings are older reproductions; not all are antiques. *214 Monmouth Ave., Spring Lake 07762, tel. 908/974–1882. 10 rooms, 2 with private bath, 8 with shared bath. Continental breakfast. Facilities: air-conditioning, piano, crib, beach tags. AE, MC, V.*

Moderate

The Carriage House. This is a pleasant private house on a quiet residential street. The rates are very reasonable for Spring Lake. *208 Jersey Ave., Spring Lake 07762, tel. 908/449–1332. 8 rooms, 6 with private bath, and a 1-bedroom apartment. Continental breakfast. Facilities: use of beach tags and towels, off-street parking. 3-night minimum stay on holiday weekends. No credit cards.*

The Colonial. This well-preserved 19th-century hotel—a real bargain in Spring Lake—has louvered doors, high ceilings, and tall windows to catch the ocean breezes. The decor is plain and clean. *1st and Sussex Aves., Spring Lake 07762, tel. 908/449–9090. 44 rooms, 15 with private bath. Continental breakfast. Facilities: some off-street parking, beach tags at reduced rates. MC, V. Closed Sept. 6–May 24.*

Camping

Pine Cone Campground (480 Georgia Rd., west end of West Farms Rd., Freehold 07728, tel. 908/462–2230).

The Arts and Nightlife

The Arts

Concerts **Count Basie Theater** (99 Monmouth St., Red Bank, tel. 908/842–9002). This restored vaudeville theater, where Count Basie got his start, now mounts concerts and theatrical presentations.

Garden State Arts Center. (Garden State Pkwy. Exit 116, Holmdel, tel. 908/442–9200). Built with revenues from Garden State Parkway tolls, the Garden State Arts Center presents a diverse array of entertainment throughout the year, ranging from classical concerts to ethnic heritage shows. Many singers and comedians who play the Atlantic City casino showrooms also perform here, usually a month or so before or after their Atlantic City appearances. Tickets for Arts Center shows are always priced lower than Atlantic City. Sightlines are uniformly good.

Monmouth County Parks concert series (tel. 908/842–4000). Free or low-priced evening concerts are presented in various parks within the county park system, June–August.

Ocean Grove Great Auditorium (Auditorium Sq., Ocean Grove, tel. 908/775–0035). It's worth attending a concert here just to marvel at this wonderful wood hall, originally constructed entirely without nails or any other kind of metal. Concerts range from inspirational religious groups to classical music recitals.

Theater **Spring Lake Theater Company** (Community House Theater, 3rd and Madison Aves., tel. 908/449–4530). Original and repertory productions are presented here.

Movies **Aberdeen:** Strathmore Twin Cinema 1 & 2 (Rte. 34, tel. 908/583–4141).

Atlantic Highlands: Atlantic Twin (82 1st Ave., tel. 908/291–0148).

Bradley Beach: Beach Cinema (110 Main St., tel. 908/774–9089).

Eatontown: Eatontown Community Theatre 1 & 2 (Rte. 36, tel. 908/542–4200).

Freehold: Freehold Cinema 4 (Rte. 9 and Pond Rd., tel. 908/780–4436); Freehold Cinema 6 (Rte. 9N, tel. 908/462–0600).

Howell: Howell Cinema Centre 4 (Rte. 9S, tel. 908/364–4544).

Long Branch: Long Branch Movies 1 & 2 (Ocean Ave., West End, tel. 908/870–2700).

Middletown: UA Middletown Theatre (Rte. 35 and Palmer Ave., tel. 908/671–1020).

Ocean Township: Middlebrook Twin (Middlebrook Shopping Center, tel. 908/493–2277); Seaview Square Cinema 1 & 2 (Rtes. 66 and 35, tel. 908/775–8810).

Red Bank: Red Bank Movies 1 & 2 (36 White St., tel. 908/747–0333).

Shrewsbury: Shrewsbury Plaza Cinema 1, 2 & 3 (Shrewsbury Ave. and Broad St., tel. 908/542–5395).

Nightlife

Nightclubs and Bars

Casablanca (309 Fisk Ave., Brielle, tel. 908/528–6466). Summertime makes this a prime social site among the sons and daughters of Brielle's yachting crowd. DJ Top-40 music.

Cafe Bar (115 Ocean Ave., Long Branch, tel. 908/229–9725). A better-than-average yuppie disco, this spot features "classic rock," DJ music, and a spacious dance floor. The bar offers a good view of the beach and Long Branch boardwalk.

Columns by the Sea (601 Ocean Ave., Avon, tel. 908/988–3213). This is a superb retreat for those whose idea of happiness is a cold drink, a shady porch, and a great view of the beach.

Legget's Sand Bar (217 1st Ave., Manasquan, tel. 908/223–3951). Here's an easygoing "barefoot" bar—wear anything more than a T-shirt and swimsuit and you're overdressed.

Green Parrot (Rte. 33, Neptune, tel. 908/775–1991). Better-than-average rock, new wave, and reggae is played here Wednesday–Saturday.

Jason's (1604 F St., South Belmar, tel. 908/681–9782). A genuine jazz club, Jason's presents live music nightly beginning at 9:30, from mid-June through August.

Rod's Olde Irish Tavern (507 Washington Blvd., Sea Girt, tel. 908/449–2020). This is an Irish bar for all occasions, for serious drinking, great barside stories, and fishermen's lies.

The Stadium (Plaza Blvd., Sea Girt, tel. 908/449–1444). This monster sports bar offers TV sets and occasional live entertainment.

The Stone Pony (913 Ocean Ave., Asbury Park, tel. 908/988–1777). The most famous rock-and-roll club on the Jersey Shore, the Pony may not be around for many more years. Fans of Bruce Springsteen, Southside Johnny Lyon, Clarence "Big Man" Clemons, and Miami Steve Van Zandt make dutiful pilgrimages, though the club's glory days as the most exciting live music club have passed. Live bands perform several nights each week May–August.

Tsunami (160 Ocean Ave., Long Branch, tel. 908/870–9292). This dressy yuppie megabar has a large dance floor. T-shirts, shorts, sandals, and tank tops are discouraged.

T-Bird's (Main St. and Asbury Ave., Asbury Park, tel. 908/502–0072). A stark, almost grim, urban rock club, T-Bird's books touring bands close to the cutting edge of live Shore music. A moderately priced restaurant menu is available, too.

Warren Lounge (901 Ocean Ave., Spring Lake, tel. 908/449–8800 or 908/449–8730). This old folks' hangout is so enjoyable that youngsters might want to fake the years. Dixieland bands, piano sing-alongs, big band swing, and breezy vocalists perform mid-May–November, Thursday–Saturday.

Werx (Sumner Ave. at the Boulevard, Seaside Heights, tel. 908/830–3555). A Shore rarity, here's a nightclub that promotes listening to music, not dancing or ignoring it. The bleacher seating is a little rude, but the quality of the bands, which range from progressive jazz to urban folk, help you forget.

4 Ocean County

Introduction

Ocean County's seaside resorts fall into three distinct areas. The first, beginning in the north at Point Pleasant and Bay Head, continues south along the narrow Barnegat Peninsula, ending at Island Beach State Park. The second, resuming across the Barnegat inlet, is Long Beach Island. Both of these islands were once a series of broken barrier islands that were filled in and linked in the late 19th century. The third resort, the coast of the mainland, has smaller villages, retirement housing, and numerous shopping areas.

Roughly equidistant from New York and Philadelphia, the islands fill in summer with vacationing families from both metropolitan areas. The more affluent own or rent houses for the season; others occupy motels and guest houses. The Shore towns have been overbuilt and the crowded conditions make car travel tedious and time-consuming during the summer season. More than any other region of the Jersey Shore, Ocean County is profoundly seasonal, with restaurants, shops, motels, and other services doing most of their business between Memorial Day and Labor Day.

Behind the barrier islands of Ocean County is the largest, broadest bay on the Shore: Barnegat Bay, the capital of the Shore's pleasure-boating enthusiasts, where people come to sail, row, powerboat, waterski, and jet-ski. On bright, breezy afternoons, Barnegat Bay becomes a moving landscape of brightly colored sails.

The bays and shoals so important to Ocean County have brought vicious storms. Both the Barnegat Peninsula and Long Beach Island were once wider, rounder, and the site of many huge 19th-century cedarwood hotels. Fires and a series of devastating northeasters destroyed many of them, and today only one, the Harvey Cedars Bible Conference Center on Long Beach Island, remains.

Storms trimmed so much from the islands that in some areas, they are less than 100 yards wide. A storm in 1962 squashed much of the Cape May and Atlantic County Shore towns and flattened hundreds of Shore vacation homes. The damage is still visible, not as wreckage, but in entire communities of garishly modern, geometric industrial-style mansions that more closely resemble spaceships than homes. Some of these are interesting period pieces, but crammed together on narrow parcels in the towns of Normandy Beach and Loveladies, they appear out of place.

When a Philadelphia newspaperman visited the island of Tucker's Beach in the late 18th century, he found dense, bramble-choked dunes that hid mysterious coves. Great stretches of cedar forests covered the higher ground. The region's few inhabitants lived in sandy caves walled in with cedar logs or in lean-tos covering hollows in the dunes. These crude habitations held a surprising array of goods: silver, gold, intricately carved woodwork, casks of French wines, and spices from the Far East. When he inquired about the origins of these treasures, the reporter was told that it was flotsam discharged from ships that "accidentally" ran aground and broke up on the shoals offshore.

Historically minded inhabitants of Ocean County say that tales of the wreckers are exaggerated, and that few inhabitants of these barrier islands were engaged in piracy. Fishing and whaling kept the early settlers alive, they claim. Still, tales of pirates and wreckers persist. The shoals off Ocean County were notorious for shipwrecks during the days when sailing ships plied the coastal trade route between the American colonies and the rum-producing islands of the Carribean. The wreckers lured ships to shore by hanging a lantern on a cow or horse and walking the animal along the dunes. Believing that this lantern was that of another ship between his ship and the shore, the captain might steer closer toward land, consequently running aground. The wreckers merely stood on the shore and waited for the waves to break up the ships and wash the booty in. The fate of the few humans who managed to survive the treacherous surf and wade to shore is not known, though some are believed to have become settlers in the Pine Barrens.

On what is now Long Beach Island, the wreckers were known as mooncussers, because they cursed cold, clear, moonlit nights when ship captains could train their telescopes on the land, spy the clumsy ruse, and steer clear of land. Somewhere on the island, the ghostly image of a sobbing woman is said to appear over the dunes on moonless nights. As the story goes, her lover, a local fisherman who engaged in occasional mooncussing, was captured offshore by the British during the Revolutionary War and drafted as a sailor aboard British merchant ships. In the dead of winter, on an appropriately cold, foggy Long Beach Island night, the woman and her father hung a lantern from a horse and lured a ship toward land. When the ship broke up and the cargo washed ashore, the woman found her lover among the bodies frozen to death in the chilling surf.

To this day, the roaring, tumbling "smasher" waves of Barnegat Peninsula and Long Beach Island are popular with surfers. The beaches are frequented by modern-day treasure hunters, who sweep the sands with metal detectors in the hope of finding old coins, keys—anything of metal that may have washed in.

Essential Information

Important Addresses and Numbers

Tourist Information **Barnegat Chamber of Commerce** (Box 362, Barnegat 08005, tel. 609/698–7170).
Brick Township Chamber of Commerce (1673 Rte. 88W, Brick Township 08724, tel. 908/458–8341).
Lakewood Chamber of Commerce (300 Main St., Box 656, Lakewood 08701, tel. 908/363–0012).
Long Beach Island (Southern Ocean County) Chamber of Commerce (265 W. 9th St., Ship Bottom 08008, tel. 609/494–7211 or 800/292–6372).
Greater Point Pleasant Chamber of Commerce (517A Arnold Ave., Point Pleasant Beach 08742, tel. 908/899–2424).
Seaside Heights Chamber of Commerce (Municipal Bldg., Box 38-R, Seaside Heights 08251, tel. 908/793–9100).
Toms River Chamber of Commerce (611 Main St., Toms River 08753, tel. 908/349–0220).

Emergencies
Medical

Point Pleasant: Medical Center of Ocean County (Osbourne Ave. and Riverfront, tel. 908/892–1100).

Toms River: Community Memorial (Rte. 37W, tel. 908/240–8000).

Lakewood: Kimball Medical Center (600 River Ave., tel. 908/363–1900).

Long Beach Island: Southern Ocean County Hospital (1140 W. Bay Ave., Manahawkin, tel. 609/597–6011).

Police and Fire

Barnegat Township (tel. 609/698–5000).

Bass River Township (tel. 609/296–2031).

Beach Haven (tel. 609/492–0505).

Berkeley Township (Bayville) (tel. 908/341–6600).

Dover Township (tel. 609/349–0150).

Eagleswood Township (West Creek) (tel. 609/296–3131).

Harvey Cedars (tel. 609/494–6509).

Little Egg Harbor Township (tel. 609/296–3666).

Lacey Township: Forked River, Lanoka Harbor, Bamber Lakes (tel. 609/693–6636).

Long Beach Township (Barnegat Light Borough) (tel. 609/494–3322).

Ocean Township: Waretown (tel. 609/693–4007).

Ship Bottom (tel. 609/494–3055).

Surf City (tel. 609/494–8121).

Stafford Township: Manahawkin, Cedar Run, Mayetta, Ocean Acres (tel. 609/597–8581).

Tuckerton (tel. 609/296–9416).

Coast Guard

Barnegat (tel. 609/494–2661).

Beach Haven (tel. 609/492–5751).

Marine Police Tel. 908/889–5050.

State Police Tel. 908/349–2596.

Publications The *Atlantic City Press,* a daily newspaper, has a zoned edition for Long Beach Island and some sections of Ocean County. The *Asbury Park Press* also covers the county, as does the *Ocean County Observer,* which is published in Toms River. Weekly papers include *The Beacon* and *Beach Haven Times* in Long Beach Island, *The Journal,* and *Ocean County Reporter.*

Arriving and Departing

By Car
From New York

The **Garden State Parkway,** a toll road, is the most convenient north–south highway. Expect summertime bottlenecks around tollbooths and along access roads leading to the island resorts on weekends. Travel time from New York City is about 1½–2 hours.

From Trenton and Philadelphia

Two limited-access highways, **I–195** and the **Atlantic City Expressway,** connect Trenton and Philadelphia to the Garden State Parkway. I–195 is preferred for Barnegat Peninsula destinations, the Atlantic City Expressway for Long Beach Island. Travel time is about 1½ hours.

You can reach Point Pleasant and Barnegat Peninsula resorts by leaving the parkway at Exit 98 (Belmar) and taking **Route 34** south. Exit 90 (Bricktown) links with **Route 88,** which also goes to Point Pleasant. The smaller, somewhat busier county **Route 528,** accessible at Exit 88 (Cedar Bridge), skirts the southern bank of the Metedeconk River, just below Point Pleasant, and connects to the Barnegat Peninsula at Mantolocking. Farther south, the towns of Seaside Heights, Ortley Beach, and Lavalette on Barnegat Peninsula are reached by the **Route 37** causeway (Parkway Exit 82) through Toms River. The only access to Long Beach Island is the Route 72 causeway (Parkway Exit 63).

The slower **Route 70,** an east–west road beginning in Camden, New Jersey (across the Delaware River from Philadelphia), is satisfactory for off-peak driving only. From Philadelphia and southern New Jersey, take Route 70 east directly to Point Pleasant (it links with Route 88 in Laurelton, just about 4 miles west of the beach). To reach southern Barnegat Peninsula, exit Route 70 at the traffic circle intersection with Route 37 east, which rolls through Toms River and ends at Seaside Heights. To reach Long Beach Island, take Route 70 east to the traffic circle intersection of Route 72 east, which cuts through the Pine Barrens to Manahawkin and, finally the Long Beach Island town of Ship Bottom. **Route 9,** which parallels the Garden State Parkway, links mainland resort towns. Travel time is 1¼–2 hours, depending on traffic conditions.

By Train **New Jersey Transit** provides daily commuter rail service to Point Pleasant from New York's Pennsylvania Station, seasonal service down the Barnegat Peninsula to Seaside Heights. Call 800/722–2222 in northern New Jersey, 800/582–5946 in southern New Jersey, 908/762–5100 from New York for information.

By Bus **New Jersey Transit** buses run up and down the Barnegat Peninsula, though some routes run only during the season. Buses also connect the mainland towns along Route 9. Commuters on Barnegat Peninsula may consider driving to the Park/Ride Bus Terminal, Highland Parkway South, Toms River (tel. 609/349–1313), for bus service to New York. The **Monmouth Bus Co.** (tel. 908/774–7780) links Point Pleasant Beach to Monmouth County resort towns.

There is no bus service to Long Beach Island. Bus passengers can take New Jersey Transit to Atlantic City, take the No. 109 local bus from Atlantic City to Manahawkin, and then call a taxi.

Ocean County Handicapped/Elderly Transportation Service (tel. 908/929–2082).

Getting Around

By Car A car is a necessity in the Ocean County beach resort towns. The causeways suffer terrific traffic jams during the summer season, especially Friday, Saturday, and Sunday afternoons.

On Barnegat Peninsula, Route 35 splits into a broad southbound and northbound street from Normandy Beach to Seaside

Park. "The Boulevard," as the long road running up and down Long Beach Island is called, incorporates a third, shared "suicide" lane in some areas, used for making left turns. Expect heavy traffic during the summer season.

By Taxi If you're without a car, the most reliable, and fastest, way to get around the Ocean County beach communities is to use one of the following taxi services.

Point Pleasant **Briggs Transportation Service** (tel. 908/892–0465).

Toms River **A Amber Taxi** (tel. 609/341–3388); **A American Taxi** (tel. 609/ 269–9000); **Caddy Cab Express** (tel. 609/698–7877); **Monnie's Yellow Cab** (Seaside Heights, tel. 908/793–0358); **Triple S Limousine Service** (Brick Township, tel. 908/920–9266).

Long Beach Island and Manahawkin **ABC Livery & Limousine** (Ship Bottom, tel. 609/361–0293); **G's Taxi** (tel. 609/597–6706); **Express Taxi & Limo** (tel. 609/597–5106).

By Trolley Long Beach Island's **Jolly Trolley** (tel. 609/494–4183) travels Long Beach Island Boulevard during the summer season daily except Wednesday morning. The trolley takes about two hours to complete its 18-mile circuit between Barnegat Light and Beach Haven. The fare is $1.

Guided Tours

Special-Interest Sightseeing Cruises The *River Belle* offers lunch, afternoon, and dinner sightseeing cruises on a Mississippi paddle-wheel-style boat. A moderately priced buffet is included in the price of some sailings, and evening cruises have live entertainment. *Broadway Basin, 47 Broadway, Point Pleasant Beach, tel. 908/892–3377. Departures daily July 1–Labor Day; Sunday brunch cruises Easter–Nov. Cost: $8.50–$35. No credit cards.*

Casino Cruises To visit Atlantic City from Ocean County, consider going by boat instead of bus or car. The *Black Whale* charter boat runs trips May–October daily to Atlantic City's marina casinos. Boats depart from the docks at Centre Street and the Bay, Beach Haven, with live entertainment and refreshments on board. The trip takes approximately 2½ hours each way, with six hours' free time at a casino. Passengers must be at least 21 years old and usually receive coin bonuses and discount coupons on casino entertainment, food, and beverages upon arrival. There is no obligation to gamble. Free parking at the dock. Call for fees and schedules: tel. 609/492–0202 or 609/492–0333.

Trolley Tours The **Long Beach Historical Society** runs weekly trolley tours of the historic district of Beach Haven and other areas on the island in the summer season. Tours cost $10 and depart Wednesday at 9 AM from the Chamber of Commerce building on the Route 72 causeway in Ship Bottom. For information, call 609/494–6828.

Exploring Ocean County

Similar sounding names make Ocean County locations confusing. Barnegat Light, a pricey, rustic borough on the northern end of Long Beach Island, is easily mistaken for Barnegat, a township on the Ocean County mainland. Beach Haven Crest, Beach Haven Park, Beach Haven Terrace, Beach Haven Gardens, Beach Haven Heights, and North Beach Haven are all little bits of Beach Haven on Long Beach Island; Beach Haven West is on the mainland. Manahawkin, on the mainland opposite Long Beach Island, is often confused with Mantolocking, on Island Beach. To ease this confusion, we've divided our listings in three areas: Barnegat Peninsula, from Point Pleasant to Island Beach State Park; Long Beach Island; and the mainland.

Numbers in the margin correspond with points of interest on the Ocean County map.

❶ Across narrow Barnegat Inlet is Long Beach Island and **Barnegat Lighthouse,** the most scenic on the Shore. Known on Long Beach Island as "Old Barney," the lighthouse was designed and completed by General George Meade in 1858. The red-and-white tower is 167 feet tall and occupies most of **Barnegat Light State Park** on the northern end of the island. At press time the lighthouse was closed for repairs, but it is expected to open in 1991. *Tel. 609/494–2016. Admission: 75¢. Open year-round dawn to dusk.*

While you're visiting the lighthouse, stop by the **Barnegat Light Museum.** The small, one-room schoolhouse protects Old Barney's original lens, with memorabilia from the island's northern end. *5th and Central Aves., Barnegat Light, tel. 609/494–3407. Admission: by donation. Open summer, daily 2–5; in winter, by appointment.*

The tiny, tony town of Barnegat Light has a rustic, woolly Cape Cod appearance, for the cedar trees and beach bramble have been left to grow wild around the mostly small houses. Be sure to wander down Barnegat Light's **East 12th Street,** a densely overgrown little avenue of simple, rustic seashore cottages, many of which are more than a century old. The high dunes and trees protected these cottages from the dozens of storms that flattened the majority of homes on the island.

❷ At Harvey Cedars, stop by the **Harvey Cedars Bible Conference Center** (Cedars Ave., on the west side of Long Beach Blvd., tel. 609/494–3107), the island's largest remaining 19th-century grand hotel. You can't go inside, but the hotel's imposing size and its cupola and gabled roof evoke an era vanquished by the modern homes.

❸ Some 12 miles south is the carefully tended town of **Beach Haven,** the island's commercial center, which might resemble any other municipality on Long Beach Island, except that a growing restoration movement among its year-round residents has led to the showcasing of Victorian architecture around the town square.

Amusement rides (tamer than those of Seaside Heights), restaurants, shopping malls, marinas, bed-and-breakfast inns, and motels ring the charming historic district, lending it a small-town charm. The only jarring note in Beach Haven comes during the summer from a few loud nightclubs, which are yielding to protests from local residents and businessmen to turn down the volume and encourage their youthful, party-hardy clientele to be more considerate.

Along the northern end of Long Beach Island the mostly residential enclaves of **Loveladies** and **Harvey Cedars** have evolved their own brand of hauteur. As outrageous as some of these ultramodern, multimillion dollar Shore palaces appear, there is no place to park the car and gawk.

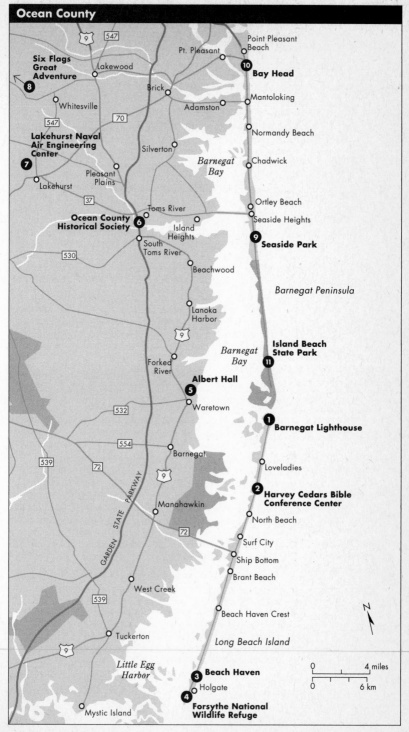

Ocean County

Six Flags Great Adventure ←
8

Lakewood

Whitesville

547

Lakehurst Naval Air Engineering Center
7

Lakehurst

Pleasant Plains

37

Toms River

Ocean County Historical Society **6**

Island Heights

South Toms River

530

Beachwood

Lanoka Harbor

9

Forked River

Albert Hall **5**

Waretown

532

554

539

72

Barnegat

9

Manahawkin

72

West Creek

539

Tuckerton

9

Mystic Island

Little Egg Harbor

GARDEN STATE PARKWAY

Pt. Pleasant

Point Pleasant Beach

10 **Bay Head**

Mantoloking

Normandy Beach

Brick

Adamston

Silverton

Barnegat Bay

Chadwick

Ortley Beach

Seaside Heights

9 **Seaside Park**

Barnegat Peninsula

Barnegat Bay

Island Beach State Park
11

Barnegat Lighthouse **1**

Loveladies

Harvey Cedars Bible Conference Center **2**

North Beach

Surf City

Ship Bottom

Brant Beach

Beach Haven Crest

Long Beach Island

N

Beach Haven **3**

Holgate

Forsythe National Wildlife Refuge **4**

| 0 | | 4 miles |
| 0 | | 6 km |

The **Long Beach Historical Society,** which has a small museum, conducts guided walking tours of the historic district and sponsors frequent evening lectures on local history and culture. *Engleside and Beach Aves., Beach Haven, tel. 609/492–0700. Museum admission: $1 adults, 25¢ children under 12. Open July and Aug., daily 2–4 and 7–9, also Tues. and Fri. 10–noon. Open Memorial Day–June and Sept. weekends, 2–4. Guided tours depart from the museum Tues. and Fri. in the summer at 10 AM. Cost: $2.*

❹ A gull would enjoy **Holgate,** a town on the southern tip of Long Beach Island that is a part of the **Forsythe National Wildlife Refuge.** The preserve was once open to the public, but when it seemed that too many humans were bothering the birds, Holgate was closed to *Homo sapiens.* The region is now inaccessible to humans. Drive over the causeway (Route 72) to the mainland.

Most of the Ocean County mainland sits on the edge of south Jersey's huge Pine Barrens Preserve (*see* Off the Beaten Track, below), which has limited development to a handful of towns clinging to Route 9. Inside the preserve, canoeing, hiking, camping, and, most recently, war games are an alternative to traditional Shore recreation. Head north up Route 9 to **Waretown.**

❺ In the plain shed of the **Albert Hall,** every summer Saturday evening locals gather to play folk music and sing Pinelands ballads. *Pinelands Cultural Society, Waretown, tel. 609/971–1593. Admission: $3 adults, 75¢ children.*

Continue east and north on Route 9 to **Toms River.** Famed "gentleman pirate" Captain William Kidd is said to have buried treasure under a tree with three branches somewhere near

❻ Toms River, where, every year, on or near April 12, the **Ocean County Historical Society** reenacts the 1782 hanging of Joshua Huddy. A Toms River resident, Huddy was allegedly involved in smuggling, privateering, and the deliberate protection of similarly employed Americans. Huddy was surprised, captured, and lynched without trial while defending the Toms River blockhouse from a band of Tory malcontents who could not contain their anger that Britain had lost the Revolutionary War. British representatives to America expressed disgust at this dastardly deed. The Ocean County Historical museum has artifacts and exhibits on the lighter-than-air dirigibles that flew from the Lakehurst Naval Air Station. *26 Hadley Ave., Toms River, tel. 908/341–1880. Open Tues.–Thurs. 1–3 PM, Sat. 10 AM–12 PM. Admission: $1.*

❼ The **Lakehurst Naval Air Engineering Center** is the site of the May 6, 1937, *Hindenburg* airship disaster that killed 35 people and seriously burned 64. The base is on the site of former Camp Kendrick, an ammunition proving ground that may have been used by the Russian Imperial government to test munitions before the Russian Revolution. **Hangar Number One** housed the *Hindenburg* and *Graf Zeppelin* lighter-than-air ships, as well as the first American rigid airship, the U.S.S. *Shenandoah.* Designated a National Historic Landmark in 1968, the hangar is supposedly haunted by the apparition of a young officer in uniform. Also at the airbase is the nondenominational **Cathedral of the Air,** designed by Paul Phillippe Cret in 1932 as a memorial to airmen lost in battle. *Rte. 547, Lakehurst, tel. 908/*

323–2527. The airbase is open to the public by appointment only.

If you have kids, you may want to take Route 547 to Route 571, which heads northwest to the town of **Jackson** and New Jersey's largest theme park, **Six Flags Great Adventure.** The admission price is a bit high, but worth it when you take advantage of Great Adventure's two distinct parks. In the 350-acre drive-through Safari Park, ostriches, giraffes, llamas, tigers, and 1,200 other wild beasts roam freely in 11 different outdoor habitats. While driving along the winding safari road, you are asked not to feed or touch the animals and to keep your car windows closed, as the aggressive monkeys and other curious animals may approach you—especially if they see you holding a brightly colored snack-food bag.

Once you've finished the safari, you should be warmed up for Great Adventure's 92-acre amusement park. Here you can experience the most terrifying roller coasters in the state (the 17-story-tall Scream Machine is a perennial favorite), a 250-foot parachute jump, and a roaring rapids ride that plunges you into cold water. For the fainter at heart, there are continuous live music shows throughout the summer. To reach Great Adventure by car from the Shore, take the Garden State Parkway to U.S. 195W, take Exit 16, and drive 1 mile south on Route 537. *Rte. 537, Jackson, tel. 908/928–3500. Admission: $23 for both safari and amusement park, $15 for children 54 inches or shorter (note: children under 54 inches are not permitted on some rides); $9 per person for safari only; parking $3. Open March 31–Apr., mid-May–mid-Sept. daily 9 AM–late evening (amusement park opens at 10 AM); open early May and late Sept. weekends only. Facilities for the handicapped.*

Retrace your path, going over Toms River to **Seaside Park,** which, with its boardwalk and amusement piers, is the region's "party city." The two amusement piers offer the best oceanfront amusements north of Wildwood. These don't compare to Great Adventure, but it's great for those who enjoy being whirled up and above the waves. From Seaside Heights, you may want to go north up the Barnegat Peninsula to **Bay Head.** Narrow Route 35 zips past mile after mile of seasonal housing. The grimness of the rental trade becomes almost chilling in Ortley Beach, where several square miles of tiny, identical "salt box" rental houses stand in row after endless row. During fall and winter, Lavallette, Chadwick, and Normandy Beach, are virtual ghost towns. In spring, they blossom quickly, and by mid-June, they are crammed with seasonal and rental residents.

In Mantolocking, the lack of zoning laws and environmental controls permitted developers to wall off the beach with Shore homes barely 3 feet apart. With restrictive parking laws, it is nearly impossible for a visitor to use the beaches.

Because the Barnegat Peninsula was the last north Shore area to get a railroad link to New York, the southern towns of Ortley Beach and Seaside Heights differ dramatically from stately Point Pleasant and Bay Head, where for several years a growing, year-round resident population has been trying to limit the number of seasonal visitors. Within the past decade, the New Jersey Public Advocate has sued the township of Bay Head to make its beach badges easier for out of towners to obtain. Both

Point Pleasant and Bay Head exude the staid, upper-middle-class exclusivity of the affluent Monmouth County resort towns, in which tourists are tolerated but not necessarily made to feel welcome. In Bay Head, look for a rambling old hotel perched on the dunes along Bay Avenue (Route 35). In a region famous for its loud rock-and-roll bars and nightclubs, **The Bluffs Hotel** harbors the county's most famous bar. Hidden under the floorboards of the ground-level hotel, the bar was the region's most notorious speakeasy. Knocking back a drink here carries with it the carefree, naughty air of Prohibition days, when spirits were prohibited everywhere but condoned in remote areas such as the Jersey Shore. The creaky hotel is now a bed-and-breakfast (*see* Lodging, below). Otherwise, head south on Route 35 to the very end of Barnegat Peninsula.

Imagine 12 miles of ocean and bay beaches with almost no evidence of human habitation. **Island Beach State Park** is a seemingly endless stretch of dunes, bramble, wild trees, and hidden coves. It is very likely what the Shore barrier islands were like when inhabited by the Leni-Lenape Indians. Island Beach is designed for the easy, economical enjoyment of day-trippers. Nowhere else in the state will you find such a perfect balance of scenic beauty, thoughtfully located facilities, wonderful waves perfect for body-surfing, and the space to enjoy all of it. Unlike municipal beaches, which require a badge for admission, Island Beach State Park charges by the carload, on a first-come basis, beginning at dawn. Once the park hits its quota of 2,083 cars, which can be at around 11 AM on summer weekends, the gates close. Closing the gates not only guarantees that everyone will have a parking space, it also keeps the crowds down. Once inside, you'll find clean, modern bathrooms with showers, changing areas, lockers for storing valuables, picnic areas, and concession stands selling refreshments. You are permitted to bring food to the beach and to build outdoor cooking fires, as long as you stay well away from dunes and conservation areas and you take all refuse out of the park. Some beaches are guarded, others are not. Also worthwhile is a visit to the **Aeolium Nature Center,** which has exhibits on the park's history and delicate ecology. *Central Ave., Seaside Park, tel. 908/793-0506. Admission: Memorial Day–Labor Day, weekdays $4 per car, weekends and holidays $5 per car; off-season, Mon. and Wed.–Sun. $2 per car, free on Tues. Fishing permits available.*

What to See and Do with Children

In addition to **Six Flags Great Adventure** (*see* Exploring Ocean County, above), the Jersey Shore has ample boardwalk amusements to delight youngsters. **Seaside Heights's two amusement piers** (tel. 908/793-6488 and 908/830-5481) offer the best rides outside of Great Adventure. The boardwalk Photon game, in which you grab a futuristic ray gun and blast away at marrauding robots, is a highlight. (Ride tickets are 50¢ each; some rides cost 4–5 tickets.) The **Water Works** water theme park (tel. 908/793-6495) is nearby. *All piers are open May and Sept., weekends; mid-June–Labor Day, daily.*

Long Beach Island has just added a new water theme park, **Thundering Surf,** right next to **Fantasy Island.** Unlike the "lunch-losers" at Seaside Heights, Fantasy Island is aimed mostly at youngsters age 10 and younger. Rides there range from $1.50 to $2. *7th St., Beach Haven, tel. 609/492-4000.*

When rain threatens, consider heading to the **Novins Planetarium** at Ocean County College. Imaginative astronomy shows are presented weekends at 2 and 8 PM. *Toms River, tel. 908/255-4000, ext. 2110. Admission: $3 adults, $1 children.*

There's also an unusual zoo at the County Humane Society Headquarters. **Popcorn Park,** on the mainland in Forked River, is a nonprofit refuge for handicapped animals. Lions, tigers, bears, deer, and other animals whose injuries and handicaps would prevent them from surviving in the wild, thrive here. This is not a petting zoo—animals are permitted to live out their lives in dignity. *1 Humane Way, Forked River, tel. 609/693-1900. Admission: $2.25 adults, $1.25 children 12 and under, $1.25 senior citizens. Open daily 11-5.*

The following Ocean County **libraries** provide free preschool and school-age story-telling hours and other educational activities.

Barnegat (700 West Bay Ave., tel. 609/698-3331).
Beach Haven (3rd and Beach Aves., tel. 609/492-7081).
Beachwood (126 Beachwood Blvd., tel. 908/244-4573).
Berkeley Township (42 Station Rd., Bayville, tel. 908/477-4513).
Brick Township (401 Chambers Bridge Rd., tel. 908/477-4513).
Island Heights (Summit and Central Aves., tel. 908/270-6266).
Jackson (Coventry Rd., tel. 908/928-4400).
Lacey Township (124 S. Main St., Forked River, tel. 609/693-8566).
New Egypt (10 Evergreen Rd., tel. 609/758-7888).
Point Pleasant (834 Beaver Dam Rd., tel. 908/295-1555).
Point Pleasant Beach (710 McLean Ave., tel. 908/892-4575).
Stafford Township (94 Stafford Ave., Manahawkin, tel. 609/597-3381).
Surf City (217 S. Central Ave., tel. 609/494-2480).
Toms River (101 Washington St., tel. 908/349-6200).
Tuckerton (Bay and Cox Aves., tel. 609/296-1470).
Waretown (112 Main St., tel. 609/693-5133).

Off the Beaten Track

The tiny hamlet of **Chatsworth,** located in the heart of the New Jersey Pine Barrens, is a very sleepy town that time and circumstance seem to have forgotten. About 25 minutes by car from Long Beach Island, a half hour from the Barnegat Peninsula, Chatsworth sits at the intersections of Routes 532 and 563 in inland Burlington County. **Buzby's General Store** (tel. 609/726-1280) in Chatsworth, is a good place to stop for a cold soft drink and a snack. In the fall, Chatsworth hosts the annual Cranberry Festival, which celebrates the local fruit harvest and also spotlights the Pine Barrens' peculiar culture and lore. Call for directions and information (tel. 609/859-9701).

En route to the Shore you can stop at a **pick-your-own farm,** where you can pluck the freshest berries, beans, peaches, and other produce and pay far less than at roadside farm markets and supermarkets. It's best to call ahead to find out what is in season and what's available for picking. Among the most popular pick-your-own farms are **DeWolf's Farm** (Colliers Mill Rd., off Rte. 539, New Egypt, tel. 609/758-2424); **Dwulet's Plant & Farm Market** (777 Parker Rd., Rte. 549, Lakewood, tel. 908/367-9803); **Hallock's U-Pick Farm** (Fisher Rd. off Rte. 528,

New Egypt, tel. 609/758–8847); **Sunny Acres** (Holmes Rd.,
Creamridge, 2 mi west of Great Adventure, tel. 609/758–8760
or 609/758–7817); **Russ Friedrich Farm** (West Millstream Rd.,
½ mi off Rte. 539, New Egypt, tel. 609/758–8298); **Emery's
Blueberries** (Long Swamp Rd., off Rte. 539, New Egypt, tel.
609/758–8514).

Shopping

Malls and shopping strips line the Route 72 approach to Long
Beach Island in Manahawkin, as well as along Route 88 in Brick
Township, which is near Point Pleasant and Bay Head. Bou-
tiques and minimalls can be found along Route 35 on the
Barnegat Peninsula and on Long Beach Island's Boulevard.

Minimalls The newest minimall is **Schooner's Wharf**, a trilevel cluster of
crafts shops, specialty stores, and fast-food cafés built next to a
reproduction of a huge schooner (9th and Bay Aves., tel. 609/
492–2800). A few blocks away, at 3rd and Bay avenues, is **Pier
18**, with souvenirs, snack, and fast-food shops. **Ship Bottom's
Pottery Barge** (21st Ave. and Long Beach Blvd., Ship Bottom,
tel. 609/494–0606) is a minimall of crafts emporia.

Specialty Stores **Everybody's General Store** in Point Pleasant Beach (515 Bay
Ave., tel. 908/892–5757) is a melange of crafts, pottery, cheese,
penny candy, and children's toys. Antiquers should investigate
the **Point Pleasant Antique Emporium** (Bay and Trenton Aves.,
tel. 908/892–2222) for a wide selection of collectibles. Long
Beach Island has a chain of sunglass stores, the **Sunglass Me-
nagerie,** in Surf City, Beach Haven, Ship Bottom, and at
Schooner's Wharf. On the mainland, **J B's Sport 'n' Craft Cove**
(601 Rte. 72, Harbour Plaza, tel. 609/698–0003) sells and ap-
praises baseball cards and memorabilia.

Flea Markets **Manahawkin Mart** (657 E. Bay Ave., Manahawkin, tel. 609/
597–1017). Friday, Saturday, and Sunday: indoor market 8–6,
outdoor market 7–3.

Route 70 Flea Market (117 Rte. 70, Lakewood, tel. 908/370–
1837). Friday at 8 AM, Saturday at 6:30 AM, Sunday at 7 AM "until
you want to go home." Indoor areas close at 4 PM.

If you've rented a house on Long Beach Island and need a crib,
a bed, a bicycle, or a TV, **Hawk's Seashore Emporium** and **Faria's** stock just about every common vacation item that vacationers tend to forget or would rather not bring with them. Call
or write to reserve items you think you'll need. A $10 deposit is
required. *Faria's: 5th St. and LB Blvd., Surf City 08008, tel.
609/494–8616; 28th St. and LB Blvd., Ship Bottom 08008, tel.
609/494–RENT. Hawk's: 2306 S. Bay Ave., Beach Haven
08008, tel. 609/492–3298.*

Sports and Outdoor Activities

Participant Sports

Beaches The **Ocean County Health Department** (tel. 908/341–9700) supplies information about the county's water quality and beach
conditions.

A visit to **Island Beach State Park** (*see* Exploring Ocean County, above), considered by many to be the most scenic natural beach on the Jersey Shore, is recommended. With the exception of Island Beach State Park, which controls beach use by charging admission, you will need a beach tag to use all Ocean County beaches during the summer season. Tags can be purchased on the beaches from inspectors, at booths near beach entrances, and at individual borough halls. **Bathhouses** serve day visitors by providing tags, lockers, changing areas, and showers for a small fee. Two bathhouses on Long Beach Island are the **Water's Edge** (135 E. 20th St., Ship Bottom, tel. 609/494–4620) and the **St. Rita Hotel** (127 Engleside Ave., Beach Haven, tel. 609/494–9192).

The contact numbers for specific Shore towns are listed below.

Barnegat Peninsula **Bay Head** (tel. 908/899–2424).

Lavallette (tel. 908/793–7477).

Normandy Beach and Ortley Beach (*see* Dover Township, Mainland).

Seaside Heights (tel. 908/793–8700).

Seaside Park (tel. 908/793–0234).

Point Pleasant Beach (tel. 908/889–2424).

Long Beach Island **Barnegat Light** (tel. 609/494–9196): public rest rooms at 10th Street and Bayview Avenue, handicapped access at 8th and 29th streets.

Beach Haven (tel. 609/492–1515): public rest rooms at Center Street Pavilion, handicapped access at 5th Street.

Harvey Cedars (tel. 609/494–2843): portable toilets at Salem Avenue, recreation center, handicapped access at 80th Street and Middlesex Avenue.

Long Beach Township (tel. 609/494–2153): public rest rooms at 6800 LB Boulevard, near Holgate; handicapped access at 68th Street, near tennis courts.

Ship Bottom (tel. 609/494–2171): portable toilets at some beach locations, handicapped access at 12th Street and at bay beach at 17th Street.

Surf City (tel. 609/494–3064): no public rest rooms, handicapped access at 20th Street.

Mainland **Berkeley Township** (tel. 908/244–7400).

Brick Township (tel. 908/477–4441).

Dover Township (includes Normandy Beach and Ortley Beach on Barnegat Peninsula) (tel. 908/341–1000).

Island Heights (tel. 908/270–6415).

Ocean Gate (tel. 908/269–3466).

Toms River (tel. 908/349–1000).

Boating Ocean County offers the best sailing and recreational boating facilities on the Jersey Shore. A summer afternoon sailing, rowing, or powerboating on the Barnegat Bay can be a delight. If it floats, you can probably rent it at **Water Sports Inc.** (3100 Long Beach Blvd., Long Beach Island, tel. 609/494–2727), which provides rentals of rowboats, paddleboats, jet-skis, motor craft and other watercraft. Rentals can be arranged on an hourly or daily basis.

Other, less diverse boat rentals dot the Ocean County island and mainland towns, some of which can supply watercraft native to the region. A *catboat* is a beamy, shallow draft-single day sailer no more than 25 feet in length, designed to negotiate back bays and creeks. The *Barnegat sneakbox*, a day sailer originally developed as a duck-hunting boat, is slipper-shape, with a rounded bottom and very low freeboard, and can move silently in calm water. The *garvey* is a flat-bottom boat with slab sides, flat transom, and scowlike bow, designed for extremely shallow waters, and once used freely by smugglers and clammers. Motorized "speed garveys" are raced on summer weekends by the East Coast Boat Racing Club (*see* Spectator Sports, below). Finally, the *Seabright skiff*, a variation on the open rowing dories used for offshore whaling, was brought to New Jersey by Scandinavian settlers and became popular with pirates and fishermen. Seabright skiffs are direct descendants of Viking ships, which had high, distinctive, curving sterns, where the steersman could sit and look over the rowers. Most Seabright skiffs built today have lower sterns to make room for motors.

Canoeing The many creeks, streams, and tributaries in the Pine Barrens provide enjoyable fair-weather canoeing. Some rental organizations provide transportation and remote pickups. Try **Art's Canoe Rentals** (1052 Rte. 9, Bayville, tel. 908/269–1413), **Camp Alboconda** (Toms River, tel. 908/349–4079), **Jersey Paddler** (900 Rte. 70, Brick Township, tel. 908/458–5777), **Mick's Canoe Rental** (Chatsworth, tel. 609/726–1380), **Mullica River Boat Basin** (Green Bank, tel. 609/965–2120), **Mullica River Marina** (Sweetwater, tel. 609/561–4337), **Pic-A-Lilli Canoe Rental** (Atsion, tel. 609/268–9831), **Pine Barrens Canoe Rental** (Chatsworth, tel. 609/726–1515), **Pineland Canoes** (Whitesville Rd., Jackson, tel. 908/364–0389), **Surf and Stream Canoe Rentals** (Rte. 571, Toms River, tel. 908/349–8919), **Winding River Park & Nature Center** (Rte. 37, Toms River, tel. 908/341–1000).

Canoeing and rowing instruction for the disabled and handicapped is available by appointment from the **Ocean County Parks Department** (1170 Cattus Island Blvd., Toms River, tel. 908/270–6960).

Fishing Numerous party and charter boats sail from Point Pleasant and Long Beach Island.

Golf These courses, all on the mainland, are open to the public: **Atlantis Country Club** (Country Club Rd., Tuckerton, tel. 609/296–2444), **Bey Lea Golf Course** (Bay Ave., Toms River, tel. 908/349–0566), **Cedar Creek Golf Course** (Forrest Hills Pkwy. at Tilton Blvd., Bayville, tel. 908/269–4460), **Lakewood Country Club** (W. County Line Rd., Lakewood, tel. 908/363–8124), **Ocean Acres Country Club** (925 Buccaneer La., Manahawkin, tel. 609/597–9393).

Health and Fitness Clubs **Lyceum** (265 W. 8th St., Ship Bottom, tel. 609/494–4394), on Long Beach Island, has Nautilus, free weights, aerobic rooms, and lockers. Memberships are available by the day, week, month, or season.

Horseback Riding **Lakewood Riding Center** (436 Cross St., tel. 908/367–6222) and **Garalee Acres** (830 Cross St., tel. 908/364–6060) both in Lakewood.

Sailing Some local marinas and yacht clubs provide sailing instruction.

Barnegat Peninsula **C&C Sailing Center** (Bay Ave., Point Pleasant, tel. 908/295–3450), **Teal Sailing Academy** (668 Main Ave., Bay Head, tel. 908/295–8225).

Long Beach Island **Aggie's Sailing School** (White's Marina, Ship Bottom, tel. 609/494–0248), **Harvey Cedars Sailing School** (6318 Long Beach Blvd., tel. 609/494–2884), **Long Beach Island Sailing School** (1812 Bay Terr., Ship Bottom, tel. 609/494–9568).

Mainland **Barnegat Bay Sailing School** (1 Corrigan Ave., Pine Beach, tel. 908/244–2106).

Scuba Diving **Four Divers, Inc.** (56 Broadway, Point Pleasant, tel. 908/899–7753), **Harbor Divers, Inc.** (73 Tiller Dr., Waretown, tel. 609/693–8999), **Triton Divers** (4404 Long Beach Blvd., Brant Beach, Long Beach Island, tel. 609/494–4400), **Underwater Discovery, Inc.** (2716 Rte. 37E, Toms River, tel. 908/270–9100).

Surfing Surfing is very popular off the Barnegat Peninsula. Waves generally average two to three feet in height, but when a good storm comes up the coast, hard-core surfers can battle eight-foot waves. For the less-balanced, body-boarding is also popular in the area. During the summer, most beaches have designated areas and/or times in which people can surf. Call beach information numbers for specific restrictions (*see* the Beaches section in Sports and Outdoor Activities, above). After Labor Day, surfing is allowed on all beaches. Surfboard rentals cost around $12–$25 per day. **Baja East** (2600 Bridge Ave., Point Pleasant, tel. 908/892–9400) sells used boards starting at $75.

Tennis Memberships may be required at private racquet clubs.

Long Beach Island **Harvey Cedars Borough Courts** (6204 Long Beach Blvd., Harvey Cedars, tel. 609/494–2843), **Holgate Courts** (West Ave., Long Beach Blvd., Holgate, tel. 609/494–2153), **St. Francis Center** (47th St. and Long Beach Blvd., Brant Beach, tel. 609/494–8861).

Mainland **Barnegat Township Tennis Courts** (Lower Shore Rd., Barnegat, tel. 609/698–6658).

War Games Five miles west of Manahawkin on the mainland are the virgin forests of the **Pinelands Recreation Area,** where you can camp, hike, take a hay ride, or embark on a field trip. The official entrance to the recreation area is on Route 72, about 10 minutes west of Manahawkin (Pinelands Recreation Area, Rte. 72, Box 420, Chatsworth, tel. 609/698–3333). Recently, simulated **war games** involving safe nonprojectile-firing infrared rifles and sensors have attracted a cult following here. The games are held daily and last two hours, weather permitting, during warmer months. The cost to take part in a war game varies with the size of group. On weekends, the cost is $16 per person for groups of 16–20 people. For smaller groups there is an additional $2 charge per person. Reservations are required.

Waterskiing **Bayside Boats** (Rte. 38 and Bay Blvd., Seaside Heights, tel. *Barnegat Peninsula* 908/793–8535), **Lawasaki Wheelhouse** (501 Atlantic Ave., Point

Pleasant, tel. 908/899–4050), **Pelican Harbor** (Rte. 37E, Pelican Island, tel. 908/793–1700).

Long Beach Island **Bayview Water Ski School** (104 W. 28th St., Ship Bottom, tel. 609/494–5405).

Mainland **Maurita's** (2800 Rte. 37, Toms River, tel. 908/270–6404), **Wet & Wild** (Pier 1, Rte. 37, Toms River, tel. 908/929–2723).

National, State, and County Parks

Island Beach State Park is the Shore's best beach. Visit it and you'll know what all of this used to be like. *Central Ave., Seaside Park, tel. 908/793–0506. Open all year. Fishing permits available. Free admission Tues. Admission: Memorial Day–Labor Day, weekdays $4 per carload, weekends and holidays $5; Labor Day–Memorial Day, $2.*

Ocean County Park (off Rte. 88, Brennan Concourse, 1 mi east of Rte. 9, Bayville, tel. 908/370–7380). Picnic areas, tennis courts, and a swimming lake are located on 300 acres of what was once a Rockefeller estate.

Berkeley Island Park (tel. 609/296–5606). This Barnegat Bay Shore park has a boat landing.

Cattus Island County Park (Fischer Blvd., off Rte. 37, Toms River, tel. 908/270–6960). Lectures, nature walks, crafts workshops, and boat and van tours of wildlife areas are offered in a 500-acre wildlife refuge. There's a small museum inside the Cooper Environmental Center, and summer nature programs are available for children.

Double Trouble County Park (off Garden State Pkwy. Exit 80, on Double Trouble Rd. W, Berkeley Township, tel. 908/349–1903). A restored village, sawmill, and cranberry bogs are here.

Lake Shenandoah Park (Brennan Concourse, across from Ocean City Park, Bayville, tel. 908/370–7380). This small park area and boat landing are on the Metedeconk River.

Spectator Sports

Boat Racing **New Jersey Offshore Powerboat Race** (tel. 908/888–8288) is a loud, exciting event that can be viewed along Point Pleasant Beach and the Island Beach peninsula, or aboard a boat in the designated ocean spectator area. More than 200,000 people watch or participate. Held in July, the race begins south of the Manasquan Inlet and goes as far south as Seaside Heights, then loops back.

The former Speed Garvey Racing Association, now called **East Coast Boat Racing Club** (tel. 908/349–7502 or 908/349–2856), races small powerboats on weekends during the summer season at various locations along Barnegat Bay.

Dining

For prices, consult the price chart in the Dining section of Chapter 1, Essential Information. Highly recommended restaurants are indicated with a star ★.

Barnegat Peninsula

Expensive   **Top o' the Mast.** A huge family-style surf-and-turf restaurant right on the beach, with great ocean views. *23rd Ave, S. Seaside Park, tel. 908/793-2444. Reservations advised. Dress: casual. Live entertainment. Children's specials. Valet parking. AE, CB, D, DC, MC, V. Open daily for lunch and dinner, Sun. brunch.*

Moderate–   **Barmore's Shrimp Box.** An unpretentious fish restaurant that
Expensive   takes most of its menu from whatever was caught by the Manasquan River fishing fleet. No reservations are taken, so expect to stand on line on busy summer weekends. *75 Inlet Dr., Point Pleasant Beach, tel. 908/899-1637. No reservations. Dress: casual. Early-bird specials. AE, D, DC, MC, V. Open Apr.–Oct., daily for dinner. Lunch and dinner Sat., Sun. brunch.*

Europa South. Good, filling Spanish and Portuguese cuisine. Gorge yourself on paella and green-sauce specialties. *521 Arnold Ave. and Rte. 35, Point Pleasant, tel. 908/295-1500. Reservations advised. Dress: casual. Early-bird specials. AE, D, DC, MC, V. Open daily for lunch and dinner, Sun. brunch.*

Filomio's. A traditional Italian family restaurant with Mediterranean decor. *15-17 Inlet Dr., Point Pleasant Beach, tel. 908/892-2723. Reservations recommended. Dress: casual. AE, MC, V. Open mid-Apr.–Oct. daily, for lunch and dinner, Sun. brunch.*

Moderate   **Dorca's.** This is Bay Head's most famous luncheonette, a bastion of the town's if-it-ain't-broke, don't-fix-it mentality. For almost 30 years, Dorca's famous home-cooked Friday suppers have been attracting crowds of tourists as well as locals from miles around. On other days, Dorca's serves big, filling breakfasts and lunches indoors and on an outdoor patio. *58 Bridge St., Bay Head, tel. 908/899-9635. No reservations. Dress: casual. No credit cards. Open Memorial Day–Labor Day, daily for breakfast and lunch, Fri. supper.*

Joe's Chadwick Diner. Joe's is an easygoing family diner, open 24 hours. No surprises on the menu, but a clown appears during the dinner hour in the summer season to keep the kids happy. Fun desserts, too. *3469 Rte. 35N at Strickland Blvd., Chadwick Beach, tel. 908/830-2288. No reservations. Dress: casual. No credit cards.*

Inexpensive–   **Co-op Seafood.** A classic Jersey Shore seafood take-out restau-
Moderate   rant, with a small dining area, owned and operated by local fishermen. Just about everything here is fresh, and on Monday and Tuesday, everything is discounted 10%. Chicken dishes, hamburgers, hot dogs, and snacks are also on the menu. Prices

Our list of Ocean County Shore restaurants was compiled with the assistance of Brooke Tarabour, restaurant columnist of the Asbury Park Press *and Ed Hitzel, food critic of the* Atlantic City Press.

vary with market rates. *Channel Dr., Point Pleasant Beach, tel. 908/889–2211. No reservations. No credit cards. Open daily for lunch and dinner.*

Long Beach Island

Expensive **Bayberry Inn.** The island's most popular surf-and-turf house could have been lifted from Colonial Williamsburg. Waitresses dress in period costumes and serve a blend of Continental and American cuisine. Expect to wait, even if you have a reservation, on busy summer weekends. *13th St. and Long Beach Blvd., Ship Bottom, tel. 609/494–8848. Reservations advised. Dress: no shorts or T-shirts; men should wear jackets. Free parking. AE, DC, MC, V. Open daily for lunch and dinner, Sun. brunch.*

Charles's Seafood Restaurant. This breezy, California-style seafood restaurant features grilled fish, a few Cajun items, pasta, veal, steak, and chicken dishes. Sauces are light, with an emphasis on fresh vegetables. *87th St. and Long Beach Blvd., Beach Haven Crest, tel. 609/492–8340. Reservations advised. Dress: casual. Children's menu. AE, MC, V. Open June–Aug., daily for dinner; May and Sept. weekends.*

Moderate– **Harvey Cedars Shellfish Company.** Steamed shrimp, clams, and
Expensive simple flatfish are served in this very casual bar. Expect a long
★ line. *7904 Long Beach Blvd., Harvey Cedars, tel. 609/494–7112. No reservations. Dress: casual. Limited off-street parking. No credit cards. BYOB. Open May–Sept.*

Owl Tree. Continental bistro cuisine is featured in this restaurant with a Victorian setting reminiscent of Cape May. *7908 Long Beach Blvd., Harvey Cedars, tel. 609/494–8191. Reservations advised. Jacket required. AE, MC, V. Open daily for lunch and dinner, with a late-night snack menu served in summer season.*

★ **Romeo's.** Pronounced roh-**MAY**-o's, this is a superb Italian restaurant, though don't be surprised if you find French, Mexican, and Cajun specials on the menu. Unpretentious and accommodating to families, Romeo's also serves the island's best Sunday brunch. They also have early-bird and all-you-can-eat specials. *100 N. Pennsylvania Ave. and Center St., Beach Haven, tel. 609/492–0025. Reservations advised. Dress: casual. MC, V. BYOB. Open daily for lunch and dinner, Sun. brunch. Closed Wed.*

Moderate **Kubel's Bar & Grille.** This surf-and-turf restaurant in stodgy Barnegat Light attracts equal numbers of natives and affluent shorebirds from Loveladies and Harvey Cedars. Waterborne passengers have "valet docking" privileges at nearby Ed's Boat Rentals. *7th St. and Bayview, Barnegat Light, tel. 609/494–8592. Reservations suggested in summer season. Dress: casual. MC, V. Open daily for lunch and dinner, Sun. brunch.*

Inexpensive– **Boulevard Clams.** This take-out seafood market has a small,
Moderate air-conditioned dining area. Specialties include clams, mussels, and flatfish, but sandwiches, pasta, and chicken are also featured on the menu. Prices of fresh fish vary with market rates. *20th St. and Long Beach Blvd., tel. 609/494–9494. No reservations. MC, V. Open daily for lunch and dinner in summer season.*

Inexpensive **Terrace Tavern.** The closest thing to a perfect Shore bar on
★ Long Beach Island, the Terrace gets a great mix of locals and

seasonal types. The bar is in an old cedarwood hotel on Long Beach Boulevard, the inside of which is dominated by hundreds of flamingos. Something about the place's good-natured Key West feeling makes you drool for frozen drinks. By all means have one, but don't neglect the grilled seafood specials. The well-prepared food is served in huge portions. *13908 Long Beach Blvd., Beach Haven Terrace, tel. 609/494–7051. No reservations. Dress: casual. No credit cards.*

Mainland

Moderate–
Expensive

Winkelmann's. This Lakewood favorite serves rich, spicy Bavarian-American fare, including schnitzel, steak, bratwurst, chicken dishes, and seafood. *945 River Rd., Lakewood, tel. 908/363–6294. Reservations advised. Dress: casual. AE, MC, V. Open daily for lunch and dinner.*

Moderate **Captain's Inn.** This is a seafood restaurant with river views. Some Continental items are also featured. *Lacey Rd., Forked River, tel. 609/693–3351. Reservations advised. Dress: casual. Entertainment on weekends. Inexpensive children's menu. AE, DC, MC, V. Open daily for lunch and dinner.*

Lodging

Room rates used to rank accommodations are for the peak summer season, June through August. Suites and rooms with ocean views can be more expensive. Acceptable low-cost accommodations are few and far between during the summer season. Rates drop significantly in the cooler "shoulder" seasons of spring and autumn and are lowest in winter. Weekend and midweek package rates also help to defer costs. All rooms in hotels and motels have a private bath, unless noted. Many small hotels, guest houses, and bed-and-breakfasts have shared baths. Children may stay with an adult at the single room rate where indicated. For prices, consult the price chart in the Lodging section of Chapter 1, Essential Information. Highly recommended lodgings are indicated with a star ★.

Motels

Barnegat
Peninsula
Expensive

Windjammer. A modest three-story beach block motel. *1st and Central Aves., Seaside Park 08752, tel. 908/830–2555. 63 rooms, 24 with efficiency kitchens. Facilities: pool, restaurant, coin laundry. Beach tags provided. AE, MC, V. Open June–Sept.*

Moderate **Bay-Berry Motel.** A tiny, clean motel a short walk from the beach. *1005 Grand Central Ave., Lavallette 08735, tel. 908/830–4442. 15 rooms. Facilities: cable TV. AE, V.*

Cadillac Motor Inn. Very close to Island Beach State Park. *201 Hiering Ave., Seaside Heights 08751, tel. 908/793–5117. 88 rooms. Facilities: pool, coffee shop. Breakfast included in some packages. AE, MC, V.*

Colonial Motel. The mood here is of a private house, not a motel, one block from the fishing marinas along the Manasquan Inlet. All rooms are heated and air-conditioned and are equipped with kitchens and TVs. *210 Arnold Ave., Point Pleasant 08742, tel. 908/899–2394. 23 rooms. Facilities: beach tags provided. AE, MC, V.*

Long Beach Island
Expensive–
Very Expensive
★

Engleside Inn. The island's best motel, with a pool, exercise room, American seafood restaurant, and barefoot bar. The inn is right on the beach. All rooms are heated and air-conditioned and most have ocean views. *30 Engleside Ave., Beach Haven 08008, tel. 609/492–1251, fax 609/492–9175. 69 rooms, 37 rooms with kitchens, 2 with whirlpools. Facilities: pool, whirlpool, exercise and massage room, meeting areas. AE, D, DC, MC, V.*

Expensive

Coral Seas. A small, intimate motel on the ocean. All rooms are heated and air-conditioned, and some have balconies overlooking the water. *Coral St. and the ocean, Box 175, Beach Haven 08008, tel. 609/492–1141. 50 rooms. Facilities: cable TV, heated outdoor pool. Charge for infants. 3-night minimum stay in summer. AE, D, MC, V. Open Apr.–Oct.*

Drifting Sands. This pleasant, woodsy motel doesn't have a pool, but it is right on the beach. All guest rooms are heated and air-conditioned, and some have ocean views and private balconies. *119 E. 9th St., Ship Bottom 08008, tel. 609/494–1123. 54 rooms, 10 with kitchenettes. Facilities: beach tags provided. 3-night minimum stay on summer weekends. AE, MC, V.*

Moderate–Expensive

Sea Spray Motel. Across the street from the beach block, this hotel features heated and air-conditioned rooms with refrigerators and two-room suites; a few rooms are equipped with small kitchens. *2600 South Bay Ave., Beach Haven Inlet 08008, tel. 609/492–4944. 52 rooms. Facilities: cable TV, heated pool. 3-night minimum stay summer weekends, 2 nights other times. AE, MC, V.*

Bed-and-Breakfasts

Barnegat
Peninsula
Expensive–
Very Expensive
★

Conover's Bay Head Inn. One of the first and best-known B&Bs in Ocean County, this is the summer home of the Conover family. An inn for nearly 25 years, it was one of a handful of accommodations responsible for the B&B renaissance along the Jersey Shore. All rooms are heated and air-conditioned, and five have ocean or bay views. A mix of antique and modern furnishings provides a relaxing, informal atmosphere. *646 Main Ave., Bay Head 08742, tel. 908/892–4664. 12 rooms, 1 with private bath. Facilities: Continental breakfast in summer, hot breakfast on Sun. and Oct.–May. Afternoon tea during spring and fall. AE, MC, V.*

Expensive

The Bluffs. Bay Head's traditional family hotel—the only one in town on the beach—is more than a century old and justifiably proud of its creaky, old-time atmosphere. About half of the guest rooms have been renovated and now have air-conditioning and modern furniture, though none have telephones or TVs. The seafood restaurant is satisfying, if a bit pricey, and the "secret" bar, a former speakeasy, is fun. *575 E. Bay Ave. (Rte. 35), Bay Head 08742, tel. 908/892–1114. 22 rooms. Facilities: cribs and cots provided free; free use of beach tags (2 per room). Continental breakfast. Free parking. AE, MC, V.*

Long Beach Island
Expensive

Victoria Guest House. Salvador Dali was once a guest of this inn, which now includes two cottages in Beach Haven's historic district. Marilyn and Leonard Miller have underlined the informal atmosphere with plenty of wicker furnishings, rag rugs, and a mix of antiques. All guest rooms are heated and have ceiling fans. A small heated outdoor pool was recently added. The beach is a block away. Activities include Saturday night wine-and-cheese parties and Wednesday night bridge parties, with lessons for those who don't know the meaning of "no-trump." *122 Amber St., Beach Haven 08008, tel. 609/492–4154. 14 rooms in 2 properties, 12 with private bath. Facilities: beach tags, chairs, towels, bicycles provided. Continental-plus breakfast, afternoon lemonade. 2-night minimum weekend stay includes late check-out. AE. Open Apr.–Nov.*

Moderate–Expensive

★ **Bayberry Barque.** A blend of antiques, reproductions, bric-a-brac, wicker, and formal furnishings grace this 19th-century house operated by Glenn and Pat Miller and Gladys Pontero. The house also features a beautiful, original stained-glass window in the stairwell. All rooms are heated and have ceiling fans. The Bayberry Barque, a block from the beach, is an easy walk from restaurants, amusements, movies, theater, nightclubs, and outdoor concerts. *117 Centre St., Beach Haven 08008, tel. 609/492–5216. 9 rooms, 2 with private bath. Facilities: beach tags provided. On-street parking. 2-night minimum stay weekends in season, 3-night minimum stay holiday weekends. AE, MC, V accepted in summer season only.*

★ **Pierrot by the Sea.** A block from the beach on Beach Haven's Victorian Centre Street, Pierrot has been lovingly restored with textbook accuracy by Catherine and Richard Burdro. Most accommodations face the ocean, and the roomy yard has a gazebo and a fountain. Guests also have use of bicycles. *101 Centre St., Beach Haven 08008, tel. 609/492–4424. 8 rooms, 2 with private bath. Facilities: full hot breakfast, afternoon tea. Bicycles provided. No smoking. 2-night minimum stay July and Aug., 3-night minimum holiday weekends. MC, V. Open Apr.–Sept.*

Moderate

Green Gables. A tiny cedar-paneled inn tucked in the Beach Haven business district, Green Gables evokes the atmosphere of a European pension, with an expensive, fixed-price dinner served nightly in the small dining room. Rooms are small but pleasant and are heated and have ceiling fans. Rita Rapella and Adolfo De Martino are the proprietors. *212 Center St., Beach Haven 08008, tel. 609/492–3553, fax 609/492–2507. 6 rooms, 1 with private bath. Facilities: beach tags provided. Children of all ages accepted. Street parking. 2-night minimum stay in summer, 3 nights on holiday weekends. MC, V.*

Mainland
Moderate

The Studio. The 1889 home of artist John F. Peto has been restored with Victorian touches and decorated with many of his original paintings. Located in Island Heights, on the Barnegat Bay, The Studio is a 10-minute drive from ocean beach resorts and offers views of the bay from its porch. Bayshore beaches and a sailboat rental are just a short walk away. Filling hot breakfasts are served in the kitchen by innkeeper Joy Smiley, Peto's granddaughter. *102 Cedar Ave., Island Heights 08732, tel. 908/270–6058. 3 rooms with shared baths. AE.*

Camping

Though neither the Barnegat Peninsula nor Long Beach Island has any campgrounds, all those listed are within a half hour's drive of beaches. **Albocondo Campgrounds** (1480 Whitesville Rd., Toms River, tel. 908/349–4079), **Atlantic City North KOA** (Stage Rd., Box 242, Tuckerton, tel. 609/296–9163), **Baker's Acres Campground** (Box 104, S. Willits Ave., Tuckerton, tel.

609/296–2664), **Brookville Campground** (Box 169, 244 Jones Rd., Barnegat, tel. 609/698–3134), **Oakgrove Campgrounds** (Rte. 9, Barnegat, tel. 609/698–3344), **Sea Pirate Light** (Rte. 9, Box 271, West Creek, tel. 609/296–7400), **Surf and Stream** (1801 Ridgeway Rd., Toms River, tel. 908/349–8919), **Turtle Run Campground** (RR2, Box 287, Wading River, tel. 609/965–5343).

The Arts and Nightlife

Concerts

Albert Hall. Folk music, especially Pinelands ballads and songs, is presented by the Pinelands Cultural Society. *Waretown, tel. 609/971–1593. Admission: $3 adults, 75¢ children. Sat. at 8 PM.*

Outdoor Concert Series. *Long Beach Island:* Weeknights in July and August. Bandshell in Bicentennial Park (Engleside and Beach Aves., Beach Haven, tel. 609/492–2883; admission free). Point Pleasant: Veteran's Memorial Bandshell (Arnold and Baltimore Aves., Point Pleasant Beach, tel. 908/899–2424).

Theater

Fine Arts Center of Ocean County College (Toms River, tel. 908/255–4000, ext. 2098). Plays, concerts, and lectures featured throughout the year.

Strand Theater (tel. 908/367–6688 or 908/367–9595). Headquarters of the Ocean County Center for the Arts, this small community theater hosts drama, musicals, concerts, and other cultural activities.

Surflight Theater. Summer-stock plays and Broadway revivals. *Beach and Engleside Aves., Beach Haven, tel. 609/492–9477. Open June–Sept. Half-price tickets for children. Handicap access.*

Movies

Long Beach Island **Beach Theatre** (Bay Ave., Beach Haven Park, tel. 609/494–1007).

Colonial Theater (Center and Bay Aves., Beach Haven, tel. 609/492–4450).

Colony Four (35th St. and Long Beach Blvd., Brant Beach, tel. 609/494–3330).

Mainland Brick Township theaters are very close to Point Pleasant and Bay Head. Toms River theaters are close to the southern Barnegat Peninsula.

Berkeley Cinema (Rte. 9, Bayville, tel. 908/269–5100).
Brick Plaza (Brick Plaza, Brick Township, tel. 908/477–3400).
Cinema Alley 1 & 2 (Rte. 37, Toms River, tel. 908/270–8899).
Circle Cinemas (1743 Rte. 88, Brick Township, tel. 908/458–5077).
Dover Theatre (Rtes. 37 and 9, Toms River, tel. 908/244–5454).
Harbor Twin (Rte. 72, Manahawkin, tel. 609/597–4949).
Mall Cinema (Kennedy Mall, Brick Township, tel. 609/477–8661).

Ocean County Mall Cinemas 1, 2 & 3 (Ocean County Mall, Hooper Ave., Toms River, tel. 908/240–5095).

Nightclubs, Bars, and Taverns

Barnegat Peninsula **The Bluffs** (575 East Ave., Bay Head, tel. 908/892–1114). Bay Head's famous "secret" bar is hidden beneath the Bluffs Hotel. A former speakeasy during Prohibition, the Bluffs gets a mixed crowd of carefully underdressed locals and vacationers.

Joey Harrison's Surf Club (1900 Ocean Ave., Ortley Beach, tel. 908/793–6625). Live rock-and-roll, with a vague air of '60s rustic. Perched right on the beach, the club is also a bathhouse and provides lockers for the day.

Pete's Bar and Grill (Rte. 35 and Delaware Ave., Point Pleasant, tel. 908/892–3382). A relaxed, easygoing tavern with laid-back bands and a better-than-average tavern menu.

Long Beach Island **Joe Pops** (2002 Long Beach Blvd., Beach Haven, tel. 609/494–0558). The island's largest rock-and-roll club, with live music most nights and a Sunday jazz jam session.

Hudson House (19 E. 13th St., N. Beach Haven, tel. 609/492–9616). A relaxed bar frequented by old-timers and fishermen.

The Ketch (529 Dock Rd., Beach Haven, tel. 609/492–3000). This big, loud, and rowdy bar has DJs on weeknights and live bands on weekends.

Quarter Deck Inn (351 W. 9th St. at the causeway, Ship Bottom, tel. 609/494–9055). DJs or live Top 40 bands Wednesday–Sunday. Tuesday is comedy night.

Touche (2 S. Bay Ave., Beach Haven, tel. 609/492–3366). A DJ dance bar, with an evening dress code.

Mainland **Slim's Cowboy Hall of Fame** (Rte. 9, Bayville, tel. 908/269–5545). Proof that you can't take the country out of the boys or girls. At Slim's you can buy cowboy clothes, drink cowboy drinks, eat cowboy steaks and chops (with some seafood also available), and hear live bands play cowboy tunes.

5 Atlantic City

Introduction

For more than a century, Atlantic City's major industry has been fleecing tourists, grandly, in the fabulous stone hotels; greedily, with inflated real-estate deals; or quickly, in the candy shops on the Boardwalk, where saltwater taffy—an innocuous corn syrup confection without a drop of salt water in it—is still sold as the Eighth Wonder of the World.

With 33 million visitors flooding the town each year and dropping about $6 million a day in the casinos, it's no wonder that Atlantic City residents have an ambivalent attitude about tourists. On the one hand, there's the old us-against-them resort mentality that reduces the humble tourist, the somewhat less humble conventioneer, and the arrogant high roller to varieties of "shoobies"—local slang for summer day-trippers who used to pack their lunches in cardboard shoe boxes. On the other hand, natives have a quirky, peculiar pride in where they live and work. They are the first to acknowledge that Atlantic City has its bad side—several, in fact—but they quickly counter that with tales of diversions and delights. You can enjoy these delights, and avoid being fleeced, by using common sense and by going native.

First, a lesson in native behavior—parking. Only a fool or someone who wants the location of a specific lot pays for parking. See our parking section on how to do it right. If you decide to be extravagant and valet park, a $1 tip to the attendant *after* your car is delivered back to you is the only anticipated gesture.

Second: crime. According to FBI statistics, Atlantic City has one of the highest per capita crime rates in the country. At night in Atlantic City, natives either drive or take a cab. Sometimes, a jitney will do (*see* Getting Around, below).

Third: local lingo. If you're in Atlantic City, you're "on the Island." Atlantic City is the largest and northernmost of four separate towns on Absecon Island, "the Island," which is different from the shopping centers and suburban sprawls "offshore" on "the Mainland" a few miles to the west. Between the Island and the Mainland is the Bay, which isn't really a bay but a marshy meadow broken by twisting creeks, several land bridges, and the Intracoastal Waterway.

On the Island, anything toward Atlantic City is "uptown." If you're heading toward Ventnor, Margate, or Longport, you're going "downbeach." Traditional compass directions become lopsided on the Island. When people tell you to go north, they really mean go away from the beach toward the bay, which actually lies to the east. To go south is to head west, toward the beach.

On the subject of street names, Arkansas Avenue is pronounced Ar-**KAN**-sas, Illinois (renamed Rev. Martin Luther King Boulevard) is Ill-uh-**NOISE,** and no one hits the first "t" in Atlantic. You're in Uhlantic City, or walking down Uhlantic Avenue. Anything south (actually west) of the beach is the Ocean.

Each casino has its own local name, though sometimes it's just a matter of when to add "the" before the title. You go to the Claridge, the Sands, the Grand, the Taj, the Castle, and the Trop. Non-the casinos are Caesars, Showboat, Harrah's (rhymes with Farrah's, never Har-**RAHs**), Trump Plaza (most certainly not the Plaza), Bally's (never Park Place), and Bally Grand (note the dropped possessive). Some nostalgic natives call Bally Grand "the Nugget," for when that casino was the Atlantic City Golden Nugget.

The casino with the most names is Merv Griffin's Resorts. It's usually called "Resorts," though some old-timers refer to it as "the Haddon Hall," from its days as a grand Boardwalk hotel.

Fourth: the ocean. Nobody swims in it, but natives, despite medical warnings, like to show off their tans.

Fifth: gambling. You'll find plenty of natives inside casinos. They're the first to tell you that the best tables at restaurants, the best rooms, and the best seats in the showroom are held routinely for gamblers. How do you get the crème de la crème if you're not a big gambler? Casino employees, who are forbidden by the state Casino Gaming Act to gamble in casinos, try to use "juice," which is Vegas slang for power, influence, or friends in high places, to get good treatment. If you don't have juice, or you don't know anyone who does, you can still get good tables in casino restaurants and good seats in a showroom without tipping (follow our advice in The Arts and Nightlife, below). In a restaurant, make your reservation as far in advance as possible and arrive on time. If you're a native, of course, you don't often eat in casinos, which tend to serve food at prices that make overpriced tourist traps look cheap (*see* Dining, below, for some great, comparatively cheap eats).

Sixth: nightlife. For late-night hangouts, nothing can beat the dealers' bars, where casino employees come for a postshift drink before they head home. Each casino adopts a bar, usually within walking distance, and if you arrive at shift change (around 11:30 PM), you'll see dealers come in, usually still in uniform and ready to tell tales about the big-money craziness they just left behind. A personal favorite is 12 South, on 12 South Indiana Avenue (between Pacific and Atlantic avenues), where dealers from Bally's, the Sands, and the Claridge congregate from 11 PM on. Aubrey's, at Arkansas and Pacific, gets Caesars people.

Of course there are times when natives want to get far away from the city, to Cape May, the pretty Victorian seashore town at the bottom of the Garden State Parkway (*see* Chapter 8, Victorian Cape May), to the Bruce Springsteen boardwalk carnival of Wildwood (*see* Chapter 7, Cape May County), or to the Forsythe Wildlife Refuge in Oceanville (*see* Chapter 6, Greater Atlantic County), where they, too, can feel like strangers in a strange land.

Essential Information

Important Addresses and Numbers

Tourist Information
Atlantic City Convention and Visitors Bureau (2304 Pacific Ave., tel. 609/348–7100 or 800/262–7395).

Atlantic City Convention Center (Boardwalk at Mississippi Ave., tel. 609/348–7000).

Atlantic County Office for the Aging and Disabled (1333 Atlantic Ave., tel. 609/345–6700, ext. 2831).

Emergencies Dial 911 for police or fire department.

Medical **Atlantic City Medical Center** (Michigan and Pacific Aves., tel. 609/344–8090). Most casinos have a nurse on duty and a doctor on call.

Beach Patrol Tel. 609/347–5312.

Coast Guard Tel. 609/344–3586.

Marine Police Tel. 609/441–3586.

Publications The daily *Atlantic City Press* covers national and local news, with an emphasis on the casino industry. Its "Friday at the Shore" section lists entertainment and sports, both in and outside of the casinos. *Whoot!,* a free weekly paper distributed at local taverns and nightclubs, also covers entertainment, with comprehensive listings of lounge acts and club bands. *Atlantic City Magazine,* on sale at newsstands and distributed free at some casino hotels, has longer feature articles about the region and good restaurant listings.

Gambling Problems **Compulsive Gambling Hotline** (tel. 800/426–2537), **Gamblers Anonymous** (tel. 609/429–6516).

Opening and Closing Times

Atlantic City is the only city in New Jersey in which bars can stay open 24 hours a day. Unlike Las Vegas, where gaming goes on 24 hours a day, Atlantic City's casinos close at 4 AM on weeknights, 6 AM on weekends and reopen at 10 AM.

Restaurants usually close their kitchens at 11 PM or substitute a light menu for late nights, though most casinos have a coffee shop or delicatessen that stays open all night.

Most stores open at 10 AM and close between 6 PM and 9 PM, depending on the season.

Guided Tours

Gray Line Tours (9 N. Arkansas Ave., tel. 609/344–0965) offers guided bus tours of Atlantic City, Smithville, Renault Winery, and Cape May. Tours are offered to groups of 20 and more, beginning at a hotel or motel. Fees range from $15 for a three-hour tour to $25 for a five-hour tour. Meals are not included but can be purchased at Smithville or other sites.

Arriving and Departing

By Plane **Atlantic City International Airport** (tel. 609/545–7895), in Pomona, gets scheduled service from **USAir** (tel. 800/331–3131), the **Trump Shuttle** (tel. 800/247–8786), and **TW Express** (tel. 800/221–2000). Cab fare is roughly $30 to Atlantic City, and the trip takes 20 minutes. Limousine service is also available from **Airport Limousine** (tel. 609/345–3244), **Blue and White Airport Service** (tel. 609/848–0770), **Casino Limousine Service** (tel. 609/646–5555), **General Limousine Service** (tel. 609/348–1777), or **Rapid Rover Airport Shuttle** (tel. 609/344–0100).

Bader Field (tel. 609/347–6680) is located on the Black Horse Pike (Albany Ave.), about a five-minute drive from Bally's Grand casino. Cab fare is about $3. Continental Express (tel.

800/525–0280) provides service here, but there has been talk of suspending flights because of low ridership.

By Helicopter **Trump Air** (tel. 609/344–6006 or 800/448–4000) provides daily flights from New York's West 34th Street Heliport to Atlantic City's Steel Pier (opposite the Taj Mahal Resort & Casino on the Boardwalk) and the Trump Castle Casino Resort in the marina section. The fare ranges from $125 to $145 each way.

By Car You reach Atlantic City from New York by crossing into New Jersey, taking the **New Jersey Turnpike** south to Exit 11, and then the **Garden State Parkway** and **Atlantic City Expressway** toll roads. From Trenton, take **I–195** east to the **Garden State Parkway** and proceed south to the **Atlantic City Expressway**. From Philadelphia, cross into New Jersey at the **Walt Whitman Bridge,** then stay on the north–south freeway (**Route 42**) until it merges with the **Atlantic City Expressway.** From Delaware and points south, the fastest route is to go north on U.S. 95 through Philadelphia to the **Walt Whitman Bridge.** Expect heavy traffic on all roads and delays at tollbooths during summer weekends.

Driving Time From New York: about 2½ hours.
From Philadelphia: 1½ hours.
From Washington, DC: 4½ hours.

By Bus **New Jersey Transit** (tel. 609/344–8181) and **Greyhound** (tel. 609/345–5403) provide scheduled express service from Philadelphia and New York City to Atlantic City's Municipal Bus Terminal on Arkansas and Atlantic avenues.

There are also line bus services direct to various casinos. Line buses target day-trippers with perks such as coupons for discounted meals and beverages, free show tickets, and a small sum of cash, delivered in coins on or near the casino floor in the hope that you'll stuff them into a slot machine and end up gambling from your own pocket.

A number of tour operators and bus companies offer these day trips to adults 21 years or older. They typically advertise in the entertainment sections of local newspapers, along with information about fees, times, and departure locations. The operators include **Allied Tours** (165 W. 46th St., New York, NY 10036, tel. 212/869–5100), **Academy Tours** (1515 Jefferson St., Hoboken, NJ 07030, tel. 212/964–6600), **Domenico Tours** (751 Broadway, Bayonne, NJ 07002, tel. 201/823–8687 or 800/554–TOUR), **Gray Line** (254 W. 54th St., New York, NY 10019, tel. 212/397–2620), and **Greyhound** (525 11th Ave., New York, NY 10018, tel. 212/971–6306 or 800/528–0447).

By Train **Amtrak** (tel. 800/872–7245) offers direct rail service to the Atlantic City Municipal Rail Terminal from Philadelphia International Airport, Philadelphia's 30th St. Station, Penn Station in New York City, and from some points along the northeast rail corridor. Round-trip rates start at $15 for the Philadelphia–Atlantic City trip.

New Jersey Transit also offers commuter service to Atlantic City, beginning at the PATCO Hi-Speed terminal in Lindenwold, New Jersey. For schedule information and fares, call 800/722–2222 in northern New Jersey, 800/582–5946 in southern New Jersey, 201/762–5100 from New York, 215/569–3752 from Philadelphia, or 800/772–2287 for TTD/TTY phone service for the hearing impaired, 6 AM–midnight.

The **Atlantic City Municipal Rail Terminal** is a long five-block walk to the Boardwalk and casino hotels. Some casinos offer free shuttle bus service; New Jersey Transit also operates a shuttle. A cab to the nearest casinos, Caesars or Trump Plaza, will cost about $2.50.

By Boat Two casinos, Harrah's Marina and Trump Castle, have limited tie-up service for waterborne gamblers (reservations required: call the casino and ask for the harbormaster). Harrah's also has an exclusive transportation arrangement with **Metromarine** (tel. 212/785–3100), which links the casino with the Five Town Metroport in Inwood, Long Island. Boats operate year-round, Wednesday–Sunday, leaving at 9:30 AM and returning at 7:30 PM. The ride takes about three hours, compared to 4½ hours by car. The $45 introductory round-trip fare gets $12.50 in coin and other bonuses, and the schedule allows for about five hours of gambling time at Harrah's.

Getting Around

By Car A car isn't necessary if you plan to stay in Atlantic City, where taxis and other forms of transportation are plentiful. If you do drive, avoid parking on dark streets far from the Boardwalk and casinos.

Parking Tips Free parking in Atlantic City is always a relief. Be warned: The Atlantic City Police Department writes 90,000 parking tickets each year, and several towing companies compete with city trucks to remove illegally parked cars—at great expense to the owner. The easiest and least expensive way to park is to head for a casino lot. Though incidents of auto theft and other crimes can occur in casino lots, they still tend to be safer than the streets. Before parking in a casino lot, read posted signs carefully to determine if parking is unlimited (that is, free without restriction, as it has been at Harrah's Marina, Showboat, TropWorld, the Taj Mahal, and Trump Castle) or free for a specified time (usually six to eight hours). Some lots require you to pay a fee when you park; your money is refunded when you return to your car and present a ticket that's been validated in the casino. Also be sure the lot is actually a casino lot. Just because it's located within sight of a casino, or even adjacent to one, doesn't guarantee that the casino will pay for your parking.

By Taxi Taxis are plentiful near the entrances to casino hotels, at the municipal bus terminal and the rail terminal. Cabs do not frequent the noncasino hotels, though doormen will call one for you. You should call a cab if you are going to restaurants that are several blocks away from the casinos or to any out-of-the-way location. **Mutual Cab** (tel. 609/345–6111), **Radio Cab** (tel. 609/345–1105), **Red Top Cab** (tel. 609/344–4101), and **Yellow Cab** (tel. 609/344–1221) have reliable service. Fares average about $5 between the Boardwalk and the marina district.

On Foot Atlantic City's Boardwalk was the nation's first elevated wood walkway, and a visit to the city isn't complete without a walk on the boards. Flat shoes are best: Narrow heels tend to wedge themselves into the cracks between the boards.

The Boardwalk, especially in the casino area, is one of the safest parts of Atlantic City. Ten of the casino hotels either front the Boardwalk or are no more than a block from it. Benches, bathrooms, and shaded pavilions are plentiful.

During the day, seedy Pacific Avenue (the first street from the Boardwalk that runs parallel to the beach) and mostly rundown Atlantic Avenue are reasonably safe. After sundown, either use the Boardwalk or take cabs or jitneys.

By Rolling Chair During the late 19th century, when it became fashionable to visit seaside resorts to recover from real and imagined ailments, an entrepreneur decided to rent wheelchairs—with pushers—to visitors who wanted to enjoy the Boardwalk at leisure. They became symbolic of the fantasy life of ease and luxury that Atlantic City evoked, and they spread to boardwalks all over the East Coast. Motorized wheelchairs put human operators out of business in the '60s, but they, too, died out as part of Atlantic City's decline. Now, rolling chairs (most of them restored wicker antiques) are back, typically stationed near the Boardwalk casino entrances. Though some chairs have posted fares of $2.50 per person per mile, many pushers try to negotiate for higher rates or hefty tips for a "tour." Settle on the fare before you leave.

By Bus and Jitney **New Jersey Transit** buses lumber along Atlantic Avenue on their way downbeach to Ventnor, Margate, and Longport or to shopping areas and residential areas in Atlantic City. Base fare is 85¢. White, 13-passenger **jitney** vans run 24 hours a day in all seasons. The jitneys zip up and down Pacific Avenue, visit both marina district casinos, and go as far south as the Atlantic City border at Jackson Avenue for $1 per person. Board jitneys at designated stops on Pacific Avenue street corners or in front of marina casinos. Pay careful attention to the route signs on the front of each jitney. Drivers tend to be courteous and helpful. Jitneys will not stop if they are full.

Exploring Atlantic City

The word "glitz" is a modern word made of unequal parts of "glitter" and "ritz," from Cesar Ritz, the famed 19th-century hotel impresario whose name became synonymous with luxury.

In Atlantic City, glitz refers to the loud, outrageous decoration of casino hotels. Not all of it is in bad taste. Glitz designers try to create environments that are stimulating, exciting, and extraordinary. The more escapist the environment, the more you may be likely to forget about the real world and the consequences of wagering your money.

Unlike amusement park glitz, which appeals to our childlike sense of wonder, casino glitz evokes more adult moods of sensuality, wealth, and power. You don't have to gamble to enjoy it—our tour goes through casinos, but there's no obligation to feed a slot machine. The tour does not enter any area that would require admission, purchase of a meal or drink, or special access, so we won't be seeing the stupendously glitzy high-roller suites or private lounges and dining rooms. Parents with children should note that only adults 21 years and older can enter a casino hotel's gambling area. Walking time is roughly 2½ hours.

Numbers in the margin correspond with points of interest on the Atlantic City map.

① Start at what was once the leader in casino glitz, the former Golden Nugget, now called **Bally's Grand,** at the Boardwalk and Boston Avenue. One of the smallest casino hotels in Atlantic City, the Grand, during its Nugget days, was the city's pre-eminent high-roller house. (The rusting girders two blocks south, by the way, are part of the bankrupt Dunes Casino project, one of three unfinished casino hotels.)

Enter Bally's Grand at the Boardwalk. Inside the door, on the right, is the flamboyant stained glass and black-and-white marble of the ice-cream parlor. The entire casino hotel once had this bright, whimsical blend of art nouveau and high-Victorian Gothic Revival.

Great casino glitz never lets your senses take a break. As you move down the sloping hallway, look in the bathrooms on your right. Behind the doors of the toilet stalls are reproductions of landscape paintings, thoughtfully set at eye level.

The casino on your left is an excellent example of a "day" casino. The overall brightness and the white-and-gold tones suggest daytime activity. The gilded palm trees evoke tropical images, but the most magnificent features are the spangled, brass-toned barrel vaults. Punctuated by outrageously swollen chandeliers, the ceiling creates a sweeping feeling of spaciousness in what is actually a very confined area.

Leave by one of the street exits and you'll see a festive, street-level mural on the casino's Pacific Avenue facade. Everyone in the painting appears happy and dignified.

Reenter the Grand by the entrance at the intersection of Boston and Pacific avenues. Observe the tiny, trailing lights under the carpeted steps, and take the escalator up to the restaurant level.

Like theme parks, theme casino hotels maximize the glitz in their restaurants. As you move through the Grand's second-floor restaurant and convention level, going toward the Boardwalk, you'll see some leftover Nugget glitz in the buffet restaurant. You'll also pass a fake Roman villa (the Italian restaurant), what looks like an opium den (the Chinese restaurant), and a gorgeously glitzy window of beveled glass. Take the escalator down, return to the Boardwalk, and walk north toward TropWorld.

② Enter the **TropWorld Casino & Entertainment Resort** from the Boardwalk at the lighted, arched entryway (the Trop takes up the two blocks between Brighton and Iowa avenues). Once inside, you feel as if you've stepped into a movie set. Old-time Atlantic City is the theme of TropWorld's expanded casino and amusement complex, which combines a retail arcade with restaurant space.

On the second-floor casino level a grand concourse divides Trop-World's dark "night" casino floor—remarkable only for the confusing, labyrinthine layout that makes it very difficult to leave—from Tivoli Pier, a $22 million, indoor miniature theme park designed to recall Atlantic City's fabled amusement piers. These piers were in fact developed as a less-than-scrupulous attempt to extend the Boardwalk toward the ocean. They were originally built to provide a landing for oceangoing vessels, some of which managed to dock when they didn't ram, collide, or otherwise destroy themselves on sandbars in the process.

Absecon Lighthouse, **21**

Bally's Grand, **1**

Bally Park Place Casino Hotel, **13**

Boardwalk, **4**

Brighton Park (Park Place), **14**

Caesar's Atlantic City, **10**

Central Pier, **17**

Claridge Casino Hotel, **15**

Convention Center, **6**

Dennis Hotel, **12**

Garden Pier, **22**

Howard's Pier, **16**

Merv Griffin's Resorts Casino Hotel, **18**

Ocean One Mall, **9**

Penthouse Casino Hotel, **8**

Ritz-Carlton Hotel, **3**

Showboat, **20**

Statue of Caesar Augustus, **11**

TropWorld Casino & Entertainment Resort, **2**

Trump Plaza, **7**

Trump Regency Hotel, **5**

Trump Taj Mahal Resort & Casino, **19**

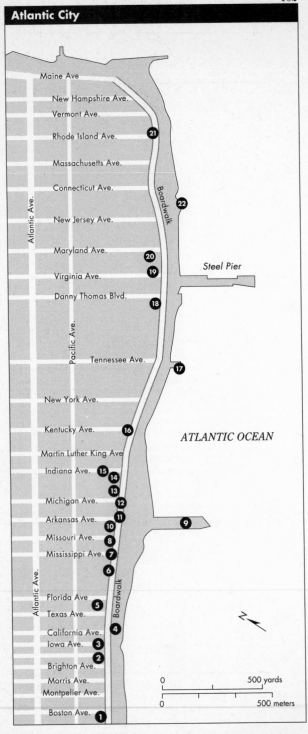

Atlantic City

The first ocean pier was Howard's Pier at Kentucky Avenue, built exactly two years after the Boardwalk. Steel Pier, the longest and most famous, was built in 1898. Applegate's Pier (currently called Central Pier), finished in 1884, at Tennessee Avenue, was bought by "Captain" John L. Young, the Donald Trump of his day, who named the pier after himself. When the pier suffered a fire, Young threw up barricades and charged strollers a dime to see the ruins.

Rising at the rear of the TropWorld concourse is a wonderful, working Ferris wheel (which should be called a Somers wheel, after a device that William Somers invented and premiered on the Boardwalk four years before George Ferris brought a similar amusement ride to the Chicago World's Fair). Tivoli Pier requires admission, so our tour stops here. TropWorld's AC Station buffet, built to resemble a railroad yard, is worth a glance on your way back to the Boardwalk.

3 The large brick building with stone flourishes at Iowa Avenue and the Boardwalk is the former **Ritz-Carlton Hotel,** the only remaining large hotel from Atlantic City's gilded past that has not been converted to a casino. It is now a condo/rental facility.

"Everyone builds his own Boardwalk," snarled a Philadelphia travel writer on an Atlantic City excursion in the late 19th century. "The shops are rented out to every variety of fakir and catchpenny show. All sorts of queer signs hang overhead, and men and women sitting around beadwork stands dressed as Indians are not Indians at all. Fraud, subterfuge, and sometimes downright rascality and villainy pervade almost every nook and corner." One of those rascals could have been the "inventor" of saltwater taffy, David Bradley, who, around 1883, claimed ocean water had swamped his candy one night.

The idea for an elevated wooden walkway was born at the Chester County House, a beachfront hotel that stood near the end of New York Avenue. The owner, Jacob Keim, was annoyed by the fact that the sand clinging to beach strollers' shoes and garments ended up on his furnishings. (This was, after all, before the invention of the vacuum cleaner.) In the spring of 1870 he and Alexander Boardman, a conductor on the Camden & Atlantic Railroad, came up with the solution. The wooden path was named after Boardman, who had not only specified that the boards be elevated, but that they have cracks between them to allow sand to fall through.

The first Boardwalk was finished on June 26, 1870. It was a temporary structure, disassembled at night and moved to accommodate changing tides and beach conditions. In 1890, a permanent, steel-girdered, 24-foot-wide Boardwalk, towering 10 feet above the sand, advanced Atlantic City into modern times. **4** This is essentially the same **Boardwalk** you see today. Each storm and fire brings improvements, the most recent being reinforced concrete and the gradual replacement of the traditional yellow pine (which quickly weathers to a dismal gray) with stronger, reddish jarrah wood.

5 Continue north. The black-glass **Trump Regency Hotel,** adjacent to the sweeping concrete arc of the Atlantic City Convention Center, was the former Atlantis Casino Hotel. When the Atlantis went bankrupt, it was purchased by Donald Trump, who closed the casino area.

❻ The **Convention Center,** still called **Convention Hall** by locals,
hosts the **Miss America Scholarship Pageant,** America's most
famous beauty contest, held every September. Originating in
1920 as the Fall Frolic International Rolling Chair Pageant, the
event drew such a crowd that the city thought a grown-up beauty pageant might draw the big crowds that thronged Asbury
Park's Baby Parade. For nearly 70 years, bringing people into
Atlantic City has been the pageant's primary but unstated pur-
pose. The pageant has had its share of scandal and criticism,
much of it justified and most of it ignored. What's nice about
Pageant Week is that the atmosphere of the city changes for a
while. People smile at each other on the Boardwalk. Pageant
families—relatives and chaperons—wear buttons depicting
their dimpled hopefuls.

The pageant consists of two days of preliminaries, usually
Wednesday and Thursday, a Friday evening Boardwalk parade, and the Saturday night televised finale. Most who have
been there agree that it's better on television: Convention Hall
develops a peculiar reek of greasy snacks from the refreshment
stands. Everything stops and the stage lights dim when com-
mercials are shown. The hall is so large that you must squint
through binoculars to tell the contestants apart. Being in the
audience does have one special thrill when, just before the televised portion begins, a handful of Miss Americas from the past
trot down the runway. Even the most die-hard cynics join the
crowd and applaud mightily. Though Miss Americas have kids,
grow fat, and die, the parade of golden oldies is the only thing in
Atlantic City that has aged well.

❼ Just past the Convention Center is **Trump Plaza,** now one of the
two Atlantic City prime high-roller houses. The sawtooth,
black-glass hotel tower was supposed to echo a similar sawtooth glass wall on New York's Trump Plaza condo/commercial
tower. The peaked red-and-brass arch at Trump Plaza's Boardwalk level grabs your eyes and pulls you in. Notice the rich,
salmon-colored marble around you. The marble, the flash-and-
brass trim with red and black accents, creates a feeling of cold,
unfriendly arrogance, especially in the hotel lobby, which you
can find if you go to your right, past the cocktail lounge (with its
absurd, stylized Trump crown) and the coffee shop (note paintings of Trump buildings thrusting high over the New York skyline).

Unlike regular hotels, which provide comfortable, spacious
lobbies for relaxation, informal meetings, drinks, or afternoon
tea, casino hotel lobbies are blatantly uncomfortable spaces
that inspire you to go somewhere else, preferably to the casino
floor. There are no chairs in Trump Plaza's lobby. The glossy,
mirrored brass columns and equally glossy marble are brutally
cold.

❽ The abandoned building next to Trump Plaza is the **Penthouse
Casino Hotel,** Atlantic City's second unfinished casino project
and a peculiar monument to human greed. Look down the dark
street of Columbia Place and you'll see a few houses, one of
which was hastily converted into a sandwich shop. These property owners held out for more money from *Penthouse* publisher
and developer Bob Guccione and found a casino being built
around them instead. The unfinished casino is currently owned
by the Trump organization.

Stand in the middle of Missouri Avenue, the street that separates the Penthouse project from Caesars, and look past Pacific Avenue to the white walls of the Trump Plaza parking garage. This is the site of the **500 Cafe** (known locally as the 500 Club or "The Five"), a nightclub that featured Frank Sinatra and many Italian entertainers until it burned down in the late '60s. In the '50s Dean Martin, then a struggling singer, teamed with Jerry Lewis, a madcap Jewish comic, to form Martin & Lewis, the volatile comedy duo that split up after a series of feuds. The 500 Cafe was one of 30 nightclubs in Atlantic City, most of which had some form of back-room gambling (the Five's gaming tables were upstairs) or off-track betting.

Before going into Caesars, the intimidating black-glass, brass-and-red trimmed casino next in line on the Boardwalk, head to ❾ **Ocean One Mall,** sprawling out into the Atlantic. Ocean One is a casino-age renovation of Million Dollar Pier, which was Atlantic City's most famous amusement pier after Steel Pier. Built in 1906 by John L. Young, the Donald Trump of his day, for the heavily promoted cost of $1 million, the pier had a large ballroom and a flamboyant, three-story Italianate villa with a sculpture garden at the rear.

In the back of Ocean One, on the first floor, is an arcade area with skeeball and other traditional Boardwalk skill games. The second floor has a reasonably good food court. Go to the third-floor restaurant level (take either the escalators or the glass elevators) and head toward the ocean. Go out the doors near the Black Forest Restaurant and walk all the way to the back of the sun deck. Turn around for an impressive panoramic view of the Boardwalk and its casino towers in an area roughly near the tower room of Young's villa. Return to the Boardwalk.

❿ **Caesars Atlantic City,** the second legal casino to open in Atlantic City, was formerly the Howard Johnson's Regency. Caesars World, Inc., the famed Las Vegas–based gambling and resort company, was so confident that the Boardwalk gambling hall would draw enough warm bodies that it left the original casino floor unheated. The current complex, much expanded, added not only heating but glitz. Enter the deco-echo casino from the Boardwalk. You'll find yourself in a warren of slot machines. Gaze left (south) at the full-scale reproduction of Michaelangelo's *David*. At the opposite (northern) end of the casino floor, almost facing *David*, is the prow of Cleopatra's Barge lounge, modeled after a larger lounge in Caesars Palace in Las Vegas. Caesars' second-floor Appian Way shopping arcade is an example of abundant marble done properly. You get the feeling of a grandly decadent imperial palace, especially in the echoing corridor near the Circus Maximus showroom. The spiral staircase leads up to the third-floor restaurant level, which has some nice themed restaurant entrances, especially the Moon gate leading to the Asian steak house. Return to the Boardwalk.

Just outside Caesars is another reproduction, this one a statue ⓫ of **Caesar Augustus** highlighted in a special red-and-brass floodlit niche at the corner of the Boardwalk at Arkansas Avenue.

Sometime in the 1890s, a young juggler from Philadelphia got a summer job performing at a Boardwalk beer garden called Fortescue's that stood on this site. For $10 per week, plus board, he had two distinct jobs. The first was attracting attention as a juggler just inside the beer garden's entrance. The second was pretending to drown at least three times a day, sometimes once an hour. His cries would be heard by stooges, who would rush out to rescue the lad, hauling him onto the beach, onto the Boardwalk, and into the beer garden, where a crowd would invariably follow. The lad lasted only a few weeks at this job, going off to join a minstrel show on Steel Pier and then moving on to vaudeville. As a vaudeville performer he kept his Atlantic City stage name, invented when his full name, William Claude Dukinfield, did not fit on the beer garden's marquee—W. C. Fields. When Fields became one of history's greatest comic film stars and was wealthy enough to buy a house with a swimming pool, he would never go in the water. When asked why, Fields was said to proclaim, "When you're paid to do it, the act loses its charm."

Just a few yards south of this corner is the marvelous facade of the Warner Theater, now a fast-food shop. This small former vaudeville house later became one of 40 Atlantic City movie theaters (today there are none within the city limits). Beyond the theater is the unfinished **Carousel Casino** project.

⑫ Beyond the mirrored-glass food-court facade at Michigan Avenue and the Boardwalk is the old, unmarked **Dennis Hotel.** The ornate brick, stone, and the copper Mansard roof are hidden under thick white paint. The Dennis, now part of Bally's Park Place, only hints at the Boardwalk's turn-of-the-century architectural opulence. Go through the arch in the food court into the Dennis's courtyard. Imagine people having tea here, relaxing in the afternoon breeze.

⑬ Return to the Boardwalk and stand back far enough to appreciate the cold, bunkerlike Boardwalk face of the **Bally Park Place Casino Hotel,** located just north of the famed Park Place. At night Bally's hexagonal hotel tower is lit with a slowly changing array of white and colored lights.

A stupendous, 93-foot escalator connects Bally's green-and-brass parklike restaurant level to the churning, deep-purple and mauve casino floor. Take the escalator up. The fountain at the top is composed of architectural fragments of the Marlborough-Blenheim Hotel, which was torn down to make way for the casino. Though Atlantic City had many larger hotels, none matched the fantastic Marlborough-Blenheim. Bally's erected a small shrine to the hotel, which you can visit by following signs on the restaurant level to the convention rooms. You'll see a single, floodlit gargoyle perched in front of photographs of the magnificent hotel. Pause here, admire what once was, and return to the Boardwalk.

Time Out   Ferrara of New York (tel. 609/340–2000), a branch of a New York Italian pastry shop, is carved out of Bally's monolithic Boardwalk facade. There's a small, inexpensive sandwich menu for lunch, and the rum-drenched, cream-filled pastries, with espresso or cappuccino, are delicious. Sit on the risers and watch the never-ending parade of Boardwalk strollers, gamblers, and rolling chairs.

⑭ **Brighton Park,** the original Park Place, is the best example of the dubious effect of casino gambling on Atlantic City. What had been a grim, gloomy city park, neglected by municipal government, was given a $7 million face-lift paid for by the Claridge and Sands casino hotels on the condition that they be allowed to build a people mover capable of siphoning gamblers off the Boardwalk. The park landscaping is open and inviting, and the new outdoor amphitheater is a focal point for small-scale cultural events. The people mover, on the other hand, is a bulky, cumbersome chute that overwhelms the park and casts much of it in shadow.

⑮ The adjacent **Claridge Casino Hotel,** the third of four remaining Boardwalk hotels from the city's golden years, was a favorite of Frank Sinatra. The building's exterior is the best restoration in the city. With the exception of an arched colonnade in one of the slot areas, however, the inside reflects none of the hotel's former grandeur.

Use the people mover on your way out of the Claridge. The so-called "museum" you glide through on the way is really just a series of photographs, most of them featuring entertainers who have performed at the Claridge or Sands. Turn right at the flowerpot, and enter the **Sands Hotel & Casino.** Then take the three-story escalator to the Sands's Food Court.

This was the first Atlantic City casino food court, and in many ways it's still the best. The row-house decor evokes inner-city, ethnic neighborhood nostalgia among older gamblers. Leave the food court, take the smaller escalator to the second floor, and look into the **Punch Bowl lounge.** This quiet, relaxing lounge is a surprising example of reverse glitz, an environment that suggests dark, masculine, upper-class New York hotel lounges rather than the frenetic casino dazzle. The Punch Bowl is named for the notoriously potent Brighton punch served in the old Brighton Hotel, an elegant Queen Anne–style wood hotel that once stood at this site. You can get a glass of the fruity punch made to order at the Punch Bowl bar. Leave the Sands, return to the Boardwalk, and continue north.

⑯ Kentucky Avenue and the Boardwalk is the site of Atlantic City's first amusement pier, **Howard's Pier,** dating from 1882. Three blocks west of the Boardwalk, Kentucky Avenue, between Atlantic and Arctic avenues, was the center of the city's black entertainment district. At its heart is the boarded-up ruin of **Club Harlem,** where nearly every major black entertainer, from Louis Armstrong to James Brown, performed. Lola Falana and Leslie Uggams were discovered here.

⑰ Near Tennessee Avenue is the Moorish Revival **Central Pier.** Destroyed many times by storms and fire, it was Atlantic City's second amusement pier, beginning as Applegate's Pier in 1884. The pier became John L. Young's first major acquisition (he originally called it Ocean Pier). When the pier burned, Young put up a fence and charged passersby 10¢ to see the destruction. Recently restored, Central Pier now has retail shops, offices, and a small amusement area that is open during the summer season.

The large parking lot at South Carolina Avenue is the site of the Chalfonte Hotel, which was connected to the Haddon Hall (now Merv Griffin's Resorts) by a covered walkway. Look across the lot to its eastern edge. The narrow street extending west from the center of the lot, about 100 yards from the Boardwalk, is **Chalfonte Alley,** Atlantic City's red-light district during the earlier part of the century. None of the celebrated bordellos remain.

⑱ Merv Griffin's Resorts Casino Hotel, the former Resorts International, was Atlantic City's first casino hotel. It opened on Memorial Day weekend in 1978, just one year after New Jersey passed its Casino Gaming Act. Griffin bought Resorts in 1989 and has restored the property using a white-and-pink color scheme and adding a twinkling "starry night" ceiling to the game room. Only a few touches of the old days remain. From the second-floor restaurant level you can see the elaborately paneled ceiling in the mezzanine.

Return to the Boardwalk. **Steeplechase Pier** (circa 1899), an amusement and performing-arts showplace (John Philip Sousa was a star act) directly opposite Resorts, was victimized by several fires. Griffin has promised to restore it, but what shape it will take, and what it will contain, have not been announced.

⑲ It's impossible to miss the **Trump Taj Mahal Resort & Casino.** At 42 stories, it's the tallest building in New Jersey, a vast glass tower. The Boardwalk facade is so spectacularly flamboyant and so visually confusing—with its riot of colorful, glistening, Moorish domes, turrets, belvederes, and absurd staircases—that if the entrances weren't marked, you wouldn't be able to find a way in.

The Taj cost $1.2 billion to build and is one of the most expensive buildings in the world. Go into the casino entrance to see if developer Donald Trump got his money's worth. You'll notice immediately that the color scheme is different. Where other casinos clobber visitors with loud, bright primary colors, the Taj tickles, with purple, peach, apricot, and pink tones, saving the primary colors for accents. The colors and a lack of spacial references help disguise the enormity of the Taj's 3-acre casino floor. Bloated chandeliers still overwhelm, and the casino's glittering barrel vaults are a steal from the original Golden Nugget.

The philosophy behind the Taj's glitz—indeed the entire property—is that more is more. The effect is exhausting. The carpet, a swirling dazzle of colors, is deliberately loud because loud carpeting disguises cigarette burns and wear and tear better than quiet, simple patterns. The Taj also reflects much of what has been learned by the casino industry, especially the importance of attracting drive-in gamblers. Go through the casino, past the lobby, outside the glassy Virginia Avenue doorway, and walk up the preposterous avenue of elephants and gratuitously gaudy facades of what are really hideously oversized parking garages.

The white tower on the north is the **Best of Life** senior citizens home. Unlike the tiny properties who refused to sell to Bob Guccione, the Best of Life building struck a deal with the Trump organization. In exchange for enduring the uncomfortable proximity to the casino, as well as the noise and dust connected with construction, the residents of the Best of Life now get free heat and electricity from the Taj Mahal, some maintenance (free exterior paint and landscaping), and a walkway leading directly to the Boardwalk.

Return to the Taj and take the tremendous escalator (just like Bally's) up to the second-floor restaurant level. The Safari

Steakhouse resembles a Banana Republic store, with its ridiculously fake tree trunks. Just as the Sands Food Court tried to seduce older, ethnic gamblers with a fake urban scene, the Taj's rock-and-roll food court yearns for yuppies, with its carseat booths, motorcycle, and Elvis effigy.

Return to the Boardwalk. The arched walkway overhead leads to the bald concrete strip of what was the famous **Steel Pier,** a spectacular low-cost family entertainment complex erected in 1898. Duke Ellington, Harry James, and Frank Sinatra were among thousands of entertainers who performed here, with such circus-act institutions as the Diving Horse, whose plunge into a tank of water vibrated the rear end of the pier. Elvis Presley was denied a date at Steel Pier because, in the much-quoted words of pier impresario George Hamid, "I didn't think anybody could be a success with a name like Elvis." Today Donald Trump owns the pier, and his plans for the structure are for additional convention space or an enclosed theme park in the next decade.

20 The **Showboat's** sloping facade hints at the front of an ocean liner. Inside, it is a rough knockoff of the old Golden Nugget. Unlike the Nugget, which used its San Francisco Victoriana to titillate high rollers, the Showboat's nautical, New Orleans decor aspires to the middle- to low-rolling crowd. The florid red wallpaper, abundant chandeliers, and hokey restaurant facades are meant to be immediately accessible and amusingly nonthreatening. Random stars in the ceiling above the main concourse cluster around the restaurant and casino entrances. The second-floor bowling center is modern and incongruously nonglitzy. Gilded steamboat smokestacks at the Showboat's auto entrance are supposed to resemble Mississippi paddle wheelers.

You may see surfers in the ocean outside the Showboat. The States Avenue beach, which the Showboat fronts, is favored by surfers on Absecon Island. Before the casino was built, this was the site of an international surfing competition. Because surfers don't gamble, the competition was discontinued because of a lack of sponsorship.

21 Wander a few yards north of the Showboat; to your left (west) you'll be able to see the cupola and tower of the **Absecon Lighthouse,** on Rhode Island Avenue off Pacific Avenue, now surrounded by low- and middle-income housing projects. The lighthouse has no published telephone number and is in a high-crime area, so a visit is not recommended.

22 To your right is **Garden Pier,** the only amusement pier owned by the city. On the pier is the Atlantic City Art League's small museum, which features modern art and historical artifacts. *Tel. 609/347–5844. Admission free. Open daily, 9:30–4.*

You can return to the southern end of the Boardwalk where our tour began by taxi from the Showboat or by jitney on Pacific Avenue across from the turnoff to the Showboat. Taxi fare is approximately $5; jitney fare is $1.

What to See and Do with Children

Beyond a day at the beach, there are no free activities for children in Atlantic City. All casinos have coin-operated video arcades similar to those on the Boardwalk and in the rear of the

Ocean One Mall. The city has two family-oriented amusement piers. **Central Pier,** on the Boardwalk at Tennessee Avenue, has 13 rides, including a carousel. TropWorld Casino's **Tivoli Pier** (Iowa Ave. and the Boardwalk, tel. 609/340–4396) indoor theme park has a micro–roller coaster, Ferris wheel, bumper cars, and other small-scale amusements, plus a small lounge with a one-hour revue-style show.

Off the Beaten Track

Inside the Atlantic City Public Library is the **Heston Collection,** a small assortment of memorabilia, old souvenirs, historic relics from the city's past, Monopoly games, books, films, and maps. *Tennessee and Atlantic Aves., tel. 609/345–2269. Admission free. Open Tues.–Thurs. 9–5. Closed Fri.–Mon.*

Gardner's Basin, an attempt to create a Mystic Seaport–style maritime village, is at best a work in progress. Though out of the way at the end of North New Hampshire Avenue on the Inlet, the tumbledown atmosphere; the proximity to commercial, sport fishing, and recreational boating docks; and the peculiar collection of boats (which include a lightship, a miniature submarine, and a speedboat) all make for a rewarding side trip. The moderately priced Flying Cloud Café (*see* Dining, below) is worth a visit. *800 North New Hampshire Ave., tel. 609/348–2880. Admission free, though some fees are charged during festivals and special events.*

Shopping

Most of the casino hotels have shopping arcades, with expensive brand-name clothes, gifts, jewelry, souvenirs, and accessories designed to catch the eyes of high rollers (who can get some of these items as gifts from the casino) or paying customers who have just won a jackpot and want to commemorate their fortune with a spending spree. The Taj Mahal has a Tiffany shop, Caesars has Gucci, and you'll find similarly expensive retail arcades at TropWorld, the Sands, and Bally's Grand.

The Boardwalk is dominated by candy shops, low-end souvenir shops, and bargain shops. **Ocean One Mall** (tel. 609/347–8082), the largest of these, stretches toward the Atlantic, opposite Caesars, and has an odd mix of typical mall chain shops, gift stores, bargain shops (Atlantic Books on the second level discounts hardbacks), an amusement arcade, a food court, and third-floor restaurants. The **Eleganza** (tel. 609/348–4894) men's shop on the Boardwalk level of the Ocean Club Condominium is glitzy and chic.

Most of the shops that remain on Atlantic Avenue have tried and failed to attract business from Boardwalk tourists. You'll find some bargains here, a few grocery stores, restaurants, liquor stores, and luncheonettes, but the pickings tend to be slim. **Giacomo** (2021 Atlantic Ave., tel. 609/345–1222) has a good selection of men's sport clothing. **Princeton Antiques** (2917 Atlantic Ave., tel. 609/344–1943) sells old books, antiques, and collectibles. **Gordon's Alley** (between Atlantic and Pacific Aves. at North Carolina Ave., tel. 609/344–5000) is a surprisingly upscale mall, with a Polo shop, gourmet food emporia, and Alley Books, a small bookshop with an intelligent selection.

Ducktown, Atlantic City's Little Italy, has some wonderful little grocery stores, such as **Bongiovanni's** (2307 Atlantic Ave., tel. 609/344–6622), and bakeries whose aromatic goods make an afternoon walk along otherwise dismal Mississippi Avenue a heady experience. Buy a loaf at **Rando's Bakery** (128 N. Mississippi Ave., tel. 609/345–6678), get some sliced cheese and deli meats at Bongiovanni's, and have a feast!

How to Gamble

Lights flash, dice bounce jauntily down a table, slot machines beep, blink, and clang. Gambling fever is in the air. Before you catch the bug, however, consider these essential rules: Don't gamble when you're in debt, drunk, irritated, or tired; never play with more money than you can afford to lose; and if you find yourself in a losing streak, stop playing—don't expect a sudden reversal in fortunes to permit you to catch up. As the New Jersey Casino Control Commission says, "Bet with your head, not over it."

Slot Machines

The slots in Atlantic City still come in nickel and dime denominations, though these are becoming rare. Quarter machines are by far the most numerous, with dollar machines, half dollar, $5, and even $25 machines after that.

Though the symbols vary—from fruit to cards—all the machines work the same way. You put from one to seven coins in the slot, pull the handle and, if the bars line up, or you get a row of cherries, jackpot signs, or the glowing cards equivalent to the appropriate jackpot, money clatters out. If you hit the big jackpot, lights flash, bells ring, buzzers buzz, sirens sound, and, faster than you might think, a slot host appears to check the machine to make sure the jackpot was hit fairly and that no one has tampered with it. Some things to remember about slot machines:

All slot machines in Atlantic City are required to return 87% of what they take in. Some, typically the large, "big Bertha" dollar machines placed at the entrances to the casinos, are set to return as much as 95%. Before you go racing off to feed them, remember that for every dollar you put in, the machine is keeping 5¢ to 13¢. You may hit a small jackpot and have all of your money, or double your money. But the longer you play, on the average, the more the machine will keep until you end up without any money. The trick is to quit when you're ahead.

The odds of winning increase with the number of coins you put in. Put one coin in and the machine will only pay out when the right combinations are arranged straight across. Put another coin in and the machine may pay out combinations on the horizontal line and on one diagonal. Another coin will increase your chances of winning. Most large jackpots can't be won unless you play the maximum number of coins per pull.

Slot machines offering the largest jackpots are arranged in rows or clusters, with large numbered signs above them. They are called Linked Progressive Slots. These "linked" machines pool their take and their jackpot. As the machines are fed, the jackpot increases incrementally. In some casinos you'll find Megabucks slot machines. These machines are not only linked to others on the casino floor, but to machines in other casinos as well. In all cases, you can only win the progressive jackpot by playing the maximum number of coins per pull.

Pulling the handle hard or soft won't affect the outcome. Most handles make a crunching sound when you pull them because slot machine companies found that people like the illusion of pulling on something that offers some resistance. In fact, the handle trips a switch and the mechanical reels are spun at a constant speed by a motor. In the machines with video screens, everything is done by computer.

In Atlantic City, slot jackpots in excess of $1,200 are paid by a cashier's check from the casino, which can then be cashed at the casino window. To receive your check, you must provide valid identification and fill out a U.S. Department of Internal Revenue Form W2G, for gambling winnings, or a 1099 form. Both forms require that you provide your name, address, and Social Security number.

Table Games

In order to play table games, you'll need chips—colorful plastic pieces exchanged for cash. (They make the play faster and neater, but they also help you lose your understanding of the value of money—a stack of chips doesn't *feel* the same way in your hand as does a wad of cash.) The lowest denomination chip in Atlantic City is the white $1 chip, followed by red ($5), green ($25), black ($100), and purple ($500). Higher denomination chips are sometimes issued in metallic plates.

Chips are available at cashier windows (known as "cages") or from any dealer. When buying chips from a dealer, wait until the game he or she is handling is finished and all bets are paid. Dealers are not permitted to change chips back into cash; that must be done at the cage.

The person who watches the dealer is the "floor man," though many floor men in Atlantic City are women. A "pit boss" watches the dealer, the floor man, and the action at a group of tables. Pit bosses can issue comps—freebies called complimentary services—to gamblers who have made significant wagers. If you want to be "comped," ask the pit boss to rate your play. The pit boss will keep tabs on the amount of money you bet: It typically takes $2,000 to $5,000 worth of wagers on your first visit to a casino to merit such comps as a free meal or show tickets.

The pit boss will not be your only observer. Look overhead and you'll see mirrored domes hanging from the ceiling. These hide television cameras, which are capable of reading the serial number on a dollar bill. Beside the cameras are mirrored areas where special cameras, or a crew of human watchers, can view individual tables from above.

Before you decide to play a table game, look at the limit of the table. The limit is the lowest minimum bet. Unlike Las Vegas, where $2-limit gambling tables are reasonably plentiful, most Atlantic City tables start with a $5 limit, which can be raised to $25 and even $100 as the casino fills.

Drinks at all Atlantic City table games are free while you are at the table. A tip of $1 per drink is customary, but not required.

Gambling chips in Las Vegas are an unofficial currency, but in Atlantic City chips from a casino have no cash value outside that casino, so cash in any you have left over. You will not be compelled to show identification or fill out an IRS form unless your winnings were extraordinary enough for the state Division of Gaming Enforcement to notice. Keep in mind that failure to report your winnings as income is a violation of Federal laws (and a picture taken of you by a camera in the cage when you cashed in your chips is available to Federal and state law enforcement agencies).

Big Six Wheel Also called the wheel of fortune, this carnival game is considered a "sucker" bet because the likelihood of losing is as high here, sometimes higher, than in a slot machine.

Betting is simple. Put your chips on the square you want. Symbols on the squares show various dollar amounts, a joker, and the casino logo. The dealer spins the wheel. If the wheel stops with the pointer on a symbol that matches your square, you're paid as follows:

Square	Pays
$1	one-to-one (even money)
$2	two-to-one (double money)
$5	five-to-one
$10	10-to-one
$20	20-to-one
Joker	45-to-one
Logo	45-to-one

Blackjack This British import is Atlantic City's most popular table game. Nobody calls it "21" here, though the object of the game is to collect cards as close in value to 21 as possible without going over. Seven players can sit at one crescent-shape table. Your position at the table has nothing to do with your odds of winning or losing.

Players place their bets. The game begins with the dealer dealing two cards, faceup, to each player, starting from the left. The dealer then deals two cards to himself, one of which is facedown. Add up the numerical values of your cards. (Face cards count as 10, aces are either 1 or 11.) If the two cards total 21, you have blackjack and you win immediately—unless the dealer also has blackjack, in which case it is a tie, and no one wins.

Players ask to be "hit" if they wish to receive additional cards. The value of those cards is added to the player's total. At any point you may decide to "stand," and receive no more cards. If you go over 21 ("bust"), you lose.

After all the players have been dealt their cards, the dealer reveals his down-facing card. The dealer must take another card at 16 or less, but cannot take additional cards if he has 17 or more. If the dealer busts, he must pay all the players whose hands are under 21. If not, all players with card totals lower than the dealer's lose.

If the dealer's "up" card is a 9 or less, blackjacks are paid immediately, 3-to-2 (that is, if you made a $50 bet, and got a blackjack, you'd be paid $75). If the dealer's up card is 10 or more, all hands must be played before bets are paid.

Never touch the cards in blackjack. Requests for cards are either stated verbally or indicated with hand gestures. Hand gestures are recommended.

Players can also decide to alter their bets and hands in the following ways:

Doubling down. If the amount of your cards is 9, 10, or 11, you can double your bet, but can only draw one additional card. If the dealer has a blackjack, you lose only your original bet, half of what you wagered.

Splitting pairs. If you have two cards, each with the same value, you can say "split." You bet the same amount again and each card is treated as the first card of a separate hand. You must play out the first hand before obtaining additional cards for the second. If you're splitting aces, you can only ask for one additional card per ace. You're not permitted to split pairs a third time in the same game. If the dealer gets a blackjack, you only lose the first of your two bets.

Take insurance. This is basically betting that the dealer will win. If the dealer's faceup card is an ace, a player can "insure" his bet by putting half the amount on the insurance line. If the dealer has a blackjack, the player keeps his money. If the dealer and the player lose, the player loses his bet.

Winning repeatedly at blackjack depends on the cards you're dealt and your knowledge of the game. Because there are several cards in a deck with the value of 10, you can expect high value cards to come more often than low. Be cautious and consider standing if you have cards totaling more than 17. This advice isn't foolproof, however. In blackjack it is quite possible to get a run of low cards followed by a run of high cards.

Card counters attempt to memorize the number and amount of cards dealt in a game so they can determine the values of cards remaining in the "shoe" (the dealer's card dispenser), and then bet and play accordingly. Many books have been written describing card-counting strategies, and you may see advertisements for blackjack strategy courses that make extravagant claims. In the first years of legalized casino gambling, many card counters used their skills to win large amounts of money. Then the casino persuaded the state to change the rules. Casinos can now use up to eight decks of cards in a blackjack shoe, with a mandatory shuffle after two-thirds of the shoe's cards have been played. This policy has made counting cards much more difficult.

Craps This is the most exciting game to watch, the closest thing Atlantic City has to a spectator sport when the boxing action is slow. The tumbling dice bring out the rowdiness in gamblers, who shout, groan, and pray as the game wears into the night.

Players and observers alike are drawn by the singsongy chatter of the "stick man," the uniformed dealer who announces the outcome of each roll while gathering the dice with a long wooden stick and returning them to the "shooter," the player who rolls the dice.

Craps may actually be the most confusing game because so many different bets can be made on each roll of the dice. To make things even more puzzling, payouts range from even money (Pass Line, Don't Pass Line, Come, Don't Come, and Field Bets 3, 4, 9, 10, and 11) to 9-to-5 (if you bet $50, you'd get $90) on point bets of 4-to-10. Confused yet? Try this: You don't have to make a bet to throw the dice, but if you decide to throw and don't think you'll win, you can bet against yourself.

The easiest way to make sense out of craps is to look at a pair of dice. Each cube, which in Atlantic City is always made of red transparent plastic with opaque white dots, has six numbered sides. Roll the dice and 36 possible combinations can come up. However, only one combination can give you 12: both sides showing 6 must be up. And only one combination will give you a two: both sides showing 1 (the famous "snake eyes"). On the other hand, you have two chances in 36 to get a value of 3 or 11. You have 3 chances out of 36 to get a 4 or 10; 4 chances to get 5 or 9; 5 chances to get 6 or 8; and 6 chances (1 + 6; 2 + 5; 3 + 4; 4 + 3; 5 + 2; 6 + 1) to get 7, the most common roll of all.

In craps, you can make three basic kinds of bets: (1) the total of the numbers that come up in a roll; (2) the combination making up the total (3 + 3 or 2 + 4, for example); or (3) one number (or group of numbers) being rolled in a sequence before another.

A game begins when a shooter picks up the dice. Before the dice are rolled, you can make the following bets:

Pass Line. Here you are betting that the shooter's first roll, called the "come out," will be a 7 or 11. If so, you're paid even money (a $10 bet would pay back $10). You lose if the shooter "craps out" by rolling a 2, 3, or 12. If the shooter rolls any other number value—4, 5, 6, 8, 9, or 10—that number becomes the shooter's "point." During subsequent rolls, Pass Line bets are paid every time the shooter rolls his point until the shooter "sevens-out" by rolling a 7. All Pass Line bets lose when the shooter rolls a 7.

Don't Pass Line. Almost opposite of the pass line, betting "the Don't" means that you think the shooter will crap out by rolling a 2 or 3 the first time (a 12 is a standoff: nobody wins). If the shooter craps out, you're paid even money. You lose if the shooter rolls a 7 or an 11. If the shooter rolls any other number, that becomes his "point." You win if the shooter rolls a 7 before he rolls his point again. If the shooter's point comes up before a 7 does, you lose. Because the chances of rolling a 7 are higher than any other number value, the Don't Pass Line has slightly better odds than the Pass Line. It's not unusual to see cynical shooters playing the Don't Line against themselves.

Place Bets. Here you want the individual number you select to be rolled before a 7. If the 7 comes, you lose. Four or 10 pay 9-to-5 ($50 bet gets $90); 5 or 9 pay 7-to-5 ($50 bet gets $70); 6 or 8 pay 7-to-6 ($60 bet gets $70).

Big Six or Big Eight. You get even money (a $10 bet is paid $10) if a 6 or 8 comes up before a 7 does.

Hard Ways. Here you're betting on exact combinations of the dice pictured at the center of the craps table. The payouts vary from 7-to-1 ($10 bet pays $70) for a Hard 4 (2 + 2) or Hard 10 (5 + 5) to 9-to-1 ($10 bet pays $90) for a Hard 6 (3 + 3) or a Hard 8 (4 + 4). Your bet stays on the table until that number value comes up. You win if the combination on the dice is the one you bet on. If you bet on a Hard 8 and 6 + 2 is rolled, you lose. You also lose if a 7 is rolled.

The following bets differ from those above in that the bet is limited to the very next roll:

The Field. You're betting that the number value of the next roll will be a 2, 3, 4, 9, 10, 11, or 12. If a 2 or a 12 comes up, you're paid 2-to-1 ($10 bet is paid $20). Three, 4, 9, 10, and 11 are paid even money.

Any Craps. You bet that the very next roll will be a 2, 3, or 12. The payout is 8-to-1 ($10 bet brings $80).

Any Seven. Here you bet that the very next roll will be a 7, paying 5-to-1 (a $10 bet brings $50).

Eleven. Much as in Any 7, you bet that the very next roll is 11. If it is, you're paid 15-to-1 ($10 bet brings $150).

The following bets are made on subsequent rolls after the shooter has made his point—that is, rolled a 4, 5, 6, 8, 9, or 10:

Come. This is similar to the Pass Line. You win if a 7 or an 11 comes up, and if the shooter rolls his point before sevening-out. You lose if the shooter "craps out" with a 2, 3, or 12. The bet pays even money.

Don't Come. The reverse of the Come bet, this Don't brings you even money if the shooter craps out on 2 or 3. You also win if the shooter rolls a 7 before rolling his point. You lose if he rolls 11, or if his point comes up, followed by a 7. A 12 is a standoff: nobody wins.

Dice are usually passed to the right after a shooter sevens-out. Anyone over 21 years of age can roll the dice, and the shooter is not obligated to bet, though it is expected that a shooter will show confidence in his or her destiny by putting money into the game.

Roulette

Roulette is a breezy, easy game. It is centered around a spinning wheel with various numbered slots, into one of which a little ball eventually falls. You can bet on any single number from one to 36 or on various combinations, as well as the green zero or the double zero. Because half the numbers (not counting zero and double zero) are in red slots, you can bet simply that the ball will fall into either a red slot or a black one. You can bet that the ball will land in a slot that is numbered even or odd; that the slot will be in either the first or the second half of 36; that the slot's number falls in the first, second, or third row of 12 on the playing field; or in groups of 6, 5, 4, 3, and 2 numbers.

Roulette's only complication is the placement of chips on the table's playing field. A difference of a half inch can mean a win or a loss. If you have any questions about a bet, ask the dealer. He or she will show you the correct position for the bet you seek.

Before playing roulette, you must buy specially colored chips from the dealer. The chips help the dealer determine who made each bet, and they don't leave the table. Every player has a different color, and the chips are for one denomination only ($5, $10, and so forth). When you're finished playing, the dealer will exchange roulette chips for casino chips.

You place your bets as the wheel is spinning. No bets can be made after the ball is released.

The Bets **Even Money.** The row closest to the players on the playing field includes squares for red numbers, black numbers, even numbers, and odd numbers. You win if, for example, you bet even numbers and the ball lands in an even-numbered slot. You lose if an odd number, 0, or 00 comes up.

Two-to-One. The row between the even money bets and the individual numbers divides the possibilities into groups of 12. You can bet in the first (1–12), second (13–24), or third group (25–36) by putting a chip in that square. Along the lower edge of the numbered field are three columns of 12 numbers each. You can bet in any of these columns. If you bet $20 on the 13–24 group and 18 comes up, for example, you will be paid $40, or double your money. You lose if the number is outside your group, or 0 or 00.

Five-to-One. You can bet a group of six consecutive numbers as long as these numbers take up two adjacent rows on the playing field. Betting 16 through 21, for example, is permitted because it includes 16, 17, and 18 in the first row, and 19, 20, and 21 in the second. Put your chip on the borderline closest to you, at the intersection of the 16 and 19 square. If you win, a $10 bet is paid $50.

Six-to-One. Here you're betting on numbers 0, 00, 1, 2, and 3 *only*. Put your chip on the borderline closest to you, at the intersection of the 1 and 0 squares. A winning bet of $10 pays $60.

Eight-to-One. This is called a "corner" bet because it covers four numbers sharing a corner. If you want to bet on 5, 6, 8, and 9, for example, place your chip at the intersection of those numbered squares. If it wins, it pays $80 on a $10 bet.

Eleven-to-One. This "row" bet covers three numbers in a row. To bet 31, 32, and 33, for example, put your chip on the borderline between number 31 and the box covering the "third 12" group.

Seventeen-to-One. This is a split, or "horseback" bet, for any two numbers sharing a common edge. Put your chip on the borderline shared by the 4 and 7.

Thirty-Five-to-One. Here you bet on any single number. Put your chip in the center of the number's square. If you win, a $10 bet would bring $350.

Baccarat

This is the ultimate high-roller game, favored by many wealthy Europeans and Asian players. The baccarat pit is always set off from the casino floor, in an alcove or surrounded by velvet ropes. Viewed from the sidelines, this game moves at a monotonously slow pace. The subtleties of the game lie in the strategy and interplay between the players.

In baccarat the winner is the first player to draw at least two playing cards that together show a number value of nine. A two-card total of nine is known as a natural. Face cards (king, queen, jack) and tens have a value of zero. When cards total more than nine, you count only the last digit of the total. Ten plus four, for example, equals four, as does six plus eight.

Instead of betting against the casino, up to eight players can choose to bet against the other players or against the player who serves as banker. Because the chances of winning are in the banker's favor, the banker tends to accumulate the most winnings, and players who bet on the bank must pay 5% of each win to the casino. Players can play alone against the bank, or the entire table can gang up on the banker: eight people betting as one, against the banker.

Rules requiring players and bankers to take additional cards seem complex, but they become easier to remember as you go along. The banker deals two cards from the shoe to the player who has made the highest wager. If a player's first two cards total anywhere from zero to five, he or she must draw a third card. If the cards total six or seven, the player must "stand" (refrain from taking another card). The banker cannot draw a card if a player has an eight, which is the second-best hand possible after a two-card total of nine, and also called a natural. (In this case, the player wins, unless, of course, the banker has a nine.)

The rules governing the banker's actions are more complex. The following chart illustrates the options for the banker after the first two cards have been dealt and the player has drawn a third card:

Banker's Hand	Banker Draws if the Player Has	Banker Stands if the Player Has
3	0, 1, 2, 3, 4, 5, 6, 7, 9	8
4	2, 3, 4, 5, 6, 7	0, 1, 8, 9
5	4, 5, 6, 7	0, 1, 2, 3, 8, 9
6	6, 7	0, 1, 2, 3, 4, 5, 8, 9
7	Banker must stand	
8, 9	Banker wins unless there is a tie	

Note that the banker must stand on six if the player decides not to take a third card.

When a banker plays, the banker collects losing bets and pays winnings one-to-one (even money). If the outcome is a tie, no one wins.

Luck

Finally, some words about luck. About the best that can be said about luck in a casino is that all the games, without exception, are designed to make you lose more often than you win. The longer you play, the more often you'll lose. In the long run, you're going to keep losing until you have no money left.

What makes gambling tantalizing is that no one can tell how long the "long run" will be. And there's always the possibility that you'll win big enough, stop, and pocket your winnings, and then swagger off for the obligatory celebratory bottle of champagne.

This doesn't happen to most people. A Japanese gambler once won $6.4 million over two days at Trump Plaza, gambling $200,000 a hand at baccarat. The man played at his own table, roped off from the casino, observed by a crowd of casino executives, consultants, and security staff. He occasionally put his fists on the felt, raised them, and opened his palms, as if he was zapping the game with cosmic energy.

Officials at the casino wondered if they should cut their losses and stop the game. They consulted a statistician, who told them that there is no such thing as a winning streak. "Sooner or later, he'll lose." Trump Plaza officials let the man continue to gamble. A few days later he'd lost all of his money and owed the casino almost $2 million. He later returned and lost $10 million.

As they say, you can't win them all.

Sports and Fitness

The Beach Atlantic City has always been proud of its beach, though cynics grumble that like the rest of the town, it has seen better days. This is one of the last beaches on the Jersey Shore that you can use without purchasing a beach badge or tag. There are no bathhouses where you can rinse off ocean brine after a swim and change your clothes. The cabanas opposite the Boardwalk casino hotels are operated by the casinos for hotel guests only. Public rest rooms are located at regular intervals on the Boardwalk between the casinos. Call for beach information (tel. 609/348–7044).

Bicycling Bicycling is permitted on the Boardwalk daily from 6 to 10 AM. You can rent bicycles at booths along the Boardwalk near Convention Hall (Mississippi Ave.) during those hours. Bicycling on Atlantic City's busy streets is permitted at all times, but the heavy traffic makes this difficult.

Fishing Surf fishing off jetties or along the northern edge of the Boardwalk (where waves rush in under your feet) is free and requires no permit. The *Captain Applegate* (tel. 609/345–4077) is one of a dozen party and charter boats departing March–November from the Frank S. Farley State Marina (Huron Ave. and the Marina).

Health Clubs and Spas All the casino hotels have a pool and exercise facility, but the **spa at Bally's Park Place Casino Hotel** is in a class by itself. Marketed as a self-contained resort, the spa at Bally's offers packages that include supervised exercise, special meals, massage, and herbal wraps. The pool has speakers that will play your favorite music while you swim. Less imposing is the health club at **Best Western Golf and Tennis World,** a short drive west of Atlantic City on the Black Horse Pike (tel. 609/641–3546).

Jogging **Boardwalk Runners** (tel. 609/641–2549) sponsors regular races and fun runs on the Atlantic City Boardwalk and throughout Absecon Island.

Tennis and Squash   **Trump Castle, Trump Plaza,** and **TropWorld** have regulation-size tennis courts. **Merv Griffin's Resorts** has squash courts on its 15th floor. (All of these are for the use of hotel guests only.) There are also municipal tennis courts adjacent to **Bader Field airport,** on the Black Horse Pike (tel. 609/347–5348).

Dining

Atlantic City casinos specialize in showplace restaurants, where high prices, glitzy decor, a champagne-heavy wine list, and obsequious service tend to overwhelm the food. A high employee turnover creates remarkable inconsistency in service and quality. Still, casino restaurants can be fun because they are so . . . much. Everything—the decor, the service, the wine list, even the arrangement of the food on the plate—is designed to impress.

Casino restaurants are demographically aimed at the kind of gamblers a casino wants to attract. At the top are the high-priced gourmet rooms, dishing out mostly rich, Continental cuisine. After that are Italian, Chinese, Japanese, and steak-and-seafood restaurants. Further down are the delicatessens, all-you-can-eat buffets, and the latest rage in casino dining, fast-food courts.

With the exception of the fast-food courts, all casino restaurants have two lines. The first, and usually the shortest, is for VIP guests, that is, gamblers who dine on the house. They are seated first at the best tables regardless of whether they have reservations. The second, longer line is for paying customers, who frequently make reservations, arrive on time, and are still asked to wait, though there may be several empty tables in the restaurant. Maître d's are required to keep some tables open so if a favored gambler arrives without notice, he or she can be seated immediately. Tipping the maître d' will not get you seated any faster.

Casinos tend to have better-than-average brunches, and all feature some version of the all-you-can-eat buffets. Reservations are not needed, but it's a good idea to arrive either very early or very late, avoiding the peak hours of noon–2 PM for lunch and 6–8 PM for dinner. Because the price goes up at 5 PM when the buffet changes to its dinner menu, you just might be able to grab a buffet dinner at its freshest and for the price of lunch if you can slip in at 4:30. Sunday brunches are expensive ($20–$35 per person), champagne-drenched extravaganzas. Reservations are always required, and you may have to wait while high rollers go in first. Try to arrive before noon, when the brunch rooms fill up and buffet tables get a war-torn look. It's customary for men to wear jackets in the more expensive casino restaurants.

Casino chefs are skilled at preparing dishes that are not on the menu, either for gamblers with finicky tastes or for paying customers who want something different. Call a few days in advance if you have a specific request that requires unusual ingredients, or simply ask the chef to design your meal himself on a night when the kitchen isn't too busy.

Tipping 15% of your restaurant bill is proper, with 5% going to the captain (who takes your order, pours your wine, and does the tableside cooking) and 10% going to the waiter (who does everything else). If you were struck dumb by fabulous service and want to be remembered as a cherished friend, an additional 5% to the maître d' will cement a lifelong relationship. Giving $1 per drink to cocktail waitresses is generous.

Dining beyond the casinos requires a degree of courage, because Atlantic City's seedy appearance does not invite exploration. When in doubt, take cabs. The adventurous will be rewarded with lower prices, more relaxed atmosphere, and food and service as good as or better than what the casinos provide.

For prices, consult the price chart in the Dining section of Chapter 1, Essential Information. Highly recommended restaurants are indicated with a star ★.

Casino Restaurants

Very Expensive   **Delfino's.** The best of the casino seafood restaurants, this is a great place for a three-pound lobster, broiled seafood, prawns, and even rack of lamb. Only one Trumpish touch intrudes: Veal loin Ivanca is named for one of Trump's children. *Trump Castle, Huron Ave. and the bay, tel. 609/441–8353. Reservations advised. Jacket required. AE, DC, MC, V.*

Ivana's. Rumors flew during the Trumps' highly publicized marital spat that Donald wanted his wife's name removed from the restaurant. Executives huddled and came up with The Orchid, which at press time had not been used. In any event this is one of the top gourmet rooms, with the buttery Escoffier French cuisine done to impressive heights. It also serves very good lamb, seafood, and veal dishes. *Trump Plaza, Mississippi Ave. and the Boardwalk, tel. 609/441–6400. Reservations advised. Jacket required. Limited free garage parking. AE, DC, MC, V.*

Le Posh. The name is an acronym for Port Out, Starboard Home, which was the preferred way to book a cabin on ocean liners. Le Posh features imaginative seafood and veal dishes and a fabulous champagne Sunday brunch that will render you motionless. *Caesars Atlantic City, Arkansas Ave. and the Boardwalk, tel. 609/348–4411, ext. 5914. Reservations advised. Jacket required. AE, DC, MC, V. Closed for lunch.*

Expensive– **Pier 7.** This seafood restaurant attempts to evoke the atmo-
Very Expensive sphere and cuisine of a San Francisco Fisherman's Wharf fish house. Most seafood is grilled or steamed. One interesting gimmick is the Hot Rock, a calorie-conscious variation on the hot-oil fondue in which you singe marinated chicken, beef, and shellfish on a heated slab of pumice. *TropWorld, Iowa Ave. and the Boardwalk, tel. 609/340–4000. Reservations advised. Dress: casual. AE, D, DC, MC, V.*

Moderate   **Carnegie Deli.** All casinos have a deli serving overstuffed sandwiches. The Carnegie is a branch of the famous New York deli, and that gives this place a sentimental edge, despite the generic old-timey decor and nostalgic photos of Atlantic City. Sandwiches cost a dollar or two more than they should, but they are so thick that one is more than enough. *Sands Casino Hotel, Indiana Ave. and Brighton Park, tel. 609/441–4000. Reservations advised for dinner. Dress: casual. Free parking with casino validation in casino garage. AE, D, DC, MC, V.*

Inexpensive   **Jib's Oyster Bar.** For fast seafood try a rich, hearty bowl of New England clam chowder. *Bally's Park Place at Boardwalk and Park Pl., tel. 609/340–2000. Limited free valet parking in lots adjacent to casino hotel. AE, D, DC, MC, V.*

Oyster Bar. This simple seafood eatery was immortalized in Louis Malle's film *Atlantic City* as Susan Sarandon's briny place of employment. The snapper soup makes for a hearty meal with a shot of sherry and a pile of oyster crackers. *Merv Griffin's Resorts at North Carolina Ave. and Boardwalk, tel. 609/344–6000. No reservations. Dress: casual. AE, DC, MC, V.*

Beyond the Casinos

Very Expensive   **Johan's Zelande.** This is Atlantic City's most expensive, haughty, and impressive restaurant, and it is not in a casino. Dutch chef Johan Vroegop cooks a prix fixe dinner and lunch, with a choice of five entrées. Expect the rich cream and butter sauces of Flemish cuisine and a good, though expensive, wine list. Tables have their own telephones. *3006 Atlantic Ave. (near TropWorld and Bally's Grand), tel. 609/347–4774. Reservations required. Jacket and tie required. Fax machine on premises. Limited free off-street parking. AE, MC, V. Open for lunch and dinner.*

★   **Knife and Fork Inn.** This is the Jersey Shore's ultimate surf-and-turf restaurant, a piece of the old Atlantic City. Families that want to do the big-deal, dress-up dinner have been coming here since 1927 (Burt Lancaster and Susan Sarandon celebrated their good fortune here in *Atlantic City.*) It has a pseudo-European château appearance outside and inside (note the tacky crossed knives and forks on the outside) and a plush Old World feeling. The menu is predictable—basic American steak, some chicken dishes, lobster, and broiled or fried fish—though everything is cooked to order, and service is attentive. There is free parking in the adjacent lot. *Albany and Atlantic Aves., tel. 609/344–1133. Reservations required. Jacket required. AE. Closed for lunch and Sun. in winter.*

Expensive   **Aubrey's.** Across Arkansas Avenue from Caesars, Aubrey's dining room lets you watch the arriving winners rushing in with smiles on their faces, passing the departing frowning losers. Seafood and steaks head the menu, and there is a good late-night breakfast menu. At night you can hear gossip at the bar from Caesars' dealers and staff. *Arkansas and Pacific Aves., tel. 609/344–1632. Reservations advised. Dress: casual. AE, DC, MC, V. Open for dinner, late snacks, and breakfast until 6 AM. Free parking. Closed for lunch.*

Dock's Oyster House. Atlantic City's oldest seafood restaurant, dating to 1897, serves satisfying surf-and-turf and rich clam chowder. The decor here doesn't suggest the good old days, but the clientele does. Dock's does a solid family business. *2405 Atlantic Ave., tel. 609/345–0092. Open Apr.–Oct., Tues.–Sun., dinner only. Reservations advised. Jacket required. Limited off-street free parking. AE, MC, V. Closed for lunch.*

Old Waterway Inn. An out-of-the-way place in the city's Venice Park section, this restaurant features good grilled seafood, pasta, steak, and Cajun dishes. You can tie your boat to the dock and admire the casino skyline. *1700 Riverside Dr., tel. 609/347–1793. Reservations advised. Jacket required. Free parking. DC, V. Closed Mon.*

**Moderate–
Expensive**

Abe's Oyster House. While it isn't as old as Dock's Oyster House, Abe's has the atmosphere of an old-time Atlantic City fish house with its high ceiling, nostalgic photos, and gurgling lobster tank. Excellent broiled and fried seafood, soft-shell crabs (seasonal), raw oysters, and clams are many of the highlights. *2031 Atlantic Ave. (at the corner of Arkansas, 2 blocks west of Caesars), tel. 609/344–7701. Reservations advised for dinner. Dress: casual. Off-street parking in adjacent lot. AE, MC, V. Open Mar.–Oct., Tues.–Sun., lunch and dinner. Closed Mon.*

Chef Vola's. Also known as "the cellar," this former private dining club hidden in the basement of a guest house (between the Trump Regency and TropWorld) is an Atlantic City secret favored by casino executives, locals, and entertainers. Now that Chef Vola has passed on, Chef Michael Esposito prepares Italian and Continental entrées. His wife, Louise, is responsible for the desserts. The dining room is informal. Tradition demands that you call in advance and say who sent you (actually, just saying you're hungry will do the trick). *111 S. Albion Pl., tel. 609/345–2022. Reservations required. Jacket required. Limited street parking. No credit cards. BYOB. Closed Mon.*

Flying Cloud Café. Hidden in Gardner's Basin, the struggling maritime tourist village, the Flying Cloud is frequented by businessmen, casino executives, fishermen, and folks who want to go as far away from the fizzy casino atmosphere as possible. The jukebox is jammed with '50s hits, and the food is sturdy Italianate surf-and-turf. Because of the location, it's best to drive or take a cab. *800 N. New Hampshire Ave., tel. 609/345–8222. Reservations advised for holiday weekends. Dress: casual. Free parking. MC, V.*

Frisanco Ristorante. This newcomer to Atlantic City's crowded Italian restaurant list serves a menu heavy in northern Italian veal and seafood dishes. *3426 Atlantic Ave., tel. 609/345–0606. Reservations advised. Jacket advised. Limited free parking. No credit cards.*

Il Bon Gi. Spicy Korean and artfully prepared Japanese cuisine in a dark-wood setting proves that there is a reason to go beyond the casinos for fine ethnic dishes. The *kimchi* (spicy pickled cabbage) is wonderfully fiery and sushi is served on weekends. *25 S. Tennessee Ave. (midway between the Sands and Merv Griffin's Resorts), tel. 609/344–0967. Reservations advised. Dress: casual. Limited lot parking across from restaurant. MC, V.*

Sabatini's. Here is another satisfying mom-and-pop Italian restaurant in the shadow of the casinos, favored by many entertainers who want to escape the casino atmosphere. Of special note are the superb veal and pasta dishes and the garlicky white clam sauce. *2210–14 Pacific Ave. (across Columbia Pl. from Trump Plaza), tel. 609/345–4816. Reservations advised. Dress: casual. AE, MC, V.*

**Moderate
★**

Angelo's Fairmount Tavern. Take a cab or drive—there's limited free off-street parking—and don't let the run-down neighborhood scare you. This is *the* classic mom-and-pop Ducktown Italian restaurant, and a favorite of local kids on their first date, casino execs, and politicians. Many of the locals remember the tiny bar's opening just after Prohibition. Lasagna, the best meatballs in Atlantic City, sausage, soups, and wine (try the fruity house red) are featured on the menu. You may have to wait a half hour and more for a table at night, but it's well worth it. *Mississippi and Fairmount Aves. (about 5 blocks west of Trump Plaza), tel. 609/344-2439. No reservations. Dress: casual but neat. Off-street parking. No credit cards.*

Rosa's Southern Dining. Southern-style fish, chicken, pork chops, and beef are made to order at Rosa's. The portions are large, the decor modern, and there is a dance floor and a cheery bar. Ignore your diet and order the superb fried chicken. *649 N. New York Ave. (just before intersection with Rte. 30), tel. 609/344-9484 or 609/347-1031. Reservations advised on weekends. Dress: informal. Limited free off-street parking. AE, MC, V. Closed Mon.*

Inexpensive–Moderate

Saigon Restaurant. Atlantic City's first Vietnamese restaurant is reasonably priced. Spring rolls, large steaming soups, and spicy, stir-fry dishes blend Oriental and French influences. *3205 Atlantic Ave., tel. 609/344-2282. Reservations advised. Dress: casual. No credit cards. BYOB.*

Inexpensive ★

White House Sub Shop. Even before Frank Sinatra made a splash at the legendary 500 Cafe nightclub, he and the boys would retire to the White House for late-night sandwiches. Sinatra once became so nostalgic for these that he dispatched his private jet to Atlantic City to bring two dozen White House subs back to his California home. A basic White House sub is sliced salami, bologna, cappacola, coteghino, and provolone cheese, with shredded lettuce, tomato, raw onions, seasonings, and shots of oil and vinegar crammed into a long Italian roll. Though many places in Atlantic City make subs, the White House retains a faithful show-biz clientele, who usually make a pilgrimage when they're in town. Look for the stretch limos blocking traffic at the corner of Mississippi Avenue about four blocks west of Trump Plaza. The wall of autographed pictures is a who's-who of Atlantic City's entertainment scene for the past 50 years. Expect crowds at lunchtime. *2301 Arctic Ave., tel. 609/345-1564. No reservations. Limited street parking. No credit cards.*

Lodging

For Atlantic City hotel and casino hotel reservations, contact the individual properties or call **Atlantic City Hotel Reservations** (tel. 800/524-1351), **Atlantic City Central Reservations** (tel. 800/524-1706), **Atlantic City Room Reservations, Inc.** (tel. 800/872-2424), or **Atlantic City Reserve-A-Room** (tel. 800/227-6667). These services require a credit card number for securing a room but do not charge a fee.

Hotels located across the street from a casino property are often easier to book, with lower prices, a slower pace, and many of the same amenities. Several reasonably priced hotels located a few minutes' drive outside the city are listed in Chapter 6, Greater Atlantic County.

Expect to pay upwards of $160 for a room in a casino hotel. Casinos also charge a 12% luxury tax on rooms in addition to the 6% room tax levied by the state. For price ranges, consult the price chart in the Lodging section of Chapter 1, Essential Information. Highly recommended properties are indicated with a star ★.

Casino Hotels

Reserving a room in a casino hotel on a weekend can be difficult, especially for holiday weekends, so make reservations as far in advance as possible. When reserving a room overlooking the Boardwalk, ask for a room that is as far above the street as possible, with an ocean view; in the marina district, request a bay view.

Casino hotels are first-class and generally well maintained, though with some peculiarities. Decor tends to be bright and flashy, and elevators tend to be slow. The goal at most properties is to impress rather than to create a feeling of comfort. Many casino hotel rooms are very small, so when gamblers are upgraded to a suite they notice the difference. Suites are more impressive than functional. Some have whirlpool tubs placed in sitting areas or pedestal televisions set in such a way that guests can trip over them at night on the way to the bathroom. In a town that prides itself on its ocean breeze, it is ironic that most windows are either sealed shut or will open just a few inches. Noise from other rooms, from the corridors, and from the street is also a problem.

All casino hotels are competent if not excellent at catering to the needs of their gambling clientele. Preferential treatment for gamblers includes timely room service, easy access to show tickets, and dining room reservations. This said, casino hotels still offer a level of service that is unmatched, despite the efforts of condo hotels and other noncasino hotels. All rooms have TV with cable and pay-per-view movies, and AM/FM radios. Most casinos have showrooms and lounges, health clubs, swimming pools and exercise facilities, 24-hour room service, valet service, concierges, beauty salons, handicapped access, valet parking, and numerous restaurants. Casinos also have cribs and can arrange for baby-sitters at an hourly rate.

The two marina casinos—Harrah's and Trump Castle—offer a slower, less-crowded pace. You're a little bit away from the action, but the Boardwalk and beach is only a 15-minute jitney ride away. Parking is free and unlimited in the marina casino garages, and both casino hotels can accommodate boat traffic.

Very Expensive   **Bally's Grand Hotel Casino.** Small, almost intimate by Atlantic City standards, the interiors at Bally's Grand are less flashy than they were in the Golden Nugget days, though the San Francisco Victorian theme can be glimpsed in the ice-cream parlor and in the ornate barrel vaults in the casino. In recent years the Grand, the southernmost casino on the Boardwalk, has lost some of its activity to larger casinos farther up the Boardwalk, which can be advantageous to those seeking a relatively quiet casino stay. *Boston and Pacific Aves., 08404, tel. 609/340–7100 or 800/257–8677. 514 rooms with bath. Facilities: gourmet restaurant, steak house, Chinese restaurant, buffet, coffee shop, fast food, and ice-cream parlor, 526-seat theater, valet parking, self-parking garage connected to casino by covered walkway. AE, D, DC, MC, V.*

Bally's Park Place Casino Hotel. A peculiar mix of old and new, this modernistic granite bunker with its pink-and-mauve, hexagonal tower is connected to the Dennis, one of the last of the old Atlantic City stone hotels. Bally's Park Place has more guest rooms than any other casino hotel in Atlantic City. Classic glitz includes the 93-foot casino escalator leading to the second-floor dining level. The casino gets a broad mix of high and low rollers. The spa is the city's best and most luxurious. *Park Pl. and the Boardwalk, 08401, tel. 609/340–2000 or 800/ 257–8555. 1,300 rooms with bath. Facilities: seafood restaurant, steak house, raw bar, delicatessen, snack bar, ice-cream parlor, Italian pastry shop, coffee shop, small shopping area, game arcade, 340-seat cabaret, full-service spa (with aerobics and exercise classes), beach cabanas, valet and self-parking. AE, D, DC, MC, V.*

Caesars Atlantic City Hotel-Casino. It's hard to believe that a little more than a decade ago, this was the Howard Johnson's Regency. Now thoroughly "Romanized" to suggest Caesars Palace in Las Vegas, Caesars Atlantic City is one of the Boardwalk's prime high-roller houses. It is located roughly in the center of the Boardwalk casino area, close to Convention Hall. The garage across Pacific Avenue is architecturally outrageous. There are also free bicycles for guests. *Arkansas Ave. and the Boardwalk, 08401, tel. 609/348–4411, 800/257–8555, or, in NJ, 800/582–7600. 645 rooms with bath. Facilities: children's play area; coin arcade; gourmet restaurant; steak house; Japanese, Chinese, and Italian restaurants; buffet; coffee shop; delicatessen; ice-cream parlor; tennis courts; 1,300-seat showroom. AE, DC, MC, V.*

Claridge Hotel and Casino. The Claridge, a low-roller house with a multilevel casino floor, is directly in front of Brighton Park, a block from the Boardwalk. It is a good choice for those who want the casino ambience without the high prices. *Indiana Ave. and the Boardwalk, 08401, tel. 609/340–3400, 800/ 582–7676, or 800/257–8585 in NJ. 504 rooms with bath. Facilities: steak house, Italian restaurant, snack bar, coffee shop, buffet, delicatessen, 550-seat showroom. AE, D, DC, MC, V.*

Harrah's Marina Hotel and Casino. The exception to the Atlantic City rule, Harrah's is a large, wholesome, open, airy facility done in restful green tones and gold accents. The casino has an unlimited free parking garage, its own miniature boardwalk, and a private marina on the Absecon Inlet, from which sightseeing boats sail during the summer months. The Bay Cabaret lounge is the city's best "little" room for comedy and cabaret theater. The Meadows gourmet restaurant has beautiful views of the Absecon bay. *1725 Brigantine Blvd., 08401, tel. 609/441–5000 or 800/242–7724. 760 rooms and suites. Facilities: gourmet restaurant, Italian and Chinese restaurants, buffet, steak house, delicatessen, coffee shop, fast-food court, small shopping arcade, indoor pool, health club, golf privileges. AE, D, DC, MC, V.*

Merv Griffin's Resorts Casino Hotel. In 1978 the former Haddon Hall became Resorts International, Atlantic City's first casino hotel. Connected by a passageway to the Trump Taj Mahal, Resorts is getting more than its share of overflow convention business, and at press time, a large interior renovation was underway. Merv Griffin occasionally performs in the casino. *North Carolina Ave. and the Boardwalk, 08401, tel. 609/344–6000 or 800/438–7424. 696 rooms in Haddon Hall and North Tower. Facilities: gourmet restaurant, steak house, Japanese and Italian restaurants, buffet, oyster bar, coffee shop, ice-cream parlor, arcade game room, shopping area. AE, DC, MC, V.*

Sands Hotel, Casino & Country Club. The Sands is a block from the Boardwalk, diagonally facing Brighton Park. The Sands is a smaller, medium- to high-roller house with a glitzy casino

floor with a tropical theme and an elegant upstairs lounge, the
Punch Bowl. A fast-food court features a branch of New York's
famous Carnegie Deli. The Sands also owns a golf course and
country club in Somers Point, which is open to hotel guests.
There is a garage on Kentucky Avenue. *Indiana Ave. at
Brighton Park, 08401, tel. 609/441–4000 or 800/257–8580. 501
rooms. Facilities: gourmet restaurant, steak house, Italian
restaurant, delicatessen, fast-food restaurants, 850-seat showroom. AE, DC, MC, V.*

Showboat Hotel & Casino. The Showboat was designed to appeal to "middle American" gamblers who don't care about
headliner entertainment and would rather bowl. The 60-lane
bowling center, installed on the second floor adjacent to the
convention ballrooms, is open 24 hours and is by far the most
modern bowling lane anywhere in New Jersey. The exterior of
the casino hotel resembles an ocean liner. There is unlimited
free garage parking with an entrance off Pacific Avenue. *Delaware Ave. and the Boardwalk, 08404, tel. 609/343–4000 or 800/
621–0200. 516 rooms. Facilities: gourmet restaurant, Chinese
restaurant, steak house, Italian restaurant, delicatessen, buffet, ice-cream parlor, pizzeria, 413-seat lounge. AE, D, DC,
MC, V.*

TropWorld Casino & Entertainment Resort. TropWorld has the
city's largest showroom, an indoor theme park complete with a
roller coaster, a high-tech fun house, and a saloon with a revue
show. The guest rooms are cool and modern in design. The
seemingly endless casino floor and the public areas are confus-
ingly laid out. The theme park requires an admission charge.
*Iowa Ave. and the Boardwalk, 08401, tel. 609/340–4000, 800/
843–8767, or 800/257–6227. 1,000 rooms in two towers. Facilities: gourmet restaurant, steak house, Italian, Chinese, and
seafood restaurants, buffet, salad bar, coffee shop, fast-food
court, ice-cream and sweet shop; shopping arcade; comedy
club; coin game room; 1,700-seat showroom. Unlimited free
parking in garage connected to casino by covered walkway.
AE, D, DC, MC, V.*

Trump Castle Casino Resort. Trump Castle has the advantage
of adjoining the 650-slip Frank S. Farley State Marina (the
largest state-owned marina in New Jersey), which the Trump
organization has leased. A recently added wing of suites—one
of which can be booked at the preposterous nightly rate of
$10,000—and an expanded ballroom allow the Castle to com-
pete with the Boardwalk casinos for major sports and entertainment events. The Castle also offers unlimited free parking,
direct Trump Air helicopter service, and one of the nicest
views of Atlantic City, from the Harbor View seafood restaurant. The guest rooms are decorated in soothing earth tones of
brown, beige, and aqua. *Huron Ave. and Brigantine Blvd.,
08401, tel. 609/441–2000 or 800/365–8786. 603 rooms and suite
wing. Facilities: gourmet restaurant; steak house, seafood restaurant; buffet; delicatessen; ice-cream parlor; health club
with pool, whirlpool, exercise room, sauna, steam rooms;
small shopping arcade. Inexpensive sightseeing boats in summer. Free cribs available. AE, DC, MC, V.*

Trump Plaza Hotel & Casino. This is the city's prime high-roller
house as well as the only casino hotel with direct access to the
Atlantic City Convention Center. Some of the suite rooms are
bilevel, and all rooms face the ocean. Most guest rooms are ultramodern in decor, but some of the suites are so rococo they
would make a French king blush. *Mississippi Ave. and the*

Boardwalk, 08401, tel. 609/441–2000 or 800/365–8786. 583 rooms. Facilities: gourmet, Italian, and Chinese restaurants; delicatessen; buffet; ice-cream parlor; health club with pool, tennis, exercise room, steam room, sauna; showroom. AE, DC, MC, V.

Trump Taj Mahal Resort & Casino. The Taj occupies more than 17 acres. You can't miss it from anywhere in the city. The 42-story tower, with its famed Alexander the Great "Big Al" suite on the top floor, is the tallest building in New Jersey. At 120,000 square feet, the casino floor is the city's largest. As if this weren't enough, the Taj also has the most convention space, about 175,000 square feet. The hotel is connected by enclosed walkways to the Showboat and Merv Griffin's Resorts casino hotels. At press time, the Taj's health club, swimming pool, and showroom had not been finished. *Virginia Ave. and the Boardwalk, 08404, tel. 609/449–1000 or 800/TAJ–Trump. 1,250 rooms. Facilities: gourmet restaurant, baccarat pit restaurant, steak house, Italian, Chinese, and seafood restaurants, coffee shop, buffet, delicatessen, fast food, ice-cream parlor, shopping arcade. AE, DC, MC, V.*

Noncasino Hotels

Diplomat Hotel. Completed in 1989, the Diplomat is across from TropWorld casino. The rooms are functional and pleasant; some have ocean views. *Chelsea Ave. and the Boardwalk, 08401, tel. 609/348–2200 or 800/548–3030. 220 rooms. Facilities: restaurant, lounge, pool. Free parking. AE, MC, V.*

Inn at the Ocean. This 1909 vacation home on a beach block about a mile south of the Boardwalk casinos has been completely remodeled as a bed-and-breakfast and furnished in wicker and pastels. Eight rooms have ocean views; most have private decks. An exercise room and a sauna are planned for the basement. Innkeeper Betty Culbert offers three nonsmoking rooms; a full hot, multicourse breakfast; and free use of bicycles, beach chairs, towels, washer and dryer. A two-night stay is required on summer weekends. *109 S. Dover Ave., 08401, tel. 609/345–1717, fax 609/484–9223. 8 rooms and 2 suites, all with private bath. Facilities: whirlpool tubs, hair dryers, cable TV. AE, MC, V.*

Radisson Flagship. This pleasing condo hotel is located across from the Boardwalk facing Brigantine and the Absecon Inlet, but it's rather far from the Showboat and the Taj Mahal, the closest casinos. Because of the somewhat grim Inlet neighborhood, taxi or car travel is recommended at night. All the accommodations have kitchens and there is a free breakfast buffet. *60 N. Maine Ave., 08401, tel. 609/343–7447. 300 1- and 2-bedroom suites. Facilities: health club with indoor pool, exercise room, whirlpool, steam room and sauna. AE, D, DC, MC, V.*

Trump Regency. The former Atlantis Casino Hotel became a Trump property in 1989. The casino area has been closed, but suites have been renovated and all rooms have been refurnished. As we went to press, planned room renovations had been scaled back because of problems in the Trump organization. The hotel is on the Boardwalk and has direct access to Atlantic City Convention Center. *2500 Boardwalk and Florida Ave., 08404, tel. 609/344–4000. 500 rooms. Facilities: showroom, convention facilities, restaurants, small shopping arcade. AE, DC, MC, V.*

The Arts and Nightlife

Casino Shows

The casinos dominate Atlantic City's nightlife with their own style of adult entertainment, which is designed to lure gamblers. Family-oriented acts—magic shows, ice revues, or theme revues—are booked around holidays.

Unless you're a regular visitor to the casino, you should purchase your tickets in advance. Tickets for most sports and entertainment events go on sale four to six weeks before the event. Seating in Atlantic City showrooms is by maître d', so your ticket won't be for a specific seat or table, though the price of your ticket will determine where you sit. The least expensive seats are usually for the back row. With the exception of the small theaters in the Bally properties and the Showboat's Mardi Gras lounge, where the shallowness of the showroom creates a feeling of intimacy, back-row seats are woefully inadequate.

Casino showrooms are designed to favor two rows of seats. Maître d's refer to the choice row, typically a crescent of plush banquettes one riser above the front-row tables, as the King's Row, with the two King's Row center banquettes as the absolute best. The second row of banquettes is the Queen's Row. Tipping a maître d' will not get you a banquette seat (most are promised to high rollers and guests of the entertainer). Some people believe that the best seats in most showrooms are in the row directly behind the Queen's Row. These are called "rail seats," because of a rail that protects those in the banquettes from the leaning arms of those seated behind them. Rail seats offer views as good as, if not better than, the King's or Queen's rows, and best of all, they tend not to be reserved. To get one, purchase the appropriately priced ticket, arrive as early as possible (showrooms open 30–45 minutes before showtime) and ask the maître d' for a rail seat.

The easiest way to buy tickets is by telephone with a credit card. Most casino hotels use Ticketron's Telecharge (tel. 800/233–4050). Some casino showrooms, such as the Taj Mahal, have shifted to Ticketmaster (tel. 800/736–1420). To avoid lines, pick up your tickets at the casino box office an hour or two before the show.

Casinos often advertise popular shows and holiday performances as sold-out, even if they're not. The casino holds back tickets in the hope that high rollers will want to see these shows and perhaps gamble in the casino afterward. Frequently casinos miscalculate demand. If you find yourself unable to find a ticket to a popular show, a day-of-show call to the box office may reveal available tickets. Tipping the maître d' rarely works. Casino hosts (smartly dressed men and women, identified by their badges, who make sure gamblers are taken care of), not showroom maître d's, have the power to give tickets away, and they can be generous when high-roller demand is low and the showroom must be filled so as not to embarrass the entertainer.

Atlantic City casino entertainment is divided into four categories:

Headliners These are usually well-known stars, such as Frank Sinatra, Bill Cosby, Eddie Murphy, Ann-Margret, Cher, Roseanne Barr, Bob Dylan. Most headliner shows feature two acts—the headliner whom you've paid to see and an opening act. If the headliner is a singer, the opening act is usually a comedian; if the headliner is a comedian, expect a singer to open the show. Headliner shows may seem spontaneous, but they are actually run like clockwork—opening acts run 15–25 minutes, the headliner's act runs 40–70 minutes, and the entire show almost never lasts more than 90 minutes.

Most Atlantic City casinos have headliner entertainment during the summer season and on holiday weekends. Tickets to these engagements average about $35 and can go as high as $200, with many of the best showroom seats reserved for favored gamblers.

Special Events Most of these one-time events are preceded by a great deal of advance advertising and hype. Visitors can choose from celebrity roasts, fashion and art shows, television show tapings, and sports, of which boxing is the most popular.

Revues These usually glitzy affairs fall into two categories: **variety shows,** featuring singing and dancing, with some comedy, magic, or acrobatic specialty acts added; and slightly shortened **Broadway musicals,** with or without a name star and presented without intermission. Revues are presented midweek, with some weekend shows (when headliners aren't performing) and an occasional matinee.

Casinos change their revue shows every few months, with two exceptions. **"An Evening at La Cage,"** a hilarious and at times poignant drag show at Bally's Park Place, is the city's longest-running revue. The show's loose, loopy humor spoofs sexual pretension. The show is highly recommended. Trump Castle's **"Tonight Live, Starring Mal Z. Lawrence"** is a spoof TV talk show that began as a clever repackaging of the standard variety show format. Thanks to the skills of the host, comedian Lawrence (Freddie Roman's replacement), the variety of specialty acts, a few David Letterman–style gimmicks, and the surprise guest (anyone from headliners appearing at other casinos to Trump himself), "Tonight Live" has evolved into that rarest of casino shows—a show that is different every night.

Tickets to revues cost about $20 and can usually be purchased on the day of the show. Before purchasing revue tickets, check local newspapers or ask at casino promotion booths (typically located near the casino cage area) for two-for-one admission coupons. Some revues require a one-drink minimum.

Lounge Entertainment Usually for no more than the price of a drink, guests can enjoy a variety of lounge acts at all the casinos. Harrah's Bay Cabaret and the Showboat's Mardi Gras have cover charges. The drinking age in New Jersey is 21, so admission is limited to adults. Seating in the Bay Cabaret, Mardi Gras, and Cleopatra's Barge (in Caesars Hotel-Casino) is by maître d'.

The **Bay Cabaret** is the most consistent and innovative casino lounge. Insulated from the noise and turmoil of the slot pit by soundproof glass and heavy curtains, the Bay Cabaret hosts mostly name comedians. The cover is usually $10.

The Showboat's **Mardi Gras Lounge,** a huge, crescent-shape room, gets some noise from the slot pit in the rear seats. The entertainment varies wildly—revue shows, unknowns, and headliners have performed here. The cover charge varies with the act.

Two casino lounges are devoted exclusively to comedy: the **Claridge Comedy Club** at the Claridge and TropWorld's **Comedy Stop at the Trop**. Both charge a cover and offer two to four up-and-coming comedians a night. The Comedy Stop's annual November three-day Comedy Showdown competition brings in comedians from all over the East Coast.

Box Office Telephone Numbers

Bally's Grand Hotel Casino (Boardwalk and Boston Ave., tel. 609/340–7200).

Bally's Park Place Casino Hotel (Boardwalk and Park Pl., tel. 609/340–2709).

Caesars Atlantic City Hotel-Casino (Boardwalk and Arkansas Ave., tel. 609/343–2550 or 800/677–7469).

Claridge Hotel and Casino (Boardwalk and Indiana Ave., tel. 609/340–3700 or 800/752–7469).

Harrah's Marina Hotel and Casino (1725 Brigantine Blvd., tel. 800/242–7724). Note: Harrah's is the only casino that doesn't use commercial telephone ticket-charge companies. Tickets to Harrah's shows can be purchased from the box office over the telephone.

Merv Griffin's Resorts Casino Hotel (Boardwalk and Arkansas Ave., tel. 609/340–6830).

Sands Hotel, Casino & Country Club (Indiana Ave. and Brighton Park, tel. 609/441–4591).

Showboat Hotel & Casino (Boardwalk and Delaware Ave., tel. 609/343–4003 or 800/621–0200).

TropWorld Casino & Entertainment Resort (Boardwalk and Brighton Ave., tel. 609/340–4020 or 800/526–2935).

Trump Castle Casino Resort (Huron Ave. and Brigantine Blvd., tel. 609/441–8300 or 800/284–8786).

Trump Plaza Hotel & Casino (Boardwalk and Mississippi Ave., tel. 800/759–8786).

Trump Taj Mahal (Boardwalk and Virginia Ave., tel. 609/449–5145).

Beyond the Casinos

Atlantic City's nightlife has not thrived in the shadow of the casinos. The few clubs that remain are exceptions to the rule; some can serve as refuges from casino atmosphere. Remember: Alcoholic beverages can be served in Atlantic City around the clock, and most clubs stay open until dawn.

Dance Clubs

Chez Paree. Also called "the Chez," this is Atlantic City's only full-size, '70s style light-show disco. *Boardwalk and New York Ave. (across from Atlantic Palace condo hotel), tel. 609/348–4313. Cover charge. Dress: no shorts, tank tops, or sandals. Open on weekends, beginning at midnight.*

Key Club. Smaller than the Chez, this bilevel dance club is located above the Brajole Café restaurant. Regulars here are mostly fortysomething, well-dressed sports fans (part of the club doubles as a sports bar) who gawk at the occasional late-night lingerie shows. *Mississippi and Atlantic Aves., tel. 609/348–3955. Dress: jackets or dressy sweaters for men, no shorts, T-shirts, or sandals. AE, DC, MC, V. Open Wed.–Sun., at 11 PM.*

Taverns **Duke Mack's.** More interesting as a dealer's bar than a night-club, Duke Mack's gets dealers and casino workers from Bally's Grand and TropWorld (it's a good place to pick up gambling stories and casino gossip). Live bands are on tap most weekend nights. *Boardwalk and California Ave., tel. 609/345–2719. No cover charge. Dress: casual. Always open.*

Irish Pub. This is Atlantic City's off-duty cop bar, unofficial Irish heritage center, purveyor of the city's cheapest lunch, and academy of serious drinking. The walls are papered with old Atlantic City newspapers, the jukebox is stuffed with nostalgic hits from the '50s to the '80s, the food is tolerable, and the Harp Lager is served in chilled mugs. There is also a tiny Irish gift shop for those who feel the old country calling. Irish folksinging is held on Friday and Saturday nights. *St. James Pl. near Central Pier off the Boardwalk, tel. 609/344–9063. Breakfast, lunch, dinner, and late-night snacks. Limited free parking in lot opposite. Open all the time.*

Grabel's. This relaxing old-folks bar is a few blocks south of the casino area in Atlantic City's Chelsea section. Live music most nights. *3909 Atlantic Ave., tel. 609/344–9263.*

Los Amigos. Atlantic City's only Tex-Mex bar and restaurant still attracts journalists who grew accustomed to the margaritas, chips, and salsa when the *Atlantic City Press*, and other media bureaus, had offices on this block. *1926 Atlantic Ave., a block west of Bally's Park Place, tel. 609/344–2293. AE, DC, MC, V. Open daily from 4 PM, noon on weekends.*

McGettigan's Saloon and Restaurant. "M'Get's" has Atlantic City's happiest Friday happy hour among young, noncasino professionals. *440 N. Albany Ave., tel. 609/344–3030. Limited free on-site lot parking. AE, MC, V.*

Twelve South. A great casino dealers bar, Twelve South gets a mixed crowd from the Sands, Claridge, and Bally's Park Place casino hotels, plus some locals, too. The dinner menu has some eclectic touches; late-night snacks are also served. *12 S. Indiana Ave., tel. 609/345–1212. Some snacks during happy hour. Limited off-street parking. AE, M, V. Open 4 PM to 8 AM.*

6 Greater Atlantic County

Introduction

Atlantic City steals too much of the attention, excitement, and intrigue away from its home county, one of the fastest-growing yet most pristine areas along the New Jersey Shore.

No other part of the state has experienced such a sudden boom, and the resulting turmoil, as the long, woodsy stretch from the southern edge of Ocean County (including a tiny slice of Burlington County) down to the banks of the Great Egg Harbor River. Jets roar into Atlantic City International Airport in Pomona, and the roads are jammed with residents, seasonal visitors, and casino-bound gamblers.

Nearly all of this activity is due to Atlantic City's rebirth as a casino center. While Atlantic City itself shows few signs of prosperity outside the doors of the casino hotels, the Greater Atlantic County area, known as the mainland to locals, has enjoyed unprecedented prosperity, as have the island town of Brigantine and the downbeach Atlantic City suburbs of Ventnor, Margate, and Longport.

Thankfully, intelligent government planning has protected vast stretches of the Pine Barrens forests and coastal marshes from the rampant development that has crowded much of the region. Minutes away from the snarled and tangled suburban sprawl around Northfield, Pleasantville, and Absecon lies the rustic peace of the Forsythe Wildlife Refuge and the Pinelands Preserve—an antidote to the jangle of slot machines and shopping-mall cash registers.

The Greater Atlantic County area also offers a less-expensive, easier-going alternative to the typical casino/beach visit. Many moderately priced motels and hotels dot the main east–west roads toward Atlantic City, where round-trip transportation can be arranged to a Boardwalk casino, usually with some discounted casino-hotel meal coupons, free show tickets, or coin bonuses thrown in. County restaurants tend to be less expensive than their Atlantic City counterparts and cater to a local clientele rather than to the high-roller or bus-tour crowds. You'll even find movie theaters and such worthwhile cultural diversions as the South Jersey Regional Theater, Stockton State College's excellent cultural series, the Atlantic County Historical Society, and the Noyes Museum.

Essential Information

Important Addresses and Numbers

Tourist Information
Atlantic City Convention and Visitors Bureau (304 Pacific Ave., Atlantic City, tel. 609/348–7100 or 800/262–7395) supplies information on the Greater Atlantic County region.

Atlantic County Office for the Aging and Disabled (1333 Atlantic Ave., Atlantic City, tel. 609/345–6700, ext. 2831).

Brigantine Chamber of Commerce (Box 484, Brigantine, tel. 609/266–3437).

Greater Mainland Chamber of Commerce (927 N. Main St., Pleasantville, tel. 609/646–0777).

Emergencies
Medical

Southern Atlantic County, Margate County, and Longport: *Shore Memorial Hospital* (New York Ave., Somers Point, tel. 609/653–3500).

Ventnor and Brigantine: *Atlantic City Medical Center* (Atlantic City Division, Michigan and Pacific Aves., Atlantic City, tel. 609/347–2054).

Atlantic County Mainland: *Atlantic City Medical Center* (Mainland Division, Jimmie Leeds Rd., Galloway Township, tel. 609/652–1000).

Western Atlantic County: *Kessler Memorial Hospital* (Rte. 30, Hammonton, tel. 609/561–6700).

Police and Fire

State Police (tel. 609/641–4250).

Absecon (tel. 609/641–0667); Brigantine (tel. 609/266–7662); Egg Harbor City (tel. 609/965–1200); Egg Harbor Township (tel. 609/926–5200); Galloway Township (tel. 609/652–3705); Hamilton Township (tel. 609/625–2211); Hammonton (tel. 609/561–4000); Linwood (tel. 609/927–5252); Longport (tel. 609/822–2141); Margate (tel. 609/822–1151); Mullica Township (tel. 609/561–4740); Northfield (tel. 609/641–3185); Pleasantville (tel. 609/641–6100); Somers Point (tel. 609/927–6161); Stockton State College (tel. 609/652–7495); Ventnor (tel. 609/822–2101).

Publications

The *Atlantic City Press,* a daily published in Pleasantville, has the best coverage of Atlantic County events as well as casino entertainment in Atlantic City. Weeklies include the *Mainland Journal,* the *Atlantic County Record, Egg Harbor City News,* and the *Hammonton News.* The monthly *Atlantic City Magazine* lists restaurants, and *Whoot!,* a free publication, covers lounges and nightclubs.

Arriving and Departing

By Plane

Atlantic City International Airport, in Pomona, gets limited scheduled service (*see* Chapter 5, Atlantic City). For arrivals into the Philadelphia and New York City airports, *see* Arriving and Departing by Plane in Chapter 1, Essential Information.

By Car

The major toll roads serving the county are the Atlantic City Expressway, which links Philadelphia to Atlantic City, and the Garden State Parkway, which runs north–south. The greater Atlantic County region is about a 90-minute drive east of Philadelphia and two hours south of New York. From Delaware and points south, take I–95 through Philadelphia to the Atlantic City Expressway. Expect heavy traffic on summer weekends.

By Train

Travelers from Philadelphia and southern New Jersey can take **New Jersey Transit's** inexpensive local service, stopping several times daily at Pleasantville and Atlantic City and departing from the PATCO Hi-Speed Line Lindenwold station. For information call 800/AC–TRAIN.

By Bus

New Jersey Transit (tel. 800/582–5946) links some of the major towns and shopping malls, though you may first have to go to Atlantic City to reach them.

Getting Around

By Car

This is the preferred way to go. Most of Atlantic County is suburban and residential. During the summer expect westbound traffic jams Friday afternoons and evenings and heavy east-bound traffic Sunday afternoon. Summer traffic can get heavy on the main roads in Brigantine and in the downbeach communities of Ventnor, Margate, and Longport.

Parking Regulations Nonresident street parking in Ventnor is limited to three hours; parking is also timed and limited in the commercial and beach-block districts of Margate, Longport, and Brigantine.

By Taxi and Limousine On the Mainland **Absecon Taxi** (tel. 609/652–7146); **Bell Taxi** (Pomona area, tel. 609/965–0209); **Bob's Taxi** (Absecon area, tel. 609/652–2661); **May's Call-a-Cab** (tel. 609/646–7600); **City Cab** (tel. 609/641–0762); **Denny's Taxi** (tel. 609/652–7146); **L&R Cab** (tel. 609/641–8473); **Pearline's Taxi** (tel. 609/646–0848).

Ventnor, Margate, Longport **Dial Cab** (tel. 609/822–9422); **South Shore Taxi** (tel. 609/823–1984).

Brigantine **Island Cab** (tel. 609/266–7500); **Joe's Taxi** (tel. 609/266–1315).

Limousines **StariNite Limousine Service** (tel. 609/767–5273 or 609/561–2714).

By Bus **New Jersey Transit** (tel. 800/582–5946) has service to Ventnor, Margate, Longport, and the Wellington Plaza shopping mall. Buses also go to Brigantine, the Shore towns along Route 9, and to the Shore Mall and Hamilton Mall.

Guided Tours

Gray Line Tours (9 N. Arkansas Ave., Atlantic City, tel. 609/344–0965) offers guided bus tours of Atlantic City, Smithville, Renault Winery, and Cape May. Tours are offered to groups of 20 and more, beginning at a hotel or motel. Fees range from $15 for a three-hour tour to $25 for a five-hour tour. Meals are not included, though they can be purchased at Smithville and other sites. Tours are offered all year and can accommodate special interests and schedules.

Exploring Greater Atlantic County

Orientation

The Mullica River, a natural boundary between northern Atlantic County and Burlington County, is usually ignored by travelers in their haste to reach Atlantic City or the Shore towns of Long Beach Island. Being ignored tends to please the residents of this area, who value their seclusion, pristine environment, and peaceful lifestyle. The traditional birthplace of the apocryphal Jersey Devil, the Mullica River basin is one of the last remaining places on the Jersey Shore that is rustic, wild, and overgrown—a perfect get-away-from-it-all locale winding through the New Jersey Pine Barrens, an environmental preserve filled with unusual flora and fauna.

Called Amintonck by the Lenni Lenape Indians, the Mullica was named for one of its 17th-century settlers, Swedish Captain Eric Palsoon Mullica, who explored it in 1645 and claimed an enormous plantation for himself along the river's northern shore between what is now Batsto and New Gretna.

The Great Bay at the Mullica's mouth has long provided a steady income for shellfishermen. But it is the remote, hidden character of the river's inner banks that made it a natural hideout for spies, pirates, privateers, and smugglers, whose need for strong, fast craft to ply their trade allowed several families of boat builders to thrive along these shores. (Three Mullica River–based companies specializing in pleasure craft—Egg Harbor Yachts and Ocean Yachts in Egg Harbor Township, and the Viking Boat Company in New Gretna—make this the capital of New Jersey's boat-building industry.) Smuggling thrived on the Mullica up to the '30s, when rumrunners raced their boats to pick up the hootch in midnight ocean rendezvous with whiskey boats floating beyond America's 3-mile territorial limit; then they spirited their precious cargo to secret coves along the Mullica before dawn.

Numbers in the margin correspond with points of interest on the Greater Atlantic County–Mullica River Area map.

❶ Our auto tour takes most of a day and begins in **Tuckerton,** a small village on Route 9. To get there, take the Garden State Parkway to Exit 58 (north of Atlantic City), then head south on Route 539, the "old Tuckerton Road." Originally called Clamtown, Tuckerton was a major port for Great Bay shellfishers, whose catches were transported by stagecoach to Trenton and, in later years, by rail to markets in Philadelphia and New York. Many of the Shore's first tourists rode east on empty clam cars returning to Tuckerton.

Turn right onto Route 9 off Route 539 (Route 9 at this point is Tuckerton's Main Street). Just south of Tuckerton's post office, turn east onto Great Bay Boulevard and continue south about 5 miles over rattling, rickety bridges to the boat landing at the very end. The view, best seen in the early mornings, shows no evidence of human habitation. The broad, sweeping meadows, marked by twisting creeks, haven't changed much in four centuries. You can imagine Eric Mullica stepping off a boat as he charted the bay.

Return to Tuckerton and follow Route 9 south. You'll cross a narrow bridge over the Bass River, one of the Mullica's tributaries. Turn west off Route 9 onto Route 542, a winding road that skirts the Wading River, another Mullica tributary and popular canoeing area. At the little village of Wading River, stay with Route 542 as it makes a sharp turn to the left, passing through the heart of Eric Mullica's old estate and on to Green Bank. Watch on the left for sudden glimpses of the tree-shrouded river. On 542, about a mile outside Green Bank, you'll pass near what was the most notorious privateer base in New
❷ Jersey. Called **The Forks,** it was little more than a ramshackle collection of wood huts and lean-tos originally located around a convergence of the Mullica and an unnamed creek. From here hundreds of raids against British ships were launched from the 1750s to the 1830s. The privateers used low, flat, open boats to row or sail into the Great Bay and wait for British convoys, which they would efficiently commandeer. Under cover of cannon fire and confusion, the raiders would either sink the ships or steer them through the Mullica's treacherous shoals to elude pursuit.

❸ Just ahead lies the dignified little village of **Batsto,** Swedish for "bathing place," though what put it on the map was the pres-

Greater Atlantic County–Mullica River Area

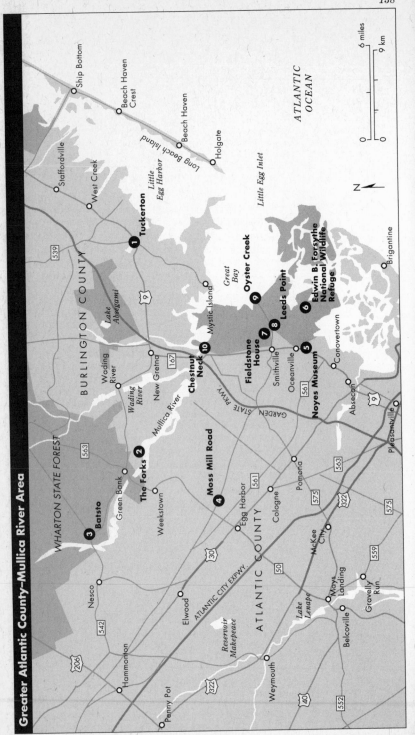

ence of iron at the bottom of bogs and streams, many of which still run rust-red. The iron was used to make weapons and ammunition during the Revolutionary War. So vital was its manufacture that General George Washington exempted all workers in Batsto from military service as long as the iron forges were going day and night. When the iron reserves were depleted, Batsto became a glass-making and lumber town. In the late 19th century the town and its lands were bought by Joseph Wharton, whose estate sold his 53,304 acres to the state of New Jersey for $3 million in 1954. The state enlarged the tract to include the 109,298-acre **Wharton State Forest,** the single largest natural preserve in the state.

Leave your car and explore. The grounds are beautiful, especially in spring and midsummer, and a peek at the Victorian splendor of the manor house is a must. Camping permits, as well as information about horseback riding, hiking, canoeing, and other outdoor activities, are available from the visitor center. *RD #4, Hammonton, tel. 609/561–3262. A $5 parking fee is collected on weekends and holidays during the summer season. Admission for tours of the manor house: $2 adults, $1 children under 12. Tours daily at 10:30, 11:30, 1:30, 2:30, 3:30.*

Drive back east on Route 542 about 5 miles to Green Bank. Turn right (south) onto Route 563 and cross the tiny bridge across the Mullica, driving 6 miles through the little village of Weekstown into Egg Harbor City. Turn left (east) onto Alternate Route 561, the **Moss Mill Road.** This old stagecoach route wanders through what was once (and some superstitious folk believe still is) the haunt of highwayman "Gentleman" Joe Mulliner, a figure of Piney folklore. Pineys, as many longtime Pine Barrens families call themselves, are of mixed stock. Originally many were escaped Hessian soldiers who broke ranks with the British and faded into the foliage, marrying settlers and living renegade lives. "Gentleman" Joe Mulliner was a Piney outlaw who frequently robbed travelers along the Moss Mill Road. The leader of a band of highwaymen, he earned his sobriquet from his legendary courtesy to female victims, whom he would deprive of possessions but let pass unmolested. According to one tale, Mulliner was so smitten by one of his lady victims that he invited her to a nearby tavern for dinner and a dance. When troops arrived he begged to be permitted to finish the dance. Colonial records, in fact, show that Mulliner was arrested in a local tavern, after which he was tried, executed, and buried. His ghost is said to be seen hovering, perhaps dancing, across Moss Mill Road on lonely nights.

Moss Mill Road ends at Smithville, once a stagecoach stop for travelers on their way to Leeds Point. Now the town is a quaint collection of shops and restaurants, most of which are in historic buildings that were moved to the site.

Time Out The **Smithville Inn** on Route 9 at Moss Mill Road is the best restaurant in the entire village of Smithville, and the Sunday American buffet brunch, with its array of crepes, kidneys, and other unusual American regional specialties, is worth a try. Ask for a table with a view of the lake.

From Moss Mill Road, turn right (south) onto Route 9 and drive about 1½ miles to Oceanville. Go past the entrance to the Forsythe Wildlife Refuge, then turn left onto Lily Lake Road,

❺ and continue to the **Noyes Museum.** Founded by the late Fred Noyes, who owned and developed the Smithville Inn, the museum's unusual mix of New Jersey folk and fine art is a peculiar, off-the-beaten-track delight. Cultural programs are scheduled frequently, and the rustic setting alone is worth a trip. *Lily Lake Rd., Oceanville, tel. 609/652–8848. Admission: $1.50. Open Wed.–Sun. 11–4.*

Return to Route 9, make a right (north), and then a quick right
❻ (east) into the **Edwin B. Forsythe National Wildlife Refuge,** one of four American wetland areas to be designated by the United Nations as having "international importance." On foot you can explore two nature trails, but far more rewarding is taking the refuge's 8.1-mile, self-guided car tour, which takes you out onto a series of earthen dikes separating a huge freshwater habitat from the salt marshes beyond. The birds flit and flutter about as you drive, some occasionally waddling across the car trail to glare at you. The speed limit is a mere 15 miles per hour, but you should go slower to take in the views, perhaps stopping to inhale the fresh air. You may leave your car and climb the observation platforms, but you may not leave any trash, food debris, or even a cigarette butt. At the eastern edge of the trail, you'll be able to see the far-off towers of Atlantic City's casinos, which actually look good from this distance. *Box 72, Oceanville, tel. 609/652–1665. Admission: $3 per car. Open dawn–dusk.*

Return to Route 9 and turn right (north). About an eighth of a mile up the road, turn right onto Route 618, Leeds Point Road, which ends in a *T*-intersection with Moss Mill Road (Alternate Route 561), the old stagecoach route. Turn right onto Moss Mill Road and drive for a quarter mile. The road forks before a
❼ **fieldstone house.** Now privately owned, the house served as a Nazi spy base during World War II. Federal agents raided the building and found a German radio and canned food and supplies labeled as belonging to the German army. No one knows if Nazi submarine U-boats supplied the base, though some U-boats were sighted off the Jersey Shore during the war. One was sunk near Long Beach Island.

❽ Turn left at the fork and enter **Leeds Point,** once a ferry stop for boat travel to various barrier islands, all of them within the Forsythe refuge and none of them inhabited. According to legend, Old Mama Leeds, an American Colonial settler living here, had an illicit liaison with a Hessian soldier. The 13th child of this union had the face of a horse, the wings of a bird, a tail, and breath so foul that it soured all the milk in the house. Mama Leeds didn't have much time to gaze upon her offspring, for the child scampered up her fireplace shortly after being born. Hence the origin of the legend of the **Jersey Devil.** Believed to be immortal, the Jersey Devil has been sighted well into this century and has been blamed for everything from stolen livestock to bad odors.

At the very end of the road is the scenic clamming village of
❾ **Oyster Creek,** where huts and shanties totter on stilts above the shallow waters of the Great Bay. Earlier in the tour we viewed the Great Bay's northern shore; this is the farthest point east on its western shore. The settlement visible in the distance is **Mystic Island,** a residential community. You may also be able to see the blue water tower of the Viking Yacht Company in New Gretna.

(10) Retrace your steps to Route 9 and drive north 5 miles to **Chestnut Neck** on the western bank of the Mullica. To cross the river you must drive onto the Garden State Parkway. The view from the bridge is beautiful but, with traffic whizzing along at 55 miles per hour, difficult to enjoy. Instead, avoid the entrance to the parkway and stay on Route 9. On your right is the **Chestnut Neck Memorial,** a tall obelisk on the probable site of an earthen fort built by colonists to guard the privateer bases and landings farther up the Mullica River. On October 6, 1778, nine British warships sailed up the Mullica and destroyed the fort, all boats anchored there, and the nearby settlement. The British didn't go farther upriver, having heard reports of reinforcements camped out near Batsto under the command of Count Casimir Pulaski. The British boasted of wiping out Chestnut Neck without losses. Nevertheless, privateer operations resumed quickly afterward. Recently underwater archaeologists have discovered several sunken hulks just off Chestnut Neck dating from the Colonial period. One vessel, showing evidence of having burned as it sank, has been identified as British, suggesting that the operation may not have been the rout the British claimed.

From here take the Garden State Parkway south to Atlantic City or north to Long Beach Island.

Wineries

Most visitors are surprised to learn that southern New Jersey has wineries. Tastings are limited to those age 21 and older. The best known is the **Renault Vineyard** (pronounced re-**NALT**), founded in 1864 by Louis Nicholas Renault. The winery also has a pleasant Continental restaurant (*see* Dining, below). *Bremen Ave., Egg Harbor City, tel. 609/965–2111. Admission: $1. Open Mon.–Sat. 10–5. Closed Sun.*

The smaller **Balic Winery** (Rte. 40 in Mays Landing, tel. 609/625–2166) also gives tours and tastings. **Tomasello's Winery** (Rte. 9 at Moss Mill Rd. in Hammonton, tel. 609/561–0567) has a shop offering free tastings in the Smithville shopping area.

What to See and Do with Children

Lucy the Elephant is a classic example of seashore surrealism. Surrounded by ugly condos, nightclubs, and restaurants is the magnificent seven-story-high elephant-shape building. Constructed in 1881 to attract potential real-estate buyers to the then wild, mostly uninhabited marshy south end of Absecon Island, the elephant has served as a tavern, a private house, and an adjunct to a hotel. In the '60s, Lucy (no one is sure how she got her name) was saved from demolition by local residents and moved two blocks south to her present location. The elephant now holds Margate's historical museum, with a gift shop, snack bar, and amphitheater in her vast shadow. Tours of Lucy the elephant are given daily in summer, weekends by appointment in the colder months. *Atlantic and Decatur Aves., Margate, tel. 609/822–6519 or 609/822–0424. Admission: $2 adults, $1 children 6–12, children 6 and under free. Concerts Thurs. evening July and Aug. Snack bar open June–Aug. Limited free parking.*

As a service to families with young children, local libraries offer **free storytelling** and reading hours—perfect entertainment for rainy days. Dates and times vary: Brigantine (1500 W. Brigantine Ave., tel. 609/266–0110); Galloway Township (30 W. Jimmie Leeds Rd., tel. 609/652–2352); Hammonton (South Egg Harbor Rd., tel. 609/561–2264); Margate (8100 Atlantic Ave., tel. 609/822–4700); Pleasantville (132 W. Washington Ave., tel. 609/641–1778); Somers Point (747 Shore Rd., tel. 609/927–7113); Ventnor (6500 Atlantic Ave., tel. 609/823–4614).

The Stockton State College Performing Arts Center (550 Jimmie Leeds Rd., Pomona, tel. 609/652–9000) presents many shows for children. The children's theater troupe, The Paper Bag Players, performs every April as part of the "Imagination" series—a program of music, dance, and theater productions from December through May. In July, children can attend "Marvelous Midday Matinees," a summer theater series with shows every Wednesday at 10 AM, noon, and 2 PM.

Storybook Land is a preschool children's theme park 10 miles west of Atlantic City that has an elaborate Christmas lighting display every December. *1671 Black Horse Pike, Cardiff, tel. 609/641–7847. Admission: $7.60. Open daily 10–5 through Sept. 9; off-season, Thurs. and Fri. 10–3, weekends 11–5.*

Off the Beaten Track

Fischer's Greenhouses is famous for its African violets and other flowering plants. Tours are free by appointment. There is a flower shop and garden center on the premises. *Blackman Rd. and Poplar Ave., Bargaintown, tel. 609/927–3399. Free admission. Open daily 9–5. No tours Sun.*

The **Marine Mammal Stranding Center and Sea Life Museum** was founded by Robert Schoelkopf, who once directed dolphin shows on Atlantic City's Steel Pier. He has since become an expert on marine creature strandings—when whales, dolphins, sharks, turtles, and other marine life somehow become disoriented and maroon themselves on beaches at low tide and require human assistance to return to open water. The small museum illustrates Schoelkopf's passionate concern for the environment and has replicas of game fish, marine mammals, and other flora and fauna. *3625 Brigantine Blvd., Brigantine, tel. 609/266–0538. Admission by donation. Open Memorial Day–Labor Day, daily 10–5; off-season, weekends noon–4.*

The famed Monopoly landmark of Marvin Gardens was misspelled deliberately by Charles Darrow, who could not use a trademarked name when he patented his real-estate game. This small, bungalow-style residential community of **Marven Gardens** is located on the border between the towns of MARgate and VENtnor (hence the spelling, Marven) just off the west side of Ventnor Avenue on Absecon Island. Note the winding streets and lack of overhead utility wires. Marven Gardens was one of the first suburban communities to bury these wires so as not to obscure the view.

Atlantic County's oldest residence, the 1720 **Somers Mansion,** sits on a bluff overlooking Egg Harbor, Ocean City, and the busy Somers Point traffic circle. It is maintained as a museum by the **Atlantic County Historical Society,** whose offices and a small museum and library are about a quarter mile north on

Shore Road. *Mansion: Shore Rd. at the Somers Point Circle, Somers Point, tel. 609/927–2212. Admission free. Open Wed.– Fri. 9–5, Sat. 10–noon and 1–5, Sun. 1–5. Historical Society: 907 Shore Rd., Somers Point, tel. 609/927–5218. Open Wed.– Sat. 10–3:30.*

The **Stockton State College Observatory** is open for sky-watch-ing on Friday evenings from 9 to 11, weather permitting. *2 mi north of Rte. 30 (White Horse Pike) on Rte. 575, Galloway Township, tel. 609/652–4520. Admission free. Open Fri. 8–10 PM.*

Shopping

Atlantic County specializes in suburban malls. The **Hamilton Mall,** the county's largest, is in Hamilton Township on the Black Horse Pike next to the Atlantic City Race Course. An-chor stores include a JC Penney, Macy's, and Sears, and there are other smaller shops as well.

The **Shore Mall,** at Tilton Road and Black Horse Pike, features Boscov's and Steinbachs department stores and the county's largest multiplex movie theater.

Smaller malls and strip shopping are plentiful along Route 9 in Somers Point and on Route 30 in Absecon and Galloway Town-ship.

Central Square, on Route 9 in Linwood, is a tony assortment of clothing stores and boutiques. The historic town of Smithville almost overflows with boutiques, such as **Carousel Fantasies** (615 E. Moss Mill Rd., Smithville, tel. 609/748–0011), which specializes in carousel horses and amusement art.

The **Lenox China** company manufactures china and giftware in its factory on Tilton Road in Pomona (tel. 609/641–3700). The factory store is open weekdays 9:30–5 and sells Lenox china at retail prices. Bargain hunters should consider calling in Octo-ber when the store has its week-long annual sale.

Sports and Outdoor Activities

Participant Sports

Beaches Between Memorial Day and Labor Day you must purchase a beach tag to enter beaches in Brigantine, Ventnor, Margate, and Longport. Season-long beach tags cost between $5 and $10 and are usually discounted if purchased before May 31; weekly tags cost between $2 and $3. Badges are available at municipal halls and from tag inspectors on the beach. Only Atlantic City's beach has public rest rooms. Information is available at *Brig-antine* (tel. 609/266–5511); *Ventnor* (tel. 609/823–7904); *Mar-gate* (tel. 609/822–0424); *Longport* (tel. 609/823–4015). The **Atlantic County Health Department** (tel. 609/645–7700, ext. 4372) supplies information about water quality and beach con-ditions in Atlantic County.

Bicycling Linwood, a town on the Atlantic County mainland, has a small bicycle path over old railroad tracks running parallel to Shore and New roads (Route 9). Bicycling is permitted on the Ventnor boardwalk every day until 10 AM. Several rental shops can be found on the main streets of Linwood, Margate, and Ventnor.

Bird-watching The **Forsythe National Wildlife Refuge** has observation platforms with excellent vantage points. Kennedy Park, off the traffic circle in Somers Point, gets some waterfowl. *Oceanville, on Great Creek Rd. off Rte. 9, tel. 609/652–1665. General admission free for walkers. 8-mi wildlife drive: $3 per car. Open daily sunrise–sunset; closed in inclement weather.*

Fishing Party boats leave from Margate Bay docks along Amherst Avenue. You can also fish off the Ventnor and Margate fishing piers or try open casting along the Longport jetty. The Margate fishing pier is located at Exeter Avenue, and the beach is the headquarters of the **Angler's Club of Absecon Island.** *Exeter Ave., at the beach, Margate City, tel. 609/823–9846. Use of the pier for members only.*

Golf The **Sands Country Club** (Mays Landing Rd., Somers Point, tel. 609/927–5072) admits guests of the Sands Hotel & Casino in Atlantic City as well as nonmembers. **Marriott's Seaview Golf Resort** has two 18-hole courses that are also open to nonguests. *Rte. 9, Absecon, 08201, tel. 609/652–1800. Admission: $65 per day. Open daily 7 AM–dark.*

Ventnor has a miniature golf course in its municipal recreation center (tel. 609/823–3086). During the winter the course is disassembled and flooded for ice skating.

Tennis Municipal courts are available in Ventnor at Suffolk and Atlantic avenues and at Surrey and Ventnor avenues (tel. 609/823–7946); and in Margate at Fremont and Jerome avenues. *Tel. 609/822–8650. Admission free. Courts open daily 10–5.*

Water Sports Boat and jet-ski rentals are available in Margate and Somers Point.

Spectator Sports

Horse Racing The **Atlantic City Race Course** features Thoroughbred racing in summer and simulcast betting in the winter season. There is a restaurant on the premises. *Rte. 40, McKee City, tel. 609/641–2190. Admission June–Sept.: $4 clubhouse, $2 grandstand; free in winter. Races June–Sept., post time 7:25 PM; closed Tues. and Sun. Winter simulcasts, post time 7:30 PM Mon.–Sat.*

Polo The game of kings is played in the relaxed, informal setting of the **Mattix Run Equestrian Center** every other Sunday after Memorial Day beginning at 1:30 PM; the season continues on alternate weekends through mid-October, weather permitting. *Polo grounds, off Rte. 9 in Smithville (a few yards south of the entrance to the Smithville shopping area), at 573 E. Moss Mill Rd., tel. 609/652–8096. Admission: $3. Free parking.*

County Parks

Birch Grove is a 275-acre county park with fishing lakes, playground, nature paths, picnic areas, miniature golf, and a small zoo. *Mill Road and Burton Ave., Northfield, tel. 609/641–3778. Admission free; miniature golf costs $2. Open daily early morning–7PM.*

Atlantic County Park is a group of parks, at various locations, that together cover more than 1,000 acres, with nature exhibits, playground and picnic areas, fishing, bike trails, a running course, and hiking. Occasionally environmental lectures and tours of ruined glassworks are given. *For information, call 609/ 625–1897.*

Dining

For price ranges, consult the dining price chart in Chapter 1, Essential Information. Highly recommended restaurants are indicated with a star ★.

New Gretna, Burlington County

Moderate– **Rosalie's New Gretna House.** Dinner theater, mystery dinners, Expensive and a good salad bar liven up this pleasant surf-and-turf restaurant in a historic stagecoach building, with some early-bird and children's specials. *Rte. 9 and N. Maple Ave., New Gretna, tel. 609/296–2400. Reservations advised. Dress: casual. Free parking. AE, MC, V. Open Wed.–Sun. for dinner. Closed Mon. and Tues.*

Inexpensive– **Allen's Clam Bar.** Nearby Tuckerton was once called Clamtown Moderate because of the rich clam beds nearby. You'll have to stand on ★ line to sample the freshest clams and oysters, raw, steamed, fried, or dunked in chowder. *Rte. 9, New Gretna, tel. 609/296– 4106. No reservations. Limited free parking. No credit cards. BYOB. Closed Mon.*

Atlantic County Mainland

Very Expensive **Ram's Head Inn.** This restaurant is a little bit pretentious, but the country-inn setting is likely to win you over. Several dining rooms overlook a forested park. The Ram's Head is renowned for its strict dress code: Men must wear a jacket. The cuisine is mostly Continental, but American steak-and-seafood entrées are also served. *9 W. White Horse Pike (near Garden State Pkwy. exit), Absecon, tel. 609/652–1700. Reservations advised. Jacket required. Valet parking. AE, DC, MC, V.*

Expensive– **Marriott's Seaview Golf Resort.** A very good Sunday brunch Very Expensive and Friday evening seafood buffet are featured at this resort. ★ The service is crisp and the dining rooms sparkle—you get the feeling you're at a very expensive wedding reception. *Rte. 9, Absecon, tel. 609/652–1800. Reservations advised. Jacket required. Free parking. AE, D, DC, MC, V.*

Renault Winery Gourmet Restaurant. Six-course American and Continental dinners are served in banquettes made of wine casks. The nicely done Coquilles St. Jacques outclasses the local wines, but the ambience is fun. *Bremen Ave. and Moss Mill Rd., Egg Harbor City, tel. 609/965–2111. Reservations required. Dress: casual. Free parking. AE, MC, V. Open for dinner only, Thurs.–Sun. Closed Mon.–Wed.*

Restaurant reviews were compiled with the assistance of Ed Hitzel, food critic of the Atlantic City Press; *J. M. Lang, food critic of the* New Jersey Monthly; *and Chuck Darrow, Atlantic City columnist for the* Camden Courier Post.

Expensive **Cousin's Country House.** In this romantic country-house setting you can almost pretend you're not at the Shore. Continental cuisine is featured, the setting is elegant, and the service is
very good. Dining here on Valentine's Day is a treat. *Fire and
Zion Rds., Egg Harbor Township, tel. 609/927–5777. Reservations advised. Dress: casual. Free parking. AE, DC, MC, V.*
Tre Figlia. This warmly satisfying northern Italian restaurant
sits on busy Route 30. Inside you'll think you'd died and gone to
New York. The decor is clean and spare, the veal and chicken
dishes superb. *50 W. White Horse Pike (Rte. 30), Pomona, tel.
609/965–3303. Reservations advised. Jacket required. Free
parking. AE, MC, V. Closed weekdays. No lunch.*

Moderate– **The Bayou.** Rich gumbo and blackened seafood are featured at
Expensive this enjoyable, informal, family-style Cajun restaurant perched
on the causeway connecting Somers Point to Longport. Cray-
ons are provided for place-mat coloring—the best works
are displayed on the walls. *Longport Blvd., Somers Point, tel.
609/927–1377. Reservations advised. Dress: casual. No credit
cards. BYOB. Closed Mon.–Wed. and for lunch; closed Oct.–
Apr.*
Mac's. This is a good, old Italian-style surf-and-turf house with
notable '60s decor, where the management pays careful attention to fresh ingredients. *908 Shore Rd., Somers Point, tel. 609/
927–4360. Summer reservations advised. Dress: casual. Limited free parking. AE, DC, MC, V. Closed for lunch.*
Oyster Creek Inn. This ultimate, out-of-the-way restaurant has
little in the way of atmosphere, but the rustic clamming village
and the sweeping view of the Great Bay are spectacular. Basic
surf, some turf, fried, broiled, or steamed. *Oyster Creek Rd.,
Leeds Point, tel. 609/652–8565. Reservations advised on weekends. Dress: casual. Free parking. MC, V.*
Via Veneto. This boutique-size Italian restaurant is located in
Linwood's Central Square shopping center. It offers bistro cuisine: pasta, salads, and light entrées. *Central Sq. (Rte. 9),
Linwood, tel. 609/927–2500. Reservations advised for dinner.
Dress: casual. Free parking. No credit cards. BYOB. Closed
lunch Sun. and dinner Mon.*

Moderate **Golden Pyramid.** Italian, Middle Eastern, and American cui-
★ sines are available under one roof. Luscious lamb dishes are
recommended, and so is what some consider to be the best hamburger in South Jersey. *34 W. Main St., Mays Landing, tel.
609/623–0800. Reservations advised. Dress: casual. Limited
free parking. No credit cards. Closed Sun.*
Señor Rattler's Cantina. Tex-Mex cuisine and mesquite-grilled
seafood are the specialties. The *chicken chingalingas* (deep-
fried chicken tortillas) are delightful with margaritas. The dining room is decorated with plants and plaster birds and has
terraces. The restaurant, with the occasional mariachi bands,
will remind you of a Mexican *tourista* hotel. *Rte. 9, 1 mi north
of Seaview Golf Resort, Oceanville, tel. 609/646–8226. Weekend
reservations advised. Dress: informal. Free parking. AE, DC,
MC, V. Closed for lunch.*

Inexpensive **The Clam Bar.** Perched on the Great Egg Harbor Bay in
★ Somers Point and also known as Smitty's, this is one of the last
of the raw bars on the Jersey Shore. Expect long lines on summer weekend evenings and longer still if you want one of the
few outdoor seats, where you can slouch at the bar, stuff yourself with raw clams and oysters or steamed shellfish, gaze at the

bay, and listen to seagulls and the gentle slap of rigging on sail-boat masts. No alcohol is served. *910 Bay Ave., Somers Point, tel. 609/927–8783. No reservations. Dress: informal. No credit cards. BYOB.*

Ventnor, Margate, Longport

Expensive **Longport Inn.** A little bit of Spring Lake near Atlantic City, this is a relaxed surf-and-turf house frequented mostly by Longport's senior citizens and affluent Irish types. Live lounge combos appear on weekend nights. The outdoor patio is a good place for a après-beach drink. The Longport features a Sunday brunch and a children's menu. *31st Ave. and Atlantic Ave., Longport, tel. 609/822–5435. Reservations advised. Jacket required for dinner. AE, DC, MC, V.*

Moderate– **Fedele's Original Ferraro's Restaurant.** The fare is rich, gar-
Expensive licky southern Italian cuisine, though the star of the show is Mama Fedele, who can be coaxed out of the kitchen in her apron to sing arias from Italian operas. *9403 Ventnor Ave., Margate, tel. 609/822–1293. Reservations advised. Dress: casual. Street parking. AE, MC, V. Closed for lunch.*
Little Rock Cafe. The Milano Modern interior here offers a re-freshing break from the typical seashore scrimshaw. The menu emphasizes fresh salads, pastas, grilled seafood, and stirfry dishes, though it varies seasonally. Chocolate black-out cake is one of the many excellent desserts. *5214 Atlantic Ave. (near the corner of Little Rock Ave.), Ventnor, tel. 609/823–4411. Reservations advised for dinner. Dress: casual. Street parking. No credit cards. BYOB.*
Sannas Bay Club. Chic and sweat-suit trendy, this California-style restaurant serves an eclectic, international menu of grilled, Cajun, Thai, Chinese, and Italian dishes. The Sannas has outdoor dining, early-bird specials, and Sunday brunch. *Monroe and Amherst Aves., Margate, tel. 609/822–5355. Reservations advised. Dress: casual. Free parking. AE, MC, V. Closed Dec.–Apr. and Mon.*

Inexpensive **Lou's Deli.** This family-style diner and delicatessen is notable for the fresh ingredients used in its fare. It is favored for Jew-ish staples such as corned-beef sandwiches, cheese blintzes, and matzo-ball soup. Lou's has early-bird specials and a chil-dren's menu. *5011 Ventnor Ave., Ventnor, tel. 609/823–2733. No reservations. Dress: casual. Street parking. No credit cards.*

Brigantine

Expensive– **Oceanfront Restaurant.** This is the only oceanside restaurant in
Very Expensive Atlantic County that isn't in a casino, and the view from the "deco-echo" grand-hotel dining room is terrific. The fare is mostly Italian, with some Continental and Cajun entrées. *14th St. at the beach, Brigantine, tel. 609/266–7731. Reservations advised for weekend dinner. Jackets advised for dinner. Free parking. AE, DC, MC, V.*

Moderate– **Frankie's Crab House and the Lagoon Restaurant.** The Lagoon,
Expensive called Lay-goon by locals and frequented by senior citizens, is Brigantine's surf-and-turf house, with some Cajun and Conti-nental entrées. On the second floor, Frankie's serves primarily seafood, with inexpensive all-you-can-eat specials. *3700 Brig-*

antine Blvd., Brigantine, tel. 609/266–7057. Reservations advised for dinner at Lagoon. Dress: jacket required (Lagoon); casual (Frankie's). Free parking. AE, DC, MC, V. Frankie's closed for lunch.

Lodging

For price ranges, consult the lodging price chart in Chapter 1, Essential Information. Highly recommended lodgings are indicated with a star ★.

Hotels

Very Expensive
★

Marriott's Seaview Golf Resort. The South Shore's grandest private country club went public some time ago and is now a hotel with an excellent 36-hole golf course set back in the quiet woods along Route 9 about a 30-minute drive from Atlantic City. The rooms are decorated in contemporary pastels, and there are flowers throughout the hotel. Some suites have patio balconies with views of golf courses and the surrounding Pine Barrens. The dining room serves a brunch and a commendable Friday night seafood buffet. The Marriott makes sense for midsize conferences that want to be near the casino atmosphere but not dominated by it. As an added convenience, room service is available. *Rte. 9, Galloway Township 08201, tel. 609/652–1800 or 800/228–9290. 298 rooms, 41 suites, all with bath. Facilities: restaurant, bar, lounge, health club, exercise and weight machines, game rooms, steam, sauna, whirlpool, 8 tennis courts, pro shop, meeting and convention rooms. AE, D, DC, MC, V.*

Motels

Moderate–Expensive

Best Western Inn at Golf & Tennis World. A five-minute drive from Bally's Grand Hotel Casino, this property offers functional hotel rooms, some of which have bay views. A good health club and racquet-sports facility are available for guests. Casino transportation is available. *4005 Black Horse Pike, West Atlantic City 08232, tel. 609/641–3546. 110 rooms with bath. Facilities: restaurant, café, indoor and outdoor pools, exercise and weight machines, whirlpool, sauna, tennis courts, meeting rooms, game room. Bicycles available. AE, CB, D, DC, MC, V.*

Comfort Inn Victorian. This motel, decorated with Victoriana, is about 20 minutes from Atlantic City, along Pleasantville's commercial strip. The inn offers a free Continental breakfast, and transportation to the casinos is available. *1175 Black Horse Pike, Pleasantville 08232, tel. 609/646–8880. 117 rooms with bath. Facilities: cable TV, heated pool, meeting rooms. AE, D, DC, MC, V.*

Comfort Inn West. An easy eight-minute drive from Atlantic City, this hotel—the first phase of a planned office and retail complex—has comfortable rooms decorated in earth tones. From some of the rooms you can see the bay. *Dover Place and Black Horse Pike, West Atlantic City 08232, tel. 609/645–1818. 190 rooms, 8 suites, all with bath. Facilities: meeting rooms, casino transportation. AE, D, DC, MC, V.*

Whittier Inn. Located on Pleasantville's commercial strip, the Whittier is 20 minutes from Atlantic City and area beaches. A

Continental breakfast is included in the room rate. *Black Horse Pike, Pleasantville 08232, tel. 609/484–1500 or 800/237–9682. 196 rooms with bath. Facilities: heated pool, meeting rooms, coin laundry, free casino transportation. AE, D, DC, MC, V.*

Moderate **Comfort Inn North.** Located about 20 minutes from Atlantic City along the busy White Horse Pike, this chain property provides transportation to the casinos. *405 E. Absecon Blvd., Absecon 08201, tel. 609/646–5000. 200 rooms with bath, 7 suites. Facilities: heated pool, meeting rooms. AE, D, DC, MC, V.*

Howard Johnson Motor Lodge. There are beautiful bay and Atlantic City–skyline views from this motel on the White Horse Pike, 10 minutes from Atlantic City. *539 Absecon Blvd., Absecon 08201, tel. 609/641–7272 or 800/654–2000. 208 rooms, 3 suites, all with bath. Facilities: restaurant, meeting rooms. Free airport transportation, casino transportation. AE, D, DC, MC, V.*

Bed-and-Breakfast

The area's only bed-and-breakfast is in Mays Landing, the Atlantic County seat and a 30-minute drive from Atlantic City.

Moderate **Inn at Sugar Hill.** This early 1880s Victorian was once the private residence of a state senator. Now an inn, with a restaurant serving excellent American regional cuisine, the Sugar Hill boasts seven working fireplaces. Rooms are furnished with mixed antiques. The veranda and some of the rooms have views of what was an important boat-building and privateer base along the Mullica River during the Revolutionary War. A Continental breakfast is included in the room rate. *Rtes. 50 and 559, Mays Landing 08330, tel. 609/625–2226. 4 rooms with shared baths, 1 suite with private bath. Smoking on first floor only. Facilities: moderately priced restaurant (lunch and dinner). No minimum stays. Off-street parking. AE, MC, V.*

The Arts and Nightlife

The Arts

Movies **Egg Harbor Township:** Towne 16 (Shore Mall, tel. 609/646–4700).
Northfield: Tilton 6 (Tilton Shopping Center, Tilton Rd., tel. 609/646–3147).
Somers Point: Point 4 (MacArthur Blvd., tel. 609/927–0131).

Theater The **South Jersey Regional Theater** (738 Bay Ave., Somers Point, tel. 609/653–0553) is an Actors Equity community playhouse.
Stockton State College Performing Arts Center (Jimmie Leeds Rd., Pomona, tel. 609/652–9000) features plays, concerts, and public lectures. The Paper Bag Players group presents children's theater.
Walter Edge Theater (Atlantic County Community College, Black Horse Pike, west of Race Track Circle, Mays Landing, tel. 609/343–5040 or 609/343–5113) showcases student theater productions, touring companies, concerts, and lectures.

Nightlife

Bars   **Gregory's Restaurant** is a laid-back Somers Point "meetery" for the twentysomething set. *900 Shore Rd., Somers Point, tel. 609/927–6665. No dress code. Free lot parking across the street. AE, DC, MC, V. Bar open 11 AM–2 AM.*

The Waterfront restaurant is best known for its crowded, dressy happy-hour buffets. Live pop bands appear some nights, and reservations are necessary in summer season. Some boat slips are available for waterborne diners. *998 Bay Ave., off Somers Point Circle, Somers Point, tel. 609/653–0099. Dress: no tank tops, flip-flops, or cutoffs. No dress code for outdoor bar. AE, MC, V. Restaurant open 11:30 AM–10 or 11 PM; bar open 11:30 AM–2 AM.*

Ventura's Greenhouse deck bar is a short distance from the Margate beach. In the summer the microbathing-suit crowd tends to congregate here. You'd think at first that the bar merely serves as a watering hole for the thirsty, but nobody goes to the beach if they're going to the Greenhouse. Why risk sand, surf, and ocean breezes blowing that absolutely perfect hair out of place? There is an inexpensive snack menu. *106 S. Benson Ave., Margate, tel. 609/822–0140. No credit cards. Deck bar closed Oct.–Apr.*

Nightclubs   **Brownie's Lodge** is a prime country-western bar with live bands and DJ music, plus Texas-style barbecues on Sunday afternoons in the summer. You'll be dressed correctly if you wear your boots and blue jeans. *244 Poplar Ave., Bargaintown, tel. 609/927–5556. AE, DC, MC, V.*

Crazy Jane's, the mainland's busiest, dressiest disco, is where live bands and DJs hold forth. *998 Bay Ave., (across from the Waterfront, Somers Point, tel. 609/653–8999. Cover charge. Dress: no casual clothes.*

Gilhooley's is one of the busiest nightclubs in Margate. On weekends there are DJs or a live band, and Wednesday is comedy night. *9314 Amherst Ave., Margate, tel. 609/823–2800. Occasional cover charge. Dress: casual. AE, DC, MC, V. Closed Sun. and Tues. in winter.*

Markers, the former Harborlights restaurant, a few blocks north of the Waterfront in Somers Point, has weekend pop bands. *520 Bay Ave., tel. 609/653–0900. No cover charge. AE, MC, V. Weekend bands usually 9 PM–1:30 AM.*

McMahon's Circle Tavern was voted best Jersey Shore rock-and-roll bar by *Atlantic City Magazine.* Loud, live bands perform nearly every night. *3313 Brigantine Blvd. at the Circle, Brigantine, tel. 609/266–8655. Cover charge. No credit cards.*

Polo Bay is the dressiest of the many dance bars and taverns along Margate's Barbary Coast. The weekday 4–7 PM happy hour, with its 25¢ drinks and free hot and cold buffet, is the island's cheapest dinner. *9300 Amherst Ave., Margate, tel. 609/823–2144. Cover charge. Jackets required (no tank tops, T-shirts, shorts, or sneakers). AE, MC, V. Open weeknights until 1 AM, weekends until 4 AM.*

Reds is one of the best "new music" dance clubs on the Shore. It features a varied schedule of live punk, hard rock, and progressive rock bands. *Washington and Atlantic Aves., Margate, tel. 609/822–1539. Cover charge. No dress code. No credit cards.*

Pool Halls   **Tilton Billiards,** not your typical smoke-and-shot joint, is an upscale establishment with 21 tournament pool tables, three billiard tables, and a snooker table. *201 Tilton Rd. (in the London Square Mall), Northfield, tel. 609/645–1181. Casual dress but no T-shirts, shorts, or sneakers. MC, V. Open daily 10 AM–midnight.*

7 Cape May County

Introduction

During the summer Cape May County's chain of barrier-island resort towns increases population by a factor of 10. Each town has its own subtle character based on the ethnic and cultural backgrounds of its vacationers and year-round residents, though the predominantly Italian population is most obvious, with their numerous restaurants and nightclubs. Alcoholic beverages cannot be sold or served in Ocean City, which began as a Methodist retreat and still retains some of its Sunday blue laws, though its residents are now much more religiously mixed than its founders could have foreseen. Wildwood and portions of Sea Isle City have a strong Italian population, with Wildwood attracting the younger thrill-seekers and Sea Isle the older, family-oriented visitors. Avalon and Stone Harbor, two towns sharing the same island, have a dominant WASP population, with Stone Harbor the more affluent of the two.

The Cape May County mainland, usually ignored by most visitors rushing down the Garden State Parkway, is surprisingly rural, resembling portions of Delaware and Maryland's Eastern Shore. Route 9, the state road running parallel to the Garden State Parkway, is dotted with shops and shopping centers, restaurants, antiques dealers, inexpensive motels, farmers' markets, wildlife refuges, and historic small towns like Cape May Court House, the Cape May County seat. The Delaware Bay shore, a 20-minute drive from the island towns, is crowded with tiny vacation homes and retirement villages. Colonized in the early part of this century as a fishing resort area, the bay shore towns suffered when, about 30 years ago, the fish population was threatened by pollution. With the reduction in pollution along the Delaware River, the fish are now coming back.

Essential Information

Arriving and Departing

By Plane The nearest airport with scheduled service is **Atlantic City International Airport** in Pomona (*see* Arriving and Departing in Chapter 5, Atlantic City). **Cape May County Airport,** located in Lower Township near Cape May Court House, does not have scheduled service. Smaller county airports are in Ocean City and Woodbine.

By Car The most convenient way to travel in Cape May County is by car. The **Garden State Parkway,** a toll road running roughly parallel to the New Jersey Shore, offers easy access to causeways connecting the island resorts to the mainland.

From New York Southbound travelers from New York City should cross into New Jersey from **I–80** to the **New Jersey Turnpike,** another toll road, changing to the **Garden State Parkway** at Exit 11. Depending on your destination, travel time is about three hours.

From Philadelphia The **Atlantic City Expressway,** another toll road, connects Philadelphia and the southern New Jersey suburbs to the Garden State Parkway; from there head south at Exit 7. Travel time is approximately 2½ hours.

From the South From south of New Jersey travelers can enter the state at the **Delaware Memorial Bridge** and take **Route 40** southeast to faster, wider **Route 55**, then south to **Route 47** and **Route 83**, which eventually merges with the **Garden State Parkway.** Travel time from the bridge is about three hours because of slow-moving traffic.

A third alternative, the ferry from Lewes, Delaware, is described in Chapter 8, Victorian Cape May.

By Train **New Jersey Transit** commuter and **Amtrak** passenger trains arrive several times daily in Atlantic City. From the Atlantic City Municipal Terminal you can hop a New Jersey Transit bus or rent a car. (*See* Chapter 5, Atlantic City, for additional details.)

By Bus **New Jersey Transit** links the island and mainland communities. Local terminals can be found in **Ocean City:** Transportation Center (10th St. and Haven Ave., tel. 609/398–9030); **Sea Isle City:** Sea Isle Variety & Bus (46th St. and Landis Ave., tel. 609/263–6832); and **Wildwood:** New Jersey Transit Bus Operations Terminal (New Jersey and Oak Aves., tel. 609/522–2491 or 522–2492). Buses pick up and discharge passengers in **Avalon** at 3rd Avenue and 46th Street, and in **Stone Harbor** at 3rd Avenue and 94th Street.

Getting Around

By Car A car is almost a necessity on the island resorts, though steps have been taken to reduce car traffic by adding trolleys in Ocean City (*see* By Trolley and Tram, below). West–east causeways connect the island resort towns to the mainland. North to south, the islands are linked by a series of toll bridges. Expect delays because of bridge openings and heavy weekend traffic.

A word of warning: Shore municipalities ticket and tow illegally parked cars with a vengeance. Fees and fines are very expensive and must be paid in cash.

By Taxi **Ocean City: H&M Taxi** (tel. 609/398–5649) and **Ocean City Yellow Cab** (tel. 609/399–4600).

Wildwood: Checker Cab (tel. 609/522–1431).

Wildwood Crest: Yellow Cab (tel. 609/522–0555).

By Trolley and Tram
Ocean City A red, antique-looking trolley travels around the island in the summer. It runs about every 25 minutes, 8:30 AM–midnight. The southern terminus is 59th Street on Central Avenue. The trolley travels north to 23rd Street, then to Wesley Avenue, 15th Street, Ocean Avenue, 9th Street, Atlantic Avenue, Battersea, and finally to the Longport/Somers Point causeway. The fare is $1.25 for adults, less for children age 12 and under and senior citizens with a Medicaid or Department of Transportation identity card (tel. 609/884–5230, ext. 222).

Wildwood Wildwood has tram cars that cruise the 2-mile boardwalk from 10 AM to midnight during the summer months. One-way fare is $1.25 per person; a book of 25 tickets is $25 (tel. 609/522–6700).

By Bicycle Touring by bike is best in early morning, when roads and boardwalks are the least busy. Most Shore towns permit boardwalk bicycling daily from 6 AM until 10 AM. Shore causeways have narrow shoulders that make riding from the islands to the mainland difficult and dangerous. The Ocean Drive bridges charge bicycle riders a 50¢ toll.

Important Addresses and Numbers

Tourist Information Avalon Chamber of Commerce (Box 22, Avalon 08202, tel. 609/967–3936).

Cape May County Chamber of Commerce (Box 74, Garden State Pkwy. Exit 11, Cape May Court House 08210, tel. 609/465–7181).

Cape May County Dept. of Public Affairs (Box 365, Cape May Court House 08210, tel. 800/227–2297).

Ocean City Public Relations Department (9th St. and Asbury Ave., Ocean City 08226, tel. 609/399–6111, ext. 222; 800/232–2465; or, in NJ, 800/BEACH–NJ).

Sea Isle City Chamber of Commerce (Box 635, Sea Isle City 08243, tel. 609/263–0909).

Stone Harbor Chamber of Commerce (Box 422, 212 96th St., Stone Harbor 08247, tel. 609/368–6101).

Greater Wildwood Chamber of Commerce (Box 823, Wildwood 08260, tel. 609/729–4000).

Wildwood Crest Department of Tourism (6101 Pacific Ave., Box 529, Wildwood Crest 08260, tel. 609/522–7788).

Wildwood Crest Tourism Commission (Rambler Rd. and the beach, Wildwood Crest 08260, tel. 800/524–2776 or, in NJ, 800/648–0236).

North Wildwood Tourism Commission (Box 814, North Wildwood 08260, tel. 609/522–4520 or 800/223–0317).

Wildwood Dept. of Tourism (Box 609, Boardwalk and Schellenger Avenue, Wildwood 08260, tel. 609/522–1407 or 800/WW–BY–SEA).

Emergencies *Medical* Northern areas: **Shore Memorial Hospital** (New York Ave., Somers Point, tel. 609/653–3500).

Southern areas: **Burdette Tomlin Memorial Hospital** (Lincoln Ave., Cape May Court House, tel. 609/463–2000).

Police and Fire Though mandated by New Jersey state law to comply by 1992, not all Cape May county municipalities have added the 911 telephone dialing service for police, fire, and emergency services.

Avalon (tel. 609/967–3411).
Cape May Court House (tel. 609/465–8700).
Middle Township (tel. 609/465–8700).
North Wildwood (tel. 609/522–2411).
Stone Harbor (tel. 609/368–2111).
West Wildwood (tel. 609/522–2411).
Wildwood (tel. 609/522–0222).
Wildwood Crest (tel. 609/522–2456).

Coast Guard (tel. 609/399–0119).
Marine Police (tel. 609/522–0393).
Marine Forecast (tel. 609/884–8419).
State Police (tel. 609/465–1496).
Weather (tel. 609/976–1212).

Publications The *Atlantic City Press* provides daily coverage of local and national events. The newspaper's "Friday at the Shore" section has restaurant and entertainment listings. The *Cape May County Herald Dispatch,* the *Gazette Ledger,* and the *Star & Wave* are free publications covering lower Cape May County. The Ocean City *Sentinel Ledger* is also distributed in island communities.

Guided Tours

Cruises   *Yankee Schooner.* Midday and sunset sightseeing cruises in the
            Intracoastal Waterway are offered on this 80-foot twin-masted
            schooner built in Atlantic City in 1982. Cruises last 3½ hours
            under full sail when conditions permit. *Box 98, Cape May, tel.
            609/884–1919 or 884–9003. Cost: $23 adults, $17 children age
            12 and younger on 11 AM cruise only. Cruises depart June–
            Aug., daily, weather permitting, at 11 AM and 4:30 PM from
            Lighthouse Pointe Marina, D-Dock, Shawcrest Island, off Rte.
            47 (Garden State Pkwy., Exit 4). Snacks and beverages
            provided. Reservations advised. AE, MC, V.*

            Big Flamingo. This large, open motorboat cruises up the Intra-
            coastal Waterway to the accompaniment of a narrated tour. Re-
            freshments are available. *6006 Park Blvd., Wildwood Crest,
            tel. 609/522–3934. Cost: $7.50 adults, $3.50 children age 12 and
            under. Departs from Captain Sims Dock mid-June–mid-
            Sept., daily 10:30 AM, 2 PM, and 7 PM. Reservations advised. No
            credit cards.*

            The Delta Lady. For sightseeing along the Intracoastal Water-
            way New Orleans style, go for a ride on this replica of a paddle-
            wheel steamer. Live Dixieland bands play on deck. *Wildwood
            Marina, tel. 609/522–1919. Cost: $6.50 adults, $3.50 children
            12 and under. Departs daily 10:30 AM, 2 PM, 7 PM. Reservations
            advised.*

            The Princess. The Thursday night Intracoastal Waterway
            cruise on the *Princess* is followed by a Hawaiian dinner at the
            Deauville Inn in Strathmere. *Kennedy Blvd. dock in Sea Isle
            City, tel. 609/263–1633 or 263–2292. Departs Thurs. 6 PM; cost:
            $25. Friday night sunset cruises from the Deauville Inn dock,
            6:30 PM; cost: $10.*

            Zeelander Cruises. Sightseeing cruises, extended charters, and
            "bed-and-breakfast" accommodations are available on this 44-
            foot ketch. You can spend your overnight at a hotel on land or on
            the boat. *Ocean City Marina, 3rd St. and Bay Ave., tel. 609/
            399–7359. Half-day ($35), full day with lunch ($75), sunset
            cruises ($30), weekend cruise to Cape May ($250). Overnight
            accommodations include full hot breakfast. Reservations re-
            quired.*

Special-Interest   The *Casino Challenger* charter boat runs daily boat trips from
         Tours   May through October to Atlantic City's marina casinos. Boats
                   depart from the Sampson Brothers Marina (228 Bay Ave., tel.
                   609/399–3111), in Ocean City and follow the Intracoastal Wa-
                   terway. The trip lasts approximately 1½ hours one-way, with
                   six hours' free time at a casino. Passengers must be 21 years old
                   and usually receive coin bonuses and discount coupons on casi-
                   no entertainment, food, and beverages upon arrival. Passen-
                   gers are under no obligation to gamble. Call for fees and
                   schedules.

Exploring Cape May County

Some time ago a public relations wizard glanced at a map of the Cape May County island resort towns and figured that if you connected the main streets to the toll bridges, you'd come up with a single stretch of roadway that would make it easier for summer visitors (who generally tended to stay in one town for their vacation) to get from one shore resort to the other. Thus was born Ocean Drive, a supposedly scenic drive stretching 60 miles from Atlantic City's Atlantic Avenue south to Victorian Cape May.

Though street names and route numbers change frequently as you travel south from Absecon Island (home of Atlantic City, Ventnor, Margate, and Longport) to Victorian Cape May, Ocean Drive is clearly marked by signs depicting a soaring gull against a blue-water background. The signs suggest freedom and wide, open spaces; Ocean Drive has precious little of both. Traffic is so thick along the drive and on causeways connecting the islands to the mainland that you are advised to come here armed with plenty of patience, especially on summer-weekend afternoons. Detailed street maps of Ocean Drive are available free at Cape May Bridge Commission tollbooths.

The 60-mile drive passes Ocean Drive's four most scenic areas: the Great Egg Harbor Bay approach to Ocean City, Corson's Inlet, the Strathmere approach to Sea Isle City, and Townsends Inlet. Natural and historic sights along the mainland are included in the tour, which when taken at a leisurely pace with plenty of stops should last about five hours.

Numbers in the margin correspond with points of interest on the Cape May County map.

Begin on Route 52, the causeway connecting the Somers Point traffic circle (in Atlantic County) to Ocean City's commercial district. Drive east and gaze at the **Great Egg Harbor Bay.** Named *Eyren Haven* (which means Egg Harbor) by Dutch explorers who found a number of birds' eggs when they paused here in the 16th century, the bay and Great Egg Harbor River were plied by pirates and privateers in the years before and during the Revolutionary War.

Privateers working for the British used Sandy Hook, at the northern end of the Jersey Shore, as their base. Privateers working for the American colonies had bases on the Raritan, Mullica, and Great Egg Harbor rivers, and in many areas around Barnegat Bay. **Mays Landing,** a ship-building town along the Great Egg Harbor River (now the Atlantic County seat), was such a popular privateer base that merchant and financier Stephen Girard, founder of the Girard Bank in Philadelphia, frequently took the stagecoach to Mays Landing to bid on stolen goods.

From time to time the British dispatched warships up the Jersey Shore rivers with orders to destroy rebel bases. These missions failed more often than they succeeded because of the shifting shoals, treacherous currents, and, in some instances, the ingenuity of the defending privateers. Samuel Snell, a Mays Landing tavern owner, was one such defender. During

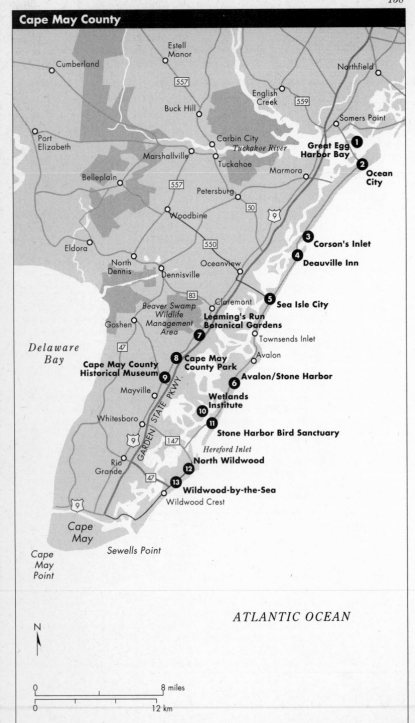

Cape May County

Northfield

Cumberland

Estell Manor

557

English Creek

559

Buck Hill

Somers Point

Port Elizabeth

Carbin City

Tuckahoe River

Great Egg Harbor Bay

1

Marshallville

Tuckahoe

Marmora

2 Ocean City

Belleplain

557

Petersburg

50

9

Woodbine

Eldora

550

Oceanview

3 Corson's Inlet

4 Deauville Inn

North Dennis

Dennisville

5 Sea Isle City

83

Claremont

Leaming's Run Botanical Gardens

Beaver Swamp Wildlife Management Area

Goshen

7

Townsends Inlet

47

Avalon

Delaware Bay

8 Cape May County Park

6 Avalon/Stone Harbor

Cape May County Historical Museum

9

Mayville

Wetlands Institute

10

Whitesboro

11 Stone Harbor Bird Sanctuary

9

147

Hereford Inlet

Rio Grande

12 North Wildwood

47

13 Wildwood-by-the-Sea

9

Wildwood Crest

Cape May

Sewells Point

Cape May Point

ATLANTIC OCEAN

N

GARDEN STATE PKWY.

0   8 miles

0   12 km

the mid-1770s he patrolled the Great Egg Harbor Bay in a tiny sloop called the *Skunk*. From a distance the *Skunk* appeared harmless, an oyster boat perhaps, listlessly dredging the shoals. Only when a British warship was within hailing distance did Captain Snell remove the canvas covering in the *Skunk*'s stern, revealing a single enormous cannon. One shot usually put the warship at the bottom of the river. During the summer of 1778 Captain Snell spied a British merchant ship meandering into Great Egg Harbor Bay. Before he could remove the canvas covering on his cannon, the British ship removed its coverings, revealing a 74-gun frigate. As the guns roared, Snell unfurled his sails and ordered his crew to start rowing—*fast*. He managed to escape the warship, but realized that his skunking days—during which he had sunk or captured 19 British vessels—were over.

2 Route 52 becomes 9th Street in **Ocean City.** Despite an influx of casino employees, Ocean City does its best to ignore Atlantic City and all the sin and vice just a few miles north. Begun as a Methodist retreat (Billy Graham got his start as a radio preacher here in the 1940s), Ocean City is one of only two dry towns (the other is Ocean Grove near Asbury Park) on the Shore.

Ocean City attracts primarily families. The island's character is mostly residential, with thousands of rental properties, which reach an almost absurd density in the south end, standing vacant during the winter and filled to the rafters every summer. Unlike most island communities, whose central business districts tend to have an overly touristy character, Ocean City's cute downtown area has a faintly nostalgic, Anytown, USA, feeling.

Drive east down 9th Street, wandering around the beach-block streets until you find parking near the boardwalk. Be sure to feed the meters and head for the boardwalk.

Ocean City's boardwalk is the most pleasant, family-oriented one of the entire Jersey Shore. The restaurants and snack shops tend to be good, and the commercialism is quietly restrained. If you enter the boardwalk at 9th Street, directly in front of you will be the **Music Pier** at Moorlyn Terrace, where concerts are held nearly every evening at 7:30 or 8 during the summer.

Most seashore towns have their share of boardwalk parades, contests, and festivals, but Ocean City's are especially silly, frivolous, and fun. Among the highlights are the April post–federal income tax salute to absurdity, the **Doo-Dah Parade;** the August **Baby Parade; Hermit Crab Race and Miss Crustacean Pageant** (with the Honorable Martin Z. Mollusk, the city's hermit crab mascot, presiding); and **Weird Contest Week,** including the **Artistic Pie-Eating Contest.** The **Night in Venice Boat Parade** is a July festival in which decorated yachts, rowboats, canoes, and kayaks float through the island's bayside lagoons. Boardwalk events typically occur near the Music Pier at Moorlyn Terrace. Ocean City's public relations office (tel. 609/399–6111, ext. 222) can provide details.

If you have small children, you may want to head first to **Gillian's Wonderland,** a small amusement area three blocks north at 6th Street. Otherwise walk south to 16th Street, look toward the ocean, and at low tide you may see the rudder and post of the *Sindia*, a four-masted bark that sank in 1901. Some of the *Sindia*'s salvage is on display in the **Ocean City Historical Museum** in Ocean City City Hall. *9th St. and Asbury Ave., tel. 609/399-6111. Admission free. Open weekdays 9-4:30.*

Once you've sampled the joys of Ocean City's boardwalk, drive west until you hit West Avenue, then make a left and proceed until West Avenue dead-ends at 55th Street; turn right and follow signs for Ocean Drive.

After looking at so many boxlike houses shuffled so close together, the first flash of green meadows and bright blue bay will refresh you. **Corson's Inlet** (tel. 609/861-2404) is a state-protected wildlife refuge, a haven for fishermen who huddle along the causeway to catch crabs and other estuary dwellers. There's a small boat ramp and beach, and you can park off the road. Be careful exploring—the undergrowth is filled with poison ivy.

Ocean City once had a straight-laced, proper, God-fearing reputation. A century ago if you asked anyone in Ocean City where a Victorian man or woman might find a little excitement and depravity, you just might have been put on the ferry back to Somers Point. Or one of the whalers who had lived on these waters and fished them might just wink an eye and tell you to meet him on the shore of Corson's Inlet at sundown. It's not for nothing that the swamp directly south of Ocean City was named **Devil's Island** (it's still on the maps).

As you continue south on Ocean Drive across the toll bridge you can't miss the three-story, cedar-paneled hotel with a simple mansard roof hugging the bayside. The former Whelen Hotel, now the **Deauville Inn,** is the tallest landmark in the ramshackle village of **Strathmere.** A century ago you'd come here for less-than-innocent merriment. Popular with fishermen, privateers, smugglers, railroad workers, and others in the know, the Whelen Hotel was at various times a speakeasy, a rum-running depot, and an illegal gambling casino. Theodore Roosevelt was among the guests who stayed in the 22 tiny rooms upstairs when it was a hotel. Though it was always in the shadow of Atlantic City, the Whelen got its share of "big name" performers in its day, including Eddie Cantor, Jimmy Durante, and Sophie Tucker.

Time Out   From Deauville walk about 100 feet to the beach, take your shoes off, and wade along the tide line. Admission to Strathmere's beach is free.

Ocean Drive in Strathmere is called Commonwealth Avenue or Route 636. It becomes Route 619 as you head south along the narrowest part of the shore, along a stretch of road and dunes that needs only one big wave to wash it all away. Once you pass the trailer camp the ocean will come so close to the road that on windy days it will hit your car. In terms of scenery, the wind, water, and densely overgrown dunes combine to form a precarious magnificence found nowhere else on the Shore, not even in the carefully preserved dunes of Cape May Point State Park. Route 619 is called Landis Avenue when it enters **Sea Isle City,** a quiet residential community that in places is reminiscent of a slightly older Ocean City. Charles K. Landis, the city's founding developer, wanted to create a miniature version of Venice here but never succeeded. Endure the slow traffic along Landis

Avenue to the end of the island and go over Townsends Inlet. Pay the 50¢ toll at the bridge.

6 Welcome to Seven Mile Beach, an imaginatively titled island that is better known as **Avalon/Stone Harbor** for the two distinct communities that share the island. Avalon, on the northern half and the older of the two towns, was founded in 1887. Turn left at 8th Street and left onto Avalon Avenue. You'll see the **high dunes** on your left, a five-block scrap of land that, aside from a few houses, has been left intact. If you can find a parking spot, leave the car and follow one of the paths to the beach. You must buy a beach tag to use the beaches of Avalon and Stone Harbor, but there's no charge for walking on the beautiful paths up and over the dunes, emerging on the clean white sand.

7 Return to your car and head south on Avalon Avenue. Turn right at 30th Street and head west off the island along Avalon Boulevard to Route 9. Directly in front of you is the beautiful **Leaming's Run Botanical Gardens,** 20 acres of painstakingly planted and tended flower gardens. The colors, composition, and varieties of plants bring as many "oohs" and "aahs" as a fireworks display. Before you reach the gardens themselves you go through 20 acres of meandering paths with high hedges and forest growth. Hidden inside is a re-created farm and a whaling village. The gardens attract hundreds of hummingbirds during late spring and early fall. Concerts are given occasionally in the gazebo, and the gift shop has a splendid collection of dried flowers. *1845 Rte. 9, Swainton, off Exit 13, tel. 609/465–5871. Admission: $4 adults, $1 children 6–12, children under 6 free. Open mid-May–Oct. daily 10–6. Guided horticultural tours, July–Aug. Thurs. 10:30 AM. Hummingbird watches throughout Aug.*

8 You can spend several peaceful hours at Leaming's Run or continue south on Route 9. After driving about 3 miles turn right onto Crest Haven Road and continue to **Cape May County Park,** a pleasantly landscaped area with a gazebo, a picnic ground, a playground, a bike trail, tennis courts, and an excellent petting zoo for kids. Free concerts are given in the summer, and the park has facilities for the handicapped. *Tel. 609/465–5271. Admission free. Open daily 9 AM–5 PM.*

9 The **Cape May County Historical Museum,** less than a mile past the park on Route 9, is an 18th-century house with a small collection of glassware, Victoriana, whaling implements, genealogical records, and a library. *Tel. 609/465–3535. Admission: $2 adults, children under 12 free. Open 10–4:30. Closed Jan.–Feb., Sun. in summer; Sun. and Mon. Mar.–May, Sept.–Dec.*

10 Continue on Route 9. Just before you enter Cape May Courthouse, whose small Main Street (Route 9) has many buildings dating from the Federal and Victorian periods, turn left (east) onto Stone Harbor Boulevard. Just before you arrive back on Seven Mile Beach Island you'll see the gray shingle **Wetlands Institute** on your right. Dedicated to enhancing environmental appreciation, this research laboratory is administered by Lehigh University and has a small nature center with a children's petting zoo. The institute conducts tours of the adjacent meadows; presents lectures on history, folklore, and ecology; and sponsors some special events. The annual **Wings and Water Festival,** held each September, celebrates Cape May County's environmental influences on culture, history, and folklore. *Stone*

Harbor Blvd., tel. 609/368–1211. Admission: $1.50 adults, 50¢ children. Open Tues.–Sat. 10–5.

Continue east on to Stone Harbor, which was founded in 1914. Stone Harbor Boulevard is now 96th Street, the Southern Shore's toniest shopping district, with many clothing boutiques, restaurants, and snack shops. Both Avalon and Stone Harbor get an upper-middle-class, WASPy crowd during the summer, and 96th Street becomes an outdoor showroom for expensive imported luxury cars.

Time Out | **Springer's Homemade Ice Cream** (tel. 609/368–4631) is inside an unpretentious old house at 3rd Avenue and 94th Street. The ice cream is delicious and comes in a dish, cone, or heaped on fruit, brownies, waffles, or pies.

⓫ Take 2nd Avenue south to the **Stone Harbor Bird Sanctuary** (tel. 609/368–5102). These few blocks in the southern part of the island, from 111th to 117th streets, are off-limits to humans and have been left completely untouched. Bird-watchers can view wildlife from observation areas.

Turn right onto 117th Street, left onto Ocean Drive, and follow Route 619 over the toll bridge to Hereford Inlet. At the traffic light at the *T*-intersection with Route 147, turn left toward Wildwood.

You zip past weather-beaten houses that seem to sag into the marshes to a place that has everything Bruce Springsteen could sing about and maybe a little more. Route 147 becomes Spruce Avenue (Route 621) when you enter **Wildwood,** which consists of five little boroughs, North Wildwood, West Wildwood, Wildwood-by-the-Sea, Wildwood Crest, and a tiny piece of Lower Township at the very end of the island. The boroughs have subtle differences, though most maintain a precarious balance of residential and commercial development.

⓬ **North Wildwood,** the borough you enter first, has two interesting sites. As you drive east toward the ocean on Spruce Street, turn left onto 1st Street to the **Hereford Inlet Lighthouse.** The Hereford Inlet Light takes up the top floor of a Victorian frame structure in what was the whaling village of Angelsea and has become a focal point for North Wildwood's civic and cultural pride. The lighthouse has a small museum, and a small area outside is set aside for concerts and outdoor events, most held during the summer season. *1st St. and Central Ave., tel. 609/729–1714. Admission free, donations accepted. Open weekdays 9–4.*

⓭ Drive south, staying on broad Central Avenue as it jogs right, then left onto New Jersey Avenue in **Wildwood-by-the-Sea.** For years this was the party town of the Southern Shore, where raucous rock-and-roll bars and the nearby boardwalk afforded the opportunity for many adolescent rites of passage. With the raising of New Jersey's drinking age to 21, many of the clubs have either closed, gone "Yup-scale" with hanging plants and less rowdy music, or now host teen dance nights, serving only soft drinks. Wildwood's heavily Italian, working-class populace favors inexpensive surf-and-turf restaurants and motels; more than 200 of these crowd the beach blocks in North Wildwood, Wildwood-by-the-Sea, and Wildwood Crest. The downtown district is suffering some of the deterioration plaguing

Long Branch, Asbury Park, and Atlantic City. A small collection of memorabilia can be found in the **George Boyer Historical Museum,** in Rooms 212 to 216 of City Hall, which is operated by the Wildwood Historical Society. *New Jersey and Montgomery Aves., tel. 609/522–1407. Admission free. Open weekdays 10–3.*

Turn right onto Schellenger Avenue and head for the boardwalk. Park in a lot, and you'll experience the single greatest concentration of outdoor **amusement rides** on the Jersey Shore. There are more than 100 stomach-crushing, gut-slamming devices on the Wildwood boardwalk, as well as an outdoor water slide and water theme park. The best rides are located in the stretch from Mariner's Landing, recognizable by its magnificent Ferris wheel at Schellenger Avenue, to Morey's Pier at 25th Street. Here the summertime seashore carnival comes to life on hot, summer Saturday nights. The screams and whirling colors of the rides, the taunting speeches of the skill games, blaring rock music from the T-shirt shops, the heady junk-food reek of cotton candy, french fries, and sizzling hot dogs, come together to create a carnival excitement that will be nostalgic for anyone who has spent his or her youth near a boardwalk. The rides start up weekends in mid-May, go into daily operation by the second week in June, revert to weekends only in September, and are closed in October.

Our tour ends here. The easiest access to the Garden State Parkway is from Rio Grande Avenue, which is about a half mile south of Schellenger Avenue. Turn right (west) onto Rio Grande Avenue. The parkway, offering access to Victorian Cape May (to the south) and the other Cape May island resorts (to the north), is a 10-minute drive away.

Other Sites and Attractions in Cape May County

Cold Spring Village, at the end of the Garden State Parkway, is a re-created pre–Civil War village, owned by Cape May County. It features crafts shows, concerts, folklore and demonstrations, a maritime museum, a restaurant, and shops. *735 Seashore Rd., Cold Spring, tel. 609/898–2300. Admission: $1.50 adults, 75¢ children 6–12, children 6 and under free. Open June–Sept., daily 10–6.*

Historic Wheaton Village. This outdoor-indoor living museum evokes the atmosphere of a 19th-century glass-making village. Facilities include a crafts shop, a bookstore, a glass museum, a restored glass factory, glass-making demonstrations, meeting areas, a restaurant, and a ¾-scale train ride for kids. Concerts and special events are scheduled during the summer. To reach the village, take Route 47 north to Millville and follow signs to Wheaton Village. Travel time from the coast is approximately 45 minutes. *Glasstown Rd., Millville, tel. 609/825–6800. Admission: $4 adults, $3.50 senior citizens, $2 children 6–17, $9 family rate. Open Apr.–Dec., daily 10–5. Closed on holidays.*

What to See and Do with Children

Most Shore municipalities have children's **recreational activities,** most of them free. Check with individual city or borough halls.

Cape May County libraries provide preschool storytelling hours and other activities for youngsters. Contact the libraries for information: Ocean City Library (6th and Ocean Sts., tel. 609/399–2434); Sea Isle City Library (125 JF Kennedy Blvd., tel. 609/263–8485); Avalon Library (251 26th Ave., tel. 609/967–4010); Wildwood Crest Library (6301 Ocean Ave., tel. 609/522–0564).

Discovery Seashell Museum and Shell Yard. This colorful collection of seashells and crafts in Ocean City has a gurgling array of tanks, all the better to show off local marine life. Many crafts and shells are for sale. *2721 Asbury Ave., tel. 609/398–2316. Admission free. Open May–Sept., daily 8–8. Closed Oct.–Apr.*

A charming five-day spectator event every June in Wildwood, the **National Marbles Tournament** (tel. 609/522–1407), attracts "mibsters" (marble shooters) from several states and occasionally from Europe.

Shopping

Natives and experienced visitors will tell you that everything costs less on the mainland. They're only partly right, and considering the time it takes to travel there and find what you want, it's easier to get what you need on the islands. Each town has at least one supermarket and downtown shopping area. Stone Harbor's 96th Street has some of the New Jersey Shore's trendiest shops and boutiques, with **Pappagallo** (237 96th St., tel. 609/368–6141) selling trendy women's fashions and **Happy Hunt,** just two blocks away (98th St. and 3rd Ave., tel. 609/368–5734), stocked with hand-painted, one-of-a-kind clothing. Ocean City's Asbury Avenue has the most practical goods. **Stainton's Department Store** (810 Asbury Ave., tel. 609/399–5511) is exactly that: a small-town department store that stocks a little bit of everything. **Kabat's Men's Shop** (720 Asbury Ave., tel. 609/399–1625) is a friendly father-and-son clothing store. While most Shore shops are open daily in the summer, Ocean City's stores are closed on Sunday.

On the mainland the largest shopping malls are in Atlantic County (*see* the Shopping section in Chapter 6, Greater Atlantic County). The **Rio Grande Mall** on Route 9 near Wildwood is small but serviceable for practical goods.

Do not pass up the nearly 30 antiques shops and farmers' markets lining Route 9 from Seaville to Rio Grande. The farmers' markets offer especially good values on fresh produce, and you haven't been to south Jersey until you've eaten a ripe, meaty Jersey tomato or chomped on an ear of white, Silverqueen corn, both in season during the summer.

Sports and Outdoor Activities

Beaches Use of beaches in Wildwood and Strathmere is free. To visit the beaches of Ocean City, Sea Isle City, Avalon, Stone Harbor, and Cape May from Memorial Day through Labor Day, you must purchase a beach tag, sold at municipal borough halls, in booths near the beaches, or on the beaches by inspectors. Many area hotels and bed-and-breakfast inns provide tags free to their guests.

For more specific information, contact the individual communities: **Ocean City** (tel. 609/399–6344), public rest rooms at 1st, 6th, 12th, and 34th streets, and at the Music Pier, the boardwalk at Moorlyn Terrace; **Strathmere** (tel. 609/628–2011), no public rest rooms; **Sea Isle City** (tel. 609/263–4461), public rest rooms at 32nd, 40th, 44th, and 85th streets; **Avalon** (tel. 609/967–8200), public rest rooms at City Hall, 3100 Dune Drive; **Stone Harbor** (tel. 609/368–5102), public rest rooms at 95th and 96th streets and 2nd Avenue; **Wildwood** (tel. 609/522–1407), public rest rooms at the boardwalk and Glenwood, Youngs, Leaming, Davis, and Schellenger avenues; in North Wildwood at 24th Street and the boardwalk.

For general information on ocean water quality and beach conditions, contact the **Cape May County Health Department** (Crest Haven Complex at the Garden State Pkwy., Cape May Court House 08210, tel. 609/465–1221).

The **Cape May Beach Quality Hotline** (tel. 609/465–2422) supplies information about all beaches in Cape May County.

Fishing Permits are not required for surf fishing, though local fees may apply at fishing piers. Party boats and charter boats too numerous to list offer half-day, full-day, and overnight bay and deep-sea fishing. Check with local bait-and-tackle shops for a list of charter boats. Bob Jackson of Cape May Court House (tel. 609/465–5671) is a shore fishing consultant who specializes in surf fishing and bait collection.

Golf **Ocean City Municipal Golf Course** (26th St. and Bay Ave., tel. 609/399–6111, ext. 219), an adequate public course, has 12 holes and is open daily during the summer season. The **Avalon Country Club** (1510 Rte. 9 North, Cape May Court House, tel. 609/465–4389), a mile south of Exit 13 on Route 9, is a public course that accepts daily and seasonal players. Also open to the public is **Stone Harbor Golf Club** (Rte. 9, Cape May Court House, tel. 609/465–9270), 1½ miles north of Stone Harbor Boulevard, Exit 10 on Garden State Parkway.

Horseback Riding Reservations are required for trail riding at the **Circle T Ranch** (210 Stagecoach Rd., Cape May Court House, tel. 609/465–7750) and **Hidden Valley Ranch** (4070 Bay Shore Rd., Cold Springs, tel. 609/884–8205).

Tennis There are two municipal courts in Stone Harbor at 82nd Street and 2nd Avenue (tel. 609/368–1210) and at 97th Street and 1st Avenue (tel. 609/368–1287). Wildwood Crest's courts are at Wistaria Road and Atlantic Avenue (tel. 609/523–0202).

Water Sports For sailing lessons, board sailing, and boat and jet-ski rentals in Ocean City, contact **Bayview Sailboats** (312 Bay Ave., tel. 609/398–3049), **Jet Ski Rentals of Ocean City** (2nd St. and Bay Ave., tel. 609/399–4017), or **Ocean City Water Sports** (3rd St. and Bay Ave., tel. 609/399–6861). For lessons and rentals in the Wildwood area, contact **Grassy Sound Marina** (N. Wildwood Blvd., North Wildwood, tel. 609/729–0337) or **Lake View Docks** (7116 Park Blvd., Wildwood Crest, tel. 609/522–0471).

Dining

*This restaurant
list was compiled
with the assistance
of Ed Hitzel, food
critic of the*
Atlantic City
Press.

A good portion of Cape May County—and a great deal of the
Shore in general—seems to have been conquered by Italian
restaurateurs.

For price ranges, consult the dining price chart in Chapter 1,
Essential Information. Highly recommended restaurants are
indicated with a star ★ .

Avalon

Expensive
★
Whitebrier Inn. This pleasant, tony place, considered the best
restaurant in Avalon/Stone Harbor, is unusually accommodating to families. Dishes include seafood, beef, and some Continental and nouvelle cuisine items. There is also an excellent
Sunday brunch. *20th St., between Ocean and Dune Aves., tel.
609/967–5225. Reservations advised for dinner. Jacket recommended. Free parking. AE, MC, V.*

Moderate
Marabella's. This breezy, bistro-style Italian place draws a
young, bustling crowd. Specialties include homemade pasta,
grilled seafood, and a late-night snack menu. *2403–89 Dune
Dr., tel. 609/967–3200. Dress: casual. Reservations not necessary. AE, MC, V.*

North Wildwood

Moderate–
Expensive
Ed Zaberer's. This consummate Jersey Shore family restaurant
is incredibly busy in the summer, serving primarily surf-and-
turf fare with Italian side dishes. The large dining room features numerous Tiffany-style lamp shades and Victoriana. A
children's menu, early-bird specials, a bar, and, in the warm
weather, outdoor dining are featured. *400 Spruce Ave., tel.
609/522–1423. Reservations advised. Dress: casual. Free parking nearby. AE, D, DC, MC, V. Closed for lunch.*

Ocean City

Moderate
The Flanders Hotel. American cuisine and surf-and-turf fare
are served in the three elegant dining rooms of this beachfront
hotel, a 1920s resort in the Spanish Colonial style. The dining
rooms have a gilded, rococo atmosphere—you'll think you're in
Atlantic City in its golden years. *11th St. and the boardwalk,
tel. 609/399–1000. Reservations advised. Jackets required for
dinner. Limited free parking. AE, MC, V.*

Inexpensive–
Moderate
Portsider. Locals and visitors frequent this family-style seafood restaurant inside Port-O-Call Hotel. Continental, veal,
and steak dishes are also offered. From the dining room you can
see the boardwalk, the beach, and the ocean. *1510 Boardwalk,
tel. 609/399–8812. Reservations advised for dinner. Dress: casual. Limited free parking. AE, DC, MC, V.*

Rio Grande

Moderate
Menz. Reasonably priced fresh seafood and some beef and
chicken dishes are the fare at this cozy mom-and-pop restaurant. The antiques and music boxes on display are authentic.
Delsea Dr. and Fulling Mill Rd., tel. 609/886–9500. Reserva-

tions advised. Dress: casual. No credit cards. BYOB. Open daily June–Aug. Closed Mon.–Wed. Sept.–May.

Sea Isle City

Moderate–
Expensive
Screnci's. Of special note at this family-style Italian restaurant are the luscious roast peppers and veal dishes. *6208 Landis Ave., tel. 609/263–2217. Reservations advised. Dress: casual. No lunch; closed Tues.*

Moderate
Busch's. Huge portions and reasonable prices are why the locals come to this simple, bare-bones seafood restaurant at the southern end of Sea Isle City. She-crab soup and deviled crabs are recommended. *87th St. and Townsends Inlet, tel. 609/263–8626. Reservations not required. Dress: casual. Open Memorial Day–Labor Day, Tues.–Sun., dinner only. AC, DC, MC, V.*

Strathmere

Moderate–
Expensive
★
Deauville Inn. This combination locals' bar, surf-and-turf house, marina, and nightclub is located in the tiniest beach-resort town on the Jersey Shore. You can tie your boat up in the marina, eat superb she-crab soup, and watch the sunset from the porch. In summer the Deauville puts on a Hawaiian luau on Thursdays and has sunset cruises on Fridays. *Ocean Dr., tel. 609/263–2080. Reservations advised. Dress: informal, but no shorts or tank tops in dining room. AE, MC, V.*

Wildwood

Inexpensive–
Moderate
★
Dragon House Restaurant. This Mandarin-style restaurant in very Italian Wildwood is considered by many to be one of the best Chinese restaurants on the Jersey Shore. *Lincoln and Pacific Aves., tel. 609/522–2320. Reservations not required. Dress: casual. Free parking. AE, MC, V. Closed for lunch and Oct.–Apr.*

★
Ravioli House. Perfect for the de rigueur postbeach pasta pigout, this restaurant is better still since just about everything is homemade, including the pastas, sauces, and meatballs. *120 E. Bennett Ave., tel. 609/522–7894. Reservations not required. Dress: casual. Limited free parking. No credit cards.*

Lodging

Wildwood is famous for its numerous '50s streamlined motels in fanciful Hawaiian, Caribbean, Oriental, Spanish, or futuristic decor. The most modern facilities are located along the beach in Wildwood Crest, and they resemble a row of miniature Miami Beach hotels. These motels are fully equipped family vacation resorts, offering planned activities for children.

In addition to properties listed, the **Ocean City Guest and Apartment House Association** (tel. 609/399–8894) can be helpful in locating available guest houses, apartments, and bed-and-breakfasts.

For price ranges, consult the lodging chart in Chapter 1, Essential Information. Highly recommended lodgings are indicated with a star ★.

Bed-and-Breakfasts

Dennisville
Moderate–Expensive
★

Henry Ludlam Inn. Henry Ludlam has a small place in New Jersey's history books as the man who started the state's first public school. His 1804 house, now a B&B, is in Federal style and sits on the shore of a 56-acre lake—"Ludlam's Pond"—where guests can use a small catamaran sailboat, a few inner tubes, a canoe, and fishing rods. There is also a gazebo with a lake view. Innkeepers Marty and Ann Thurlow have furnished the house with various antiques in mixed woods. The inn is located in Dennisville, a 20-minute drive from Stone Harbor and close to antiques shops on Routes 47 and 9. The inn has feather mattresses, is fully heated and air-conditioned, and provides complete hot breakfasts. *Rte. 47, RD #3, Box 298, Woodbine 08270, tel. 609/861–5847. 6 rooms, 4 with private bath, 3 with working fireplaces. Free use of Avalon/Stone Harbor beach tags and towels. Smoking permitted in common room only. Saturday night 6-course dinner ($30 per person, no alcoholic beverages served). 2-night weekend minimum stay July–Aug. Free off-street parking. AE, MC, V.*

North Wildwood
Moderate–Expensive
★

Candlelight Inn. Paul DiFilippo and Diane Buscham are the owners of this 1905 Queen Anne home, which has the distinction of being Wildwood's first bed-and-breakfast. They've furnished it with period antiques and crafts, including a piano and an 1855 Empire sofa in the parlor. Notable touches are the original stained-glass windows and brass gaslight fixtures. You can spend many a restful hour on the hammock and porch swing. The inn is three blocks from the beach and the boardwalk and serves a full hot breakfast. Some rooms are air-conditioned, others have ceiling fans, and all are heated. *2310 Central Ave., 08260, tel. 609/522–6200. 9 rooms, 7 with private bath, shared bathrooms have whirlpool. Facilities: outdoor hot tub, sun deck. Smoking on veranda only. Murder-mystery weekends. 3-night minimum stay weekends in July and Aug. AE, MC, V.*

Ocean City
Moderate

BarnaGate Bed and Breakfast. This trim, pleasant 1896 guest house near the Ocean City Tabernacle is furnished with country Victorian pieces, some of which are family heirlooms. The color scheme is in light pastels, peach, rose, and mauve. Frank Barna is especially proud of the handmade quilts. All rooms are heated and have ceiling fans, and a Continental breakfast is served. *637 Wesley Ave., 08226, tel. 609/391–9366. 5 rooms, 1 with private bath. Free beach tags. Smoking on veranda. 2-night minimum stay holiday weekends. Street parking only. MC, V.*

Bradbury's Guest House. Originally a private house, now with a modern addition, Bradbury's sports a spacious porch shaded by awnings and trees. All the furnishings are contemporary. Carolyn and George Bradbury operate the inn, which is close to downtown and within walking distance of the beach and restaurants. Bradbury's also accepts children of all ages. Five of its rooms are air-conditioned, and the Bradburys serve a Continental breakfast. *1009 Wesley Ave., 08226, tel. 609/398–1008. 7 rooms with private bath. Free beach tags. Smoking on veranda only. 2-night minimum stay weekends, 3-night minimum stay holiday weekends. Off-street parking. No credit cards.*

The Enterprise. Built as a small hotel in 1890, the Enterprise has been almost completely renovated. Stephen and Patty Hydock are your hosts at this downtown inn, 2½ blocks from the beach and very close to restaurants. The rooms are heated and air-conditioned, and a full hot breakfast is served. *1020 Central Ave., 08226, tel. 609/398–1698. 10 rooms, 8 with private baths, 2 suites; 1 room has a whirlpool. Free beach tags. Smoking permitted. 2-night minimum stay weekends, 3-night minimum stay holiday weekends. MC, V.*

New Brighton Inn Bed and Breakfast. Dan and Donna Hand run this Queen Anne Victorian in a residential neighborhood near the tabernacle and Memorial Park. The inn has country-Victorian antiques in all of its renovated rooms and is within walking distance of the beach. All rooms are heated and two have air-conditioning. A Continental breakfast is served on the sun porch. *510 5th St., 08226, tel. 609/399–2829. 4 rooms, 2 with private bath. Free beach tags. Smoking on veranda only. No minimum stay. Street parking. MC, V. Closed weekdays Oct.–May.*

Hotels

Avalon
Very Expensive
★

Golden Inn Hotel and Conference Center. The best hotel and small meetings facility on the island, this property has a good surf-and-turf restaurant, an excellent health club, a superb beachfront location, cable TV, and it is fully heated and air-conditioned. *Oceanfront Ave. and 78th St., 08202, tel. 609/368–5155 or 800/426–4300. 152 rooms, 75 with kitchens, all with bath; 15 suites with bath. Facilities: restaurant, raw bar, heated pool, art gallery, gift shop. Free use of bicycles. Transportation to Atlantic City casinos. AE, MC, V.*

Ocean City
Expensive–Very Expensive

The Flanders Hotel. One of the last grand hotels on the Jersey Shore, the Flanders operates as if the past 70 years never happened. The exterior is the Spanish Colonial–style architecture that was all the rage before Art Deco took over. Inside are old woods, antiques, and a polished, sleepy look you may associate with a '20s resort hotel. The large hotel sits on the boardwalk, and most rooms have ocean views. The elegant dining rooms serve an especially good brunch (*see* Dining, above). Modified American and European meal plans are available. All rooms are heated and air-conditioned, and afternoon tea is served. *Boardwalk and 11th St., 08226, tel. 609/399–1000 or 800/345–0211. 213 rooms, 1 penthouse suite, all with bath. Facilities: restaurant, heated pool, sun deck, sauna, miniature golf, shuffleboard, shopping arcade with barbershop and beauty parlor. Free parking. AE, MC, V.*

Expensive

Port-O-Call. The '60s-motel look of this boardwalk hotel, the most modern of its size on the island, appears a bit dated now, but the service is still very good and the ocean views are marvelous. The rooms are fully heated and air-conditioned, and all have TV, refrigerators, and coffee-makers. *1510 Boardwalk, 08226, tel. 609/399–8812. 98 rooms. Facilities: restaurant, sun terrace, pool, sauna, lockers. Children 6 and under stay free. Free cribs and beach. Limited free parking. AE, CB, DC, MC, V.*

Wildwood Crest
Expensive–Very Expensive

Grand Hotel Resort and Convention Center. The "little" brother of Grand Victorian in Cape May, this property mixes some Victorian reproductions in bright modern motel furnishings. Make sure you specify which facility you want when you call. Hotel rooms are heated and air-conditioned, and each has a TV, phone, and even an efficiency kitchen. *Stanton Ave. and the beach, 08260, tel. 609/729–6000 or 800/257–8550. 196 rooms*

*with bath, 22 suites with kitchens, most with ocean views, all
with bath. Facilities: restaurant, indoor and outdoor pools,
pool bar, whirlpool, nightclub, meeting rooms. AE, DC, MC,
V.*

Motels

Avalon
Very Expensive

Concord Suites. A former motel has been renovated into a modern, suite facility. All rooms are two-bedroom suites, with pull-out couches. Rooms have efficiency kitchens, TV, and phones, and all are heated and air-conditioned. *7800 Dune Dr., 08202, tel. 609/368–7800 or 800/443–8202. 90 rooms with bath. Facilities: café, lounge. 2 pools, wading pool. Free beach tags. Free parking. MC, V.*

Windrift Resort Motel. All the rooms at this Avalon beachfront motel are heated and have air-conditioning, refrigerators, and cable TV. There are four efficiencies and two-bedroom suites. You can dance between courses at the on-site restaurant. *79th St. and the beach, Box 271, 08202, tel. 609/368–5175. 93 rooms. Facilities: restaurant, piano bar, beach bar, heated pool, wading pool, sun decks. Free beach tags. 3-night minimum stay in summer, 4-night minimum stay holidays and holiday weekends. Free parking. MC, V. Closed Nov.–Feb.*

Expensive

Desert Sand Motor Inn Resort Complex. A better-than-average health club and restaurant. *79th St. and Dune Dr., 08202, tel. 609/368–5133 or 800/458–6008. 89 rooms, 22 with kitchens, all with bath; 15 suites with bath. Facilities: 2 heated pools in health club, meeting rooms. Free parking. No credit cards. Closed Dec.–Feb.*

Wildwood Crest
Very Expensive

Pan American Motor Inn. A playground and organized children's activities make the Pan American a good choice for families. *Crocus Rd. and the beach, 08260, tel. 609/522–6936. 78 rooms, 49 efficiencies, all with bath. Facilities: restaurant, meeting room, heated pool, wading pool, sauna, coin laundry. No credit cards.*

The Singapore. Most rooms in this motel decorated in Oriental style have ocean-facing balconies and refrigerators. All rooms are heated and have air-conditioning and TV. Room service is available. *Orchid Rd. and the beach, 08260, tel. 609/522–6961. 56 rooms, 24 with kitchens, all with bath. Facilities: restaurant, heated pool, wading pool, sauna, shuffleboard, meeting areas, coin laundry. Cribs available. AE, DC, MC, V. Closed Nov.–Apr.*

*Expensive–Very
Expensive*

Royal Hawaiian. All rooms are heated and equipped with TV and air-conditioning. *Ocean and Orchid Aves., 08260, tel. 609/522–3414. 86 rooms, 58 with kitchens, most with balconies and oceanfront views, all with bath. Facilities: pool, wading pool, sun deck, sauna, coin laundry. MC, V. Closed mid-Oct.–mid-May.*

Expensive

Beau Rivage Motor Inn. This oceanfront motel is convenient for families; most rooms have kitchens. The rooms are heated and air-conditioned, and all have TV. *9103 Atlantic Ave., 08260, tel. 609/729–2121. 49 rooms with bath. Facilities: restaurant, sun decks, heated pool, wading pool. Picnic tables. Cribs and baby-sitting service available. MC, V. Closed mid-May–mid-Oct.*

Port Royal Motor Inn. Some two-room suites in this motel sleep four; a few rooms sport balconies. The rooms have air-conditioning, TV, and are heated in cooler weather. *6805 Ocean*

Ave., 08260, tel. 609/729–2000. 100 rooms, 50 with kitchens, all with bath. Facilities: restaurant, heated pool, wading pool, sauna, coin laundry, meeting and game rooms. Cribs and playground. 7-day minimum stay in season. Garage parking extra. No credit cards. Closed Oct.–mid-May.

Moderate–Expensive   **Admiral Motel.** Though most of the accommodations in these two motels have efficiency kitchens, the rooms in the west building are newer. All rooms, however, are heated and equipped with air-conditioning. *Ocean Ave. and Rambler Rd., 08260, tel. 609/522–7704. 171 rooms with bath. Facilities: 2 restaurants, indoor and outdoor pools, coin laundry, grills available. Cribs and planned activities for children. AE, MC, V. Closed Nov.–Apr.*

Camping

Avalon Campground (492 Shore Rd., Clermont 08210, tel. 609/624–0075 or 522–3747).

Beachcomber Camping Resort (462 E. Seashore Rd., Cape May 08204, tel. 609/886–6035).

Big Timber Lake Camping Resort (Box 366, Cape May Court House 08210, tel. 609/465–4465 or 800/542–CAMP).

Cedar Lake Campground (Box 7, Dennisville 08214, tel. 609/785–0712).

Dennisville Lake Campground (Box 36, Dennisville 08214, tel. 609/861–2561).

Driftwood Campground (478 Shore Rd., Cape May Court House 08210, tel. 609/624–1899).

Fort Apache Camping Resort (Rte. 47 and Fulling Mill Rd., Rio Grande 08242, tel. 609/886–1076).

Frontier Campground (84 Newbridge Rd., Ocean View 08230, tel. 609/390–3649).

Hidden Acres (RD 1, Box 354, A-30, Cape May Court House 08210, tel. 609/624–9015 or 800/874–7576).

North Wildwood Camping Resort (240 W. Shellbay Rd., Cape May Court House 08210, tel. 609/465–4440 or 800/752–4882).

Oak Ridge Campground (516 S. Shore Rd., Box 598, Marmora 08223, tel. 609/390–3458).

Ocean View Resort Campground (Rte. 9, Box 607, Ocean View 08230, tel. 609/624–1675).

Pine Haven Campground (Rte. 9, Box 606, Ocean View 08230, tel. 609/624–3437).

Sea Grove Campground (Rte. 9, Box 603, Ocean View 08230, tel. 609/624–3529 or 800/432–6629).

Seashore Campsites (720 Seashore Rd., Cape May 08410, tel. 609/884–4010).

Shady Oaks Campground (62 Rte. 50, Ocean View 08230, tel. 609/390–0431).

Tamerlane Campground (Box 510, Ocean View 08230, tel. 609/624–0767).

Whippoorwill Campground (810 S. Shore Rd., Marmora 08223, tel. 609/390–3458).

The Arts and Nightlife

The Arts

Concerts
Ocean City

Concerts by the Ocean City Pops Orchestra, Dixieland bands, and string bands and other live family entertainment take place almost every night at the **Music Pier** (Moorlyn Terr. and the boardwalk between 8th and 9th Sts., tel. 609/399–6111, ext. 222). A nominal admission is charged to most events. Free concerts are usually on Sunday nights.

Sea Isle City

Free family-oriented concerts are performed at the **Boardwalk Promenade** (tel. 609/263–4461) in July and August on Wednesdays at 7 PM.

Wildwood

Free summer concerts take place in **Gazebo Park** (Rambler Rd. and the beach) and at the **boardwalk bandshell** (tel. 609/522–1407).

Movies

Current movies can be seen at these theaters: the **Strand 5** (9th St. and the boardwalk, Ocean City, tel. 609/398–6565); the **Stone Harbor Twin** (96th St., Stone Harbor, tel. 609/368–7731); the **Rio Twin** (Rio Grande Shopping Center, Stone Harbor, tel. 609/522–2429); and the **Ocean Theater** (2700 Boardwalk, Wildwood, tel. 609/522–6719).

Nightlife

Most bars and nightclubs operate from May to September, unless noted.

Bars and Nightclubs
Avalon/Stone Harbor

Jack's Place (36th St. and Ocean Dr., tel. 609/967–5001) features middle-of-the-road bands on weekend nights. Pop bands and cabaret acts appealing to the thirtysomething set can be found at **Fred's** (314 9th St., Stone Harbor, tel. 609/368–5591).

Sea Isle City

A young, rock-and-roll crowd heads to the **Dead Dog Saloon** (39th St. and Landis Ave., tel. 609/263–1500), as well as to the rock club **Ocean Drive** (3915 Landis Ave., tel. 609/263–2903). People dress up to go dancing to DJ-spun records at **Shenanigan's** (3815 Landis Ave., tel. 609/263–6430), which also has an occasional comedy night.

Wildwood

Club Casbah (Spicer and Atlantic Aves., tel. 609/522–8444) is a comedy club with three acts per show. **The Playpen** (3400 Pacific Ave., tel. 609/729–3919) is an enormous nightclub that has live bands most nights.

Dining and Dancing

The **Willard Room** in the **Deauville Inn** (Ocean Dr., Strathmere, tel. 609/263–2080), a former bordello and speakeasy, is the weekend place for dining and dancing; on Thursday nights in the summer they put on a Hawaiian luau. Big bands perform at Avalon's **Golden Inn** (78th St. and Dune Dr., tel. 609/368–5115) on weekend nights. Reservations are required.

8 Victorian Cape May

Introduction

Cape May is, in some places, a carefully and lovingly re-created fantasy of a Victorian vacation resort. In others, it is just as garish and tacky as any other seashore town. What makes Cape May a superb, adult-oriented destination, though, is its ineffable atmosphere, which becomes quite literal in the late afternoon when the scents of fresh spices, simmering garlic, and other delightful fumes from the city's eclectic, bistro-style restaurants mix with the seashore ocean brine to melt the resistance of the most die-hard dieter.

The atmosphere is whimsical, genteel, slightly daft: an Edward Gorey sensibility that gazes firmly backward to the Victorian era, which, for all its faults, became a stylebook for the wealthy 19th-century American gentry.

Believed to be the oldest ocean resort in New Jersey, Cape May was first sighted by the Dutch explorer Captain Cornelius Mey, who modestly named the entire peninsula for himself in 1620, though the spelling was subsequently updated. (One of the city's inns, Captain Mey's Inn, commemorates this fact.) Early settlers were fishermen and whalers who came by boat from Philadelphia and villages along the Delaware Bay. Today the commercial fishing port, located on a causeway linking Cape May to the island resort of Wildwood Crest, is the third largest on the East Coast, blessing Cape May's restaurants with the freshest seasonal seafood.

By the early 1800s, Cape May's guest houses had expanded into huge Federal-style hotels, which clung to the beach beside summer mansions for vacationing rich from Philadelphia, Wilmington, and Washington, DC. Fires and storms periodically ravaged the town, but an astonishing variety of structures managed to survive, including the 2 square miles of visually extravagant, gaudily appointed Italianate wood frame cottages, houses, bed-and-breakfast inns and late-19-century mansions in the city's historic district.

In the first few decades of this century, Cape May lost most of its luster to Atlantic City, and, in the '50s, to Wildwood. A catastrophic 1962 hurricane forced the city fathers to take stock of what they had. They used America's first Urban Development Grant to create an outdoor pedestrian street, the Washington Mall, leaving the old buildings that fronted Washington Street intact. This inspired a revival of the old Victorian buildings, many of which have become inns, that spread throughout the town. Buildings were not only restored to their original shape, but strict rules were passed covering everything from exterior paint to windowshades.

At about the same time, Cape May attracted a group of restaurateurs, most of them from Philadelphia, who found the combination of fresh seafood, locally grown vegetables, and low rents enough of an incentive to try their luck in a town that was still too far down the Garden State Parkway for most tourists. When one restaurant, the Mad Batter on Jackson Street, succeeded with a bizarre hybrid menu of Oriental and classic American and Continental dishes, others followed. Now Cape May has the single largest district of unusual restaurants in New Jersey, all within walking distance of each other.

Other Jersey Shore towns, most notably Spring Lake in Monmouth County, have more striking examples of restored Victorian architecture, but nowhere on the Jersey Shore do the restaurants, the shops, the architecture, and the character of the residents combine so well. This is not a Colonial Williamsburg, where actors wander about in costume. Cape May's distinctive atmosphere, a blend of Victorian whimsy and a serious veneration of restored architecture, was created entirely by a group of residents who fought incredible opposition from developers and purveyors of Jersey Shore "honky-tonk." Those who live here are as proud of what Cape May isn't as they are of what it is.

Unfortunately, the restoration/preservation spirit has not been shared by everyone, though some motels and condominiums have recently added pseudo-Victorian touches to their facades and imitation antique furniture in their rooms. On Beach Drive, junky souvenir shops stand in the shadow of some of the city's best restaurants.

Cape May's beach, a flat stretch of dark sand, is adequate for sunning though not as dramatic as those farther north. Swimming, bicycling, fishing, and birding in the nearby state park are also popular with vacationers. The city's busy summer season extends from June 15 to the end of September, when most inns require a three- to four-night minimum stay. The brisk Victorian Week, usually at the beginning of October, combines madcap frivolity with serious lectures on Victorian history and restoration. Most Cape May restaurants and inns are closed in January, February, and March.

Experiencing Cape May almost requires staying in a guest house, bed and breakfast, or small restored hotel. Some innkeepers have assembled museum-quality period furnishings, and many act as unofficial hosts to the city. For teenagers who find Cape May a little too sedate, a trip to Wildwood's amusement piers is recommended (*see* Exploring Cape May County in Chapter 7, Cape May County).

Other possible side trips, accessible by car, include the Leaming's Run Botanical Gardens in Swainton, Cold Spring Village, and the *Yankee Schooner* sunset sailing cruise, which are all described in Chapter 7. Atlantic City is an easy 40-minute trip up the Garden State Parkway. Instead of driving and enduring the crowds and congestion typical of Atlantic City on a summer night, take one of the casino buses that leave Cape May regularly. For about $15 per person, you get round-trip transportation to an Atlantic City casino hotel (where you stay for about six hours), package discounts on meals or show tickets, and $5–$10 in coins for slot machine gambling.

Essential Information

Important Addresses and Numbers

Tourist Information **Welcome Center** (405 Lafayette St., Cape May, NJ 08204, tel. 609/884–9562) has maps and information on Cape May city events and tourist activities. The center does not have rates for guest houses, bed-and-breakfasts, motels, or hotels, nor does it make reservations.

Cape May Convention and Visitors Bureau (Box 403, Cape May 08204, tel. 609/898–0280).

Cape May City Chamber of Commerce (Box 109, Cape May 08204, tel. 609/884–5508).

Emergencies   **Cape May Beach Patrol** (tel. 609/884–9520). Good source for beach and ocean swimming conditions.

Fire Department (tel. 609/884–9510).

Marine Weather Forecast (tel. 609/884–8419).

Police (tel. 609/884–9500 or 911 within Cape May City limits).

Medical   **Burdette Tomlin Memorial Hospital** (Lincoln Ave., Cape May Court House, tel. 609/463–2000) is about a 15-minute drive north of Cape May.

Opening and Closing Times

Cape May rolls up the pavement early. Most restaurants close their kitchens at 10 PM. Taverns have last call at 1 AM and are closed at 2 AM.

Tours

Guided Tours   The **Mid-Atlantic Center for the Arts,** or MAC, as it is known locally, is a nonprofit organization originally established to preserve and restore the Emlen Physick Estate. When money was needed, residents volunteered to lead walking tours of the city. Those tours have inspired a series of tours, performances, and seasonal events designed to educate visitors, preserve architecture, and enhance the cultural climate of Cape May.

MAC tours are offered daily from June 15 to Labor Day and on weekends in the cooler months. Tours are also scheduled during special events, such as **Victorian Week,** a 10-day festival during the first half of October. This is MAC's city-wide celebration combining plays, concerts, banquets, and serious seminars on Victorian art, culture, and restoration. For details contact the Mid-Atlantic Center for the Arts (Box 340, Cape May 08204, tel. 609/884–5404). *This Week in Cape May*, a free local, tourist-oriented publication, lists MAC tours and other special events; it's available at most restaurants, shops, inns, and hotels.

The MAC tour of the **Physick Estate,** which helped inspire Cape May's restoration and renovation movement, includes explanations of Victorian morals and manners, costumes, toys, and tools. *1048 Washington St. Cost: $4 adults, $1 children 3–12 and military in uniform. Tours last about 75 min beginning every 45 min in the summer season, 10:30–3. Closed Fri. and weekdays in spring and fall.*

MAC's **"Cape May's Hey Day"** explores the district east of Ocean Street, including the large Congress Hall Hotel area. **"High Victorian"** covers Columbia Avenue, Hughes Street, and the area around the Chalfonte Hotel. Tours vary but most emphasize history and architecture. *Cost: $4 adults, $1 children 3–12 and military in uniform. Weather permitting, tours depart June–Aug. daily at 10:30 AM, spring (March–May) and fall (Sept.–Oct.) weekends and holidays at 10:30 AM from the Information Booth in Washington Mall.*

Three half-hour MAC **trolley tours** offer relief for the footsore, and children enjoy the relatively swift ride. The **"Historic East End"** (Columbia Avenue, Hughes Street, and Ocean Street), the **"Historic West End"** (Congress Hall and vicinity), and the **"Historic Beach Drive"** (Cape May's oceanfront cottages and mansions) tours emphasize architecture and history, and they are recommended for those who have just arrived and want a quick overview of the city. Tours begin at the Physick Estate. *Cost: $4 adults, $1 children. A combined Physick Estate interior and trolley tour costs $10 for adults, $5 for children.*

"Mansions by Gaslight" is an evening MAC tour of the Physick Estate and three Cape May inns: the Abbey, the Mainstay, and the Humphrey Hughes House. A trolley provides transportation among the sites, with MAC guides and individual innkeepers providing information about history, renovation, Victorian furnishings, design, and antiques. *Cost: $12 adults, $6 children. Tours operate Wed. 7:30–10:30 PM in the summer and on holiday weekends throughout the year.*

"Jewels in the Crown" is a MAC tour that takes in the Chalfonte, Christian Admiral, Congress Hall, the Inn of Cape May, and the Virginia. *Cost: $12 adults, $6 children.*

The **"Victorian Sampler"** MAC tours, given throughout the year, include interiors of five restored inns or private homes. Subjects include history, restoration, antiques, and furnishings. Some innkeepers provide refreshments. *Weekends 4–6 PM. Cost: $10 adults, $6 children.*

The **Cape May Carriage Company** provides half-hour horse-and-buggy tours of the historic district, departing from Ocean Street and the Washington Mall. *Tel. 609/465–9854. Cost: $6 adults, $3 children. Tours spring and fall, weekends 9:30–12:45 and 6:30–9:45; summer, daily 9:30–12:45 and 6:30–9:45.*

Special-Interest Tours Many guided **nature walks** are scheduled at **Cape May Point State Park** (tel. 609/884–2159), a half-hour beach walk or a quick 10-minute car ride west of Cape May City. The park is open dawn to dusk. Find it either by heading south along the beach, passing the huge, old concrete gun emplacement, or by driving south on Sunset Boulevard, turning left on Lighthouse Road, and passing the Cape May Point Lighthouse as you enter.

Doing Business in Cape May

Cape May is becoming popular for small meetings, conferences, and as an executive retreat. While individual inns and motels can be quite accommodating, the best small hotel in the historic district for business purposes is the Virginia, with its corporate board room, catering and service staff, and its fax and computer support services. The Grand Hotels (actually three motels) has the largest meeting and convention space of any Cape May hotel, as well as the most rooms; it also has fax service, full catering, and a health spa. Both properties are open all year. **Details Destination Management** (Box 2188, Cape May 08204, tel. 609/884–3355) is a business support service offering local assistance to meeting planners.

Arriving and Departing

By Plane The nearest scheduled air service is at Atlantic City's **Bader Field** or **Atlantic City International Airport** in Pomona. (*See* Chapter 5, Atlantic City, for a list of airlines.)

By Car Cape May is located at the end of the **Garden State Parkway,** a toll road that roughly parallels the New Jersey Shore.

From New York City Southbound travelers from New York City should cross into New Jersey at I–80 to the **New Jersey Turnpike,** another toll road, and change to the **Garden State Parkway** at Exit 11. Travel time is 3½ hours.

From Philadelphia The **Atlantic City Expressway** toll road connects Philadelphia and the southern New Jersey suburbs to the **Garden State Parkway;** for Cape May go south. Travel time is approximately three hours.

From Delaware Traffic originating south of New Jersey can enter the state at the **Delaware Memorial Bridge,** then take rural **Route 40** south to faster, wider **Route 55** south to **Route 47,** eventually merging with the parkway and going into Cape May. Travel time from the bridge is about three hours due to slow-moving traffic. Another alternative is to drive to Lewes, Delaware, where you can hop the ferry to Cape May (*see* By Ferry, below).

By Bus **New Jersey Transit** (tel. 800/722–2222 in northern NJ, 800/582–5946 in southern NJ, 201/460–8444 from NY, 215/569–3752 in Philadelphia) provides the only scheduled bus service.

By Ferry The **Cape May–Lewes Ferry** leaves several times daily from the somewhat small, out-of-the-way town of Lewes, Delaware. (Lewes was a notorious Dutch settlement that supplied many pirates during the Colonial period.) The trip takes about 70 minutes and is a novel but thoroughly appropriate way to reach Cape May; it also makes a diverting day trip. Ferry boats are large and can accommodate minivans and recreational vehicles as well as cars, motorcycles, and bicycles. Lewes's small Victorian section is a short drive from the ferry dock. The one-way car fee, including the driver, is $16, $4 for each additional passenger, $2 for children under age 6. Fees and departure times vary; for details call the Cape May–Lewes Ferry (tel. 609/886–2718 in NJ, 302/645–6313 in DE).

Getting Around

On Foot The best way to explore the historic district is on foot. Cape May's boardwalk was destroyed by a storm in 1962 and was replaced by a stone-and-concrete embankment called the Promenade. You can also walk from the beach into the Cape May Point State Park wildlife refuge, one of the prettiest beach walks in New Jersey.

By Bicycle A bike is highly recommended for a trip to Cape May Point, Sunset Beach, and areas outside of town. Several bicycle rental shops are available. The **Village Bicycle Shop** (tel. 609/884–8500) is located in the Acme parking lot just across Ocean Street from the Washington Mall.

By Bus The local **New Jersey Transit Bus Terminal** is at 609 Lafayette Street. The **Cape May Chamber of Commerce** (tel. 609/884–5508) provides schedule information. For day trips to Atlantic City casinos, call the **Casino Bus Co.** (tel. 609/884–4343) for prices and departure information.

By Taxi **Jones Taxi** (tel. 609/884–5888) services the local area.

By Car A car is not necessary for exploring the historic district, where parking is difficult during the summer. You will, however, need a car (or be forced to depend on a taxi) for the somewhat distant restaurants and charter fishing in the Fisherman's Wharf area or a drive to Wildwood and other sites of interest in Cape May County.

Cape May is especially vigilant about ticketing parking violators. Meters are checked hourly during the summer season— even during inclement weather, and cars parked in front of driveways or in no-parking zones are towed at considerable expense to the owner. Free on-street parking can be found on Bank Street and surrounding streets west of Lafayette.

Exploring Victorian Cape May

Orientation

Cape May City is at the end of the Garden State Parkway, just over the bridge that spans the Cape May Canal. On the south side of the bridge is **Fisherman's Wharf,** a tight tangle of seafood restaurants, a fish market (at the Lobster House restaurant), and docks for pleasure boating, sport fishing, and party-boat and commercial fishing.

The majority of restaurants and B&Bs are in or near the **historic district,** which was designated a historic landmark by the federal government in 1977. Two streets handle traffic to the historic district. **Lafayette Street,** which leads directly from the Cape May Canal Bridge, has some historic homes but mostly skirts the historic district and joins West Perry Street and Sunset Boulevard to Cape May Point. The north–south traffic on Lafayette Street tends to be faster than on prettier **Washington Street,** which you will find by taking the first left turn off the bridge onto Sidney Street (signs point toward BEACHES) and then a right. Washington Street ends at Ocean Street, the beginning of the **Washington Mall,** a pedestrian mall that is the historic district's primary shopping area.

The historic district is roughly a square mile, bounded by Franklin, Columbia, and Gurney streets to the north; Beach Drive to Congress Street on the east; Congress and West Perry streets on the south; and Lafayette Street to the west. This district is in an area that was destroyed in an 1878 fire and was rebuilt shortly thereafter.

The two most beautiful streets for historic architecture and atmosphere are **Columbia Avenue** and **Hughes Street,** between Decatur and Franklin streets. Columbia is "veranda boulevard," so named for its many Italianate and Gothic Revival inns and guest houses, most sporting open porches. Hughes is the quieter and more residential street, with older, more varied architectural styles. **Jackson Street,** between Beach Drive and the Washington Mall, is also quite charming, though the rumbling delivery trucks serving the mall and the Jackson Street hotels and restaurants can be distracting.

Despite the construction of stone seawalls and jetties and a number of other frantic measures, Cape May's beaches are eroding rapidly, and with the exception of the turbulent surf off Cape May Point State Park, are not especially scenic or dramatic. Wide **Beach Drive** separates the beach blocks from the ocean. The quieter areas are north of Pittsburgh Avenue, beyond the beachfront motels.

Tour 1: Cape May Historic District

This 90-minute walking tour features Cape May's restored Victorian architecture and covers roughly 3 miles.

Numbers in the margin correspond with points of interest on the Tour 1: Cape May Historic District map.

❶ Begin at the **Emlen Physick Estate** (1048 Washington St.), Cape May's masterpiece of restored architecture. Philadelphia architect Frank Furness designed this 1879 stick-style mansion as a summer home for Philadelphia physician Emlen Physick. The stick style is reminiscent of the heavy-beam construction of the Tudor style; the decorative exterior woodwork reflects the heavier structural supports within. Note that the chimneys are wider at the top. A guided tour of the estate and the small museum inside is recommended (*see* Guided Tours, above).

Turn left and walk down Washington Street toward the Washington Mall. After crossing Jefferson Street, on your right is the curved driveway at 720 Washington Street. The stately,
❷ dignified **George Allen House** (circa 1864) is a private house designed by Samuel Sloan in the bracketed-villa style. (Brackets are the decorated exterior braces that support a second-floor porch or roof.)

Turn left onto Franklin Street, then right onto Hughes Street. These streets, along with nearby Columbia Avenue, are considered Cape May's prettiest. Along Hughes Street are several splendidly restored homes; most are private. Stop at 655
❸ Hughes Street, the Gothic Revival **J. Stratton Ware House** (circa 1860), and admire the elaborate decorative details. The doily-like trim finishing the central, third-floor dormer window is called a vergeboard, another popular feature of Victorian architecture.

❹ At 609 Hughes Street is the soberly colonial **Albert Henry Hughes House** (1838), one of Cape May's oldest houses, now operated as a B&B. Rumor has it that Robert E. Lee spent a summer here.

Cross Ocean Street, passing Captain Mey's Inn. Continue on Hughes Street, turn right onto Decatur Street, turn left just before the Washington Mall onto Carpenter's Lane, then left on Jackson Street. There are several similar houses on Jackson that declare their individuality with different color schemes, decorations, and details. Note the differences between 45 Jack-
❺ son Street, the Second Empire–style **Christopher Gallagher**
❻ **House** (1883), and the **George Hildreth House**, 17 Jackson Street (now Poor Richard's Inn).

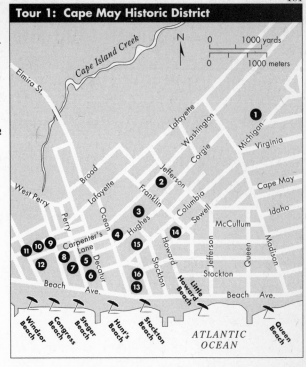

Tour 1: Cape May Historic District

Between the Gallagher House and Poor Richard's Inn (on the left side of the street as you walk toward the ocean) are five of the **Seven Sisters** (circa 1891–92), seven identical houses designed in the Renaissance Revival style by Philadelphia architect Stephen Button; they are now guest houses and private homes. What is visible is the back of the houses—they face inward on Atlantic Terrace, which you can enter on the gravel driveway leading to the right.

Continue down Jackson Street to Beach Avenue. Cross to the Promenade, where Cape May's boardwalk stood before it and much of the city were devastated in a 1962 storm. Between Jackson and Perry streets you can see the Seven Sisters facing the ocean around Atlantic Terrace. Turn right at Perry Street. The decorative glass tiles on the stick-style guest house at 9 Perry Street on your right came from a vast glass villa that was part of the 1876 Philadelphia Centennial Exposition. The enormous colonnaded edifice on your left is the Congress Hall Hotel (*see* below). Just before the Washington Mall, on your right at 33 Perry Street, is the Eldridge Johnson House (circa 1882), a Gothic Revival residence known throughout Cape May as the **Pink House** (now converted for commercial use). Note the incredibly intricate white-gingerbread trim against the house's cheery bright pink color.

Turn left along the rear of Congress Hall. This street, called Congress Place, has Cape May's most eccentric cottage. The **Henry Hunt House**, at 209 Congress Place, is an 1891 Queen Anne cottage with absurdly proportioned gables and a belvedere perched like a birdcage above the porch. It is now a private residence.

Note the similarity of the Hunt House's neighbors, the American bracket–style **Joseph Evans House** at 207 Congress Place, and the **E. C. Knight House** at 203 (circa 1881–83). They are considered to be among architect Stephen Button's finest achievements.

Cross Congress Place onto Congress Street. Directly in front of you is the fringed cupola atop the **Neafie-Levy twin house** (circa 1865) at 28–30 Congress Street. Turn left, cross Beach Drive, and turn left onto the Promenade. From here you get the best view of **Congress Hall** (circa 1879), the third building on this site to have this name (its predecessors were destroyed by fires). Abraham Lincoln and Ulysses S. Grant stayed here. When Benjamin Harrison was president, he made Congress Hall his summer White House in 1890 and 1891. John Philip Sousa gave concerts on the broad lawn and composed the "Congress Hall March" in the hotel's honor.

Continue walking east on Beach Drive. The Queen Anne–style **Colonial Hotel** (circa 1894) was the site of the coming-out party of Wallis Warfield, later the Duchess of Windsor. Walk on, turn left onto Jefferson Street, make your first left onto Stockton, and then make a right on Howard Street. The long, *L*-shape, white, gingerbread-trimmed building at Howard Street and Sewell Avenue is the **Chalfonte Hotel.**

Turn left onto Columbia Avenue, Cape May's showcase street, where many similar Victorian structures sport elaborate decoration. **The Mainstay Bed-and-Breakfast,** at 635 Columbia Avenue, is the former Jackson's Clubhouse, an 1872 men's gambling club. Note how the verandas on the various inns just past the Mainstay are precisely aligned. Across the street is the 1869 John McCreary House, now the **Abbey Bed & Breakfast,** Cape May's best example of Gothic Revival architecture (*see* Lodging, below).

Turn left onto Gurney Street to the **Stockton Place Row Houses** (circa 1869), named in honor of the Stockton Inn. Historical records mention that renting the Baldt House (26 Gurney St.) for the summer season would have cost $2,000 in 1890. You can end the walking tour here, or, to sample more of the varied delights of Cape May architecture, follow this route: Turn left onto Kearney Street, walk four blocks to Jefferson Street, and turn left on Jefferson; walk six blocks to Corge Street and turn left; walk to Madison and turn left again. Follow Madison to Washington Street, where you'll turn right and return to the Emlen Physick Estate.

Tour 2: Cape May Point

Numbers in the margin correspond with points of interest on the Tour 2: Cape May Point map.

Designed for bicyclers—or motorists who can endure the oppressive horn blasts from drivers in a hurry—this 7-mile tour includes a portion of Cape May's historic district, the Coast Guard Training Academy, Cape May Point, Cape May Point State Park, and Sunset Beach. Done at an easy pace with plenty of stops, the tour can take most of a day. Pack a lunch either from a restaurant or from the Wawa Food Market at Broad and

Bank streets. You don't need to pack any fresh fruit because the tour passes a farmers' market.

You can tour some of the inns, hotels, or private residences during MAC house tours, for which admission is charged. If you ask at inns that are not included on MAC tours, innkeepers may permit you to look around.

❶ Begin at the **Washington Mall,** at Ocean and Washington streets. The sober, stone building, now **McDowell's Gallery** gift shop, was once Cape May's City Hall. Go east on Ocean Street toward the ocean. At 202 Ocean Street is Captain Mey's Inn (*see* Lodging, below), one of several large houses owned by doctors in 1890, giving Ocean Street the local name "doctors' row." Pass the restful, green **Queen Victoria Bed & Breakfast** and then **Cheeks clothing shop** (101 Ocean St.), which is an original Victorian storefront. As you near Beach Drive, look to your left to see the magnificent twin turrets of the **Colonial Hotel** (circa 1894), now called **The Inn of Cape May** (*see* Lodging, below). Diamond Jim Brady, John Philip Sousa, and Henry Ford are reputed to have stayed here. Turn left onto Beach Drive and go south.

Pause as you pass Jackson Street to look at the Acroteria Huts. An acroterion is a symmetrical decoration at the apex of a roof, in this case on the huts. Continue down Beach Drive. Between Perry and Congress streets stop to admire the long, colonnade of **Congress Hall** (*see* Tour 1: Cape May Historic District, above). Continue west on Beach Drive and turn right on Broadway. Notice the aqua roof and buff shingles of the bungalow-style 1883 rental house at 8 Broadway, which was moved to Cape May from Cold Spring Village in 1900. The structure at 416 Broadway on your left just before the traffic light was originally a farmhouse. The front of the house is an 1874 addition to a 1690 whaler's cottage. Turn left at the traffic light onto Sunset Boulevard (Route 606). Watch out for fast-moving trucks on Sunset Boulevard.

❷ At the **farmers' market** on Sunset Boulevard you can purchase fresh fruit for your picnic. At the intersection of South Bayshore Road, you'll see a small pink cottage on your left. After the devastating 1962 storm destroyed the bottom of this house, the debris was cleared away, and what had been the top floor was settled onto the foundation. To your right, you'll see the wildlife refuge. Walk your bicycle across Sunset Boulevard and turn left at Sea Grove Avenue, a quiet, narrow, tree-lined road; Cape May Point is ¼ mile ahead at this point.

❸ Sea Grove was the original name of **Cape May Point,** which was founded as a Presbyterian religious retreat by Philadelphia department store owner John Wanamaker in 1874. Turn left at Lighthouse Avenue. At the intersection of Lighthouse and Coral avenues on your right is an open-roof structure that shelters the remains of the British blockade ship **H.M.S. *Martin,*** which was attacked and burned by American forces in 1813. The ship drifted and was buried in the sands; it was not discovered until 1954. Continue down Lighthouse Avenue to Cape May Point State Park on your left.

❹ The **Cape May Lighthouse** is on your right. Built in 1859, it is 165 feet high and is the third lighthouse to be built on this site. It also has the distinction of being the oldest lighthouse still under U.S. Coast Guard commission as a navigational aid

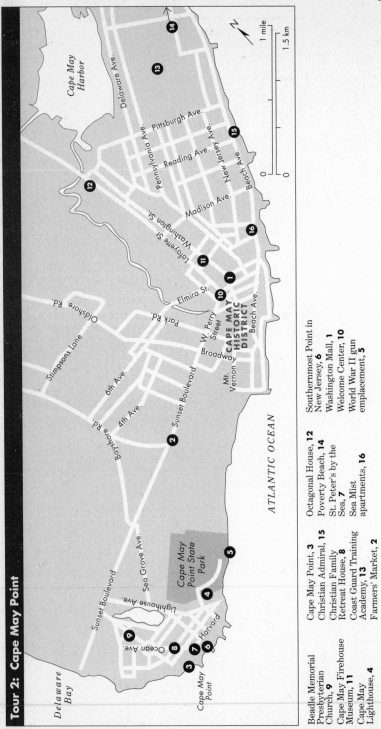

Tour 2: Cape May Point

184

Delaware Bay

Cape May Harbor

ATLANTIC OCEAN

1 mile
1.5 km

CAPE MAY HISTORIC DISTRICT

Cape May Point State Park

Beadle Memorial Presbyterian Church, **9**
Cape May Firehouse Museum, **11**
Cape May Lighthouse, **4**

Cape May Point, **3**
Christian Admiral, **15**
Christian Family Retreat House, **8**
Coast Guard Training Academy, **13**
Farmers' Market, **2**

Octagonal House, **12**
Poverty Beach, **14**
St. Peter's by the Sea, **7**
Sea Mist apartments, **16**

Southernmost Point in New Jersey, **6**
Washington Mall, **1**
Welcome Center, **10**
World War II gun emplacement, **5**

(Sandy Hook Light, 127 miles to the north, is the oldest lighthouse still standing, but it is no longer used for navigation). You climb 199 steps to the top for Cape May's most spectacular 360-degree view. *Tel. 609/884–8656. Admission: $3 adults, $1 children 12 and under. Open May–Oct., daily 9–6; off-season weekends 9–6.*

Give yourself some time to explore the park. The Nature Center has a small museum, with a photograph of how the point appeared in the '40s compared with one taken relatively recently. The pace of beach erosion is frightening. Guided nature walks and self-guided tours, with an emphasis on waterfowl, are available. Continue toward the beach, keeping clear of the dunes. This is one of the most dramatic beaches on the Jersey Shore, with dark, powdery sand. Tides are too rough for swimming, but you can get your feet wet here (and wash them in the outdoor faucet near the Nature Center). If you look north, you'll see a peculiar concrete structure supported by pilings **5** that thrust out of the water. This was a **World War II gun emplacement** that guarded the entrance to the Delaware Bay. When the guns were installed, the bunker was several hundred yards inland from the beach, buried completely in the sand. Now, thanks to many storms, it is completely exposed and has become a popular fishing platform and observation point. From the bunker you'll have the best view of the lighthouse. The wood frame structure near the lighthouse is St. Mary's by the Sea, the former Shoreham Hotel and now a summer retreat for the Sisters of the Convent of the Sacred Heart.

After leaving the park make a right and go to Lincoln Avenue, passing the front of St. Mary's by the Sea. At Lehigh Avenue, make a right and then a left onto Harvard Avenue, a one-way street. If possible, leave your car or bicycle at one of the entrances to the beach. Notice how the sand here differs from the powdery grit just a hundred yards behind you. Here, where the Delaware Bay and Atlantic Ocean meet, you are at the **6** **southernmost point in New Jersey**.

Continue west along Harvard Avenue, which becomes Ocean Avenue as it jogs right. At the corner of Ocean and Lake notice **7** the small, stick-style church, **St. Peter's by the Sea.** The church is believed to have been built in 1876 for the Philadelphia Exposition and moved here a few years later. The church is open May–September for religious services only.

Turn left onto Lincoln Avenue, passing the Cape May Point Volunteer Fire Company and Post Office. At the next intersection, on your far left, is the impressive 1872 Croll Blackburn House, now a private home. Turn right onto Cape May Avenue. **8** At the corner of Cape and Yale avenues is the **Christian Family Retreat House.** It was John Wanamaker's summer home, and President Harrison's family lived here during his two summers in Cape May.

Continue north on Cape May Avenue, going halfway around the now-empty Pavilion Avenue Circle (an octagonal pavilion used for religious services once stood here). Pick up Cape Avenue, passing the **Beadle Memorial Presbyterian Church,** a blend **9** of Gothic Revival, Queen Anne, and stick-style architecture, on your left. On your right is Lake Lilly. Continue to Sunset Boulevard, walk across Sunset Boulevard, then turn left and head west toward Sunset Beach. The observation tower on your left was erected as part of a Delaware Bay defense system during World War II.

Time Out   You can break out your packed lunch at **Sunset Beach,** where the waters of the Delaware Bay calmly lap the pebbled beach and the sunsets are spectacular. The **Sunset Beach Grill** is a small, inexpensive snack bar at the eastern end of the parking area.

The wreck directly offshore is the U.S.S. *Atlantus*, a concrete ship constructed shortly after World War I. It sank in a storm in 1926. Notice also the large pebbly beach. "Cape May Diamonds"—polished lumps of quartz—have been found here.

Head east up Sunset Boulevard toward Cape May City. At the first traffic light, Sunset Boulevard becomes West Perry Street. Turn left onto Lafayette Street (at the sign pointing toward the 🔟 Garden State Parkway). The **Welcome Center** (417 Lafayette St., tel. 609/884–9562) is located in the former Cape Island Presbyterian Church; note the Moorish domed cupola on the ⑪ top. At Franklin Street, turn right. The **Cape May Firehouse Museum,** on the corner of Franklin and Washington streets, houses antique fire-fighting equipment. The stained-glass windows in the Church of the Advent on the opposite corner date to 1867. Turn left onto Washington Street. *Tel. 609/884–9512. Admission free. Open May–Sept., daily 10–4.*

On your left as you head north on Washington Street is the Washington Inn (801 Washington St.), the Duke of Windsor Inn (817 Washington St.), and, on your right, the **Emlen Physick Estate** (*see* Tour 1: Cape May Historic District, above). Observe how the historic structures on Washington Street become more modern the farther north you go. At the very end of Washington Street bear left, then turn left onto Lafayette Street. On ⑫ the left, at 1286 Lafayette Street, is a rare **octagonal house** (circa 1875).

Turn left onto Sidney Street, left again on Washington Street, and right onto Texas Avenue. Then take another right onto Pittsburgh Avenue, site of some of the most boring residential architecture in all of Cape May. Turn left at the sign for the ⑬ **U.S. Coast Guard Training Academy** (tel. 609/884–8451, ext. 206). Access to the academy is limited, though visitors are permitted to attend Friday parade graduation ceremonies.

Continue back down Pittsburgh Avenue toward the ocean and turn left onto New Jersey Avenue. Then turn right at the dead ⑭ end and pause, looking north. This is **Poverty Beach,** believed to be named for the poor hotel workers who were forced to use this beach on what was then the far northern edge of town. In 1903, Poverty Beach was considerably wider—so much so that it contained a 2-mile auto course extending from Madison Avenue to the opening of the Cape May Canal. In 1905, **Henry Ford** entered a 60-horsepower Beach Skimmer auto in a race with Louis Chevrolet, A. L. Campbell, and Walter Christie. Campbell, in an 80-horsepower car, won. Chevrolet came in second, Christie third, and Ford last. Ford, who had been counting on the prize money to pay his hotel bill at the Stockton Hotel, was annoyed at losing. The desk clerk refused to accept stock in Ford's fledgling automobile company in lieu of payment. Ford tried to sell a touring car that he had been using to tow the Skimmer, but no one wanted to buy a car from the man who had lost the race. He finally sold it for $400 to Daniel Focer, a railroad engineer, and promised that Focer would have the first Ford dealership in America. Ford made good on his promise. In 1937, J. E. Mecray, one of Focer's partners in the dealership, was run over by an automobile in Ocean City. The car that killed him was a Ford.

Go south on Beach Drive, passing the eccentric Colvmns by the Sea Bed & Breakfast (*see* Lodging, below), and stop at the **⑮ Christian Admiral,** the imposing eight-story stone-and-brick French Baroque hotel, now used for religious retreats. The faux-marble columns in the domed lobby are made of iron. If you stand under the middle of the dome and whisper, your voice will echo throughout the dome. Continue south on Beach Drive past the olive and pale green Morning Star Villa (circa 1884) at 1300 Beach Drive, now an apartment building. Next to it is the William Weightman House (circa late 1870s), now the Angel of the Sea Bed & Breakfast (*see* Lodging, below). Both the Morning Star Villa and the William Weightman House were relocated to this site.

As you head south on Beach Drive, notice the World War II observation tower thrusting out of what is now The Grand Hotels at Philadelphia Avenue and Beach Drive (*see* Lodging, below). You'll pass more motels and Cape May's most flamboyant **⑯ oceanfront structure, the Sea Mist apartments** at 927 Beach Drive. The Sea Mist, which has five levels of porches and is topped by a circus-tent belvedere, resembles a wedding cake. The large, four-story, shingle-style Hotel Macomber on the southwest corner of Beach Drive and Howard Street occupies a portion of what was once the site of the enormous Stockton Inn (demolished in 1911), where Henry Ford stayed during the Poverty Beach race.

Turn right onto Gurney Street, passing the almost identical **Stockton Place Row Houses** (circa 1871) (*see* Tour 1: Cape May Historic District, above). On your left, at the intersection of Gurney and Columbia, is the flamboyant Gothic Revival John McCreary House, now The Abbey Bed & Breakfast (*see* Lodging, below). Turn left onto Columbia Avenue, which is called Veranda Boulevard, and walk past The Mainstay (*see* Tour 1: Cape May Historic District, above, and Lodging, below). Turn left on Ocean Avenue and return to the Washington Mall.

What to See and Do with Children

Arcade amusements on the Promenade and **miniature golf courses** near Beach Drive are popular diversions for families with young children. For boardwalk entertainment on a larger—and rowdier—scale, we recommend an evening excursion to Wildwood's amusement piers (*see* Chapter 7, Cape May County). The piers are a 15-minute car trip away, and public parking is plentiful. Teens enjoy Wildwood's boardwalk and underage club nights—where there is live entertainment but no liquor.

The **Cape May County Art League,** in the carriage house on the Physick Estate at 1050 Washington Street (tel. 609/884–8628), offers workshops in art, crafts, puppetry, music, and dance for children kindergarten ages and up and also for teens and adults.

The **Mid-Atlantic Center for the Arts** (MAC, tel. 609/884–5404) offers supervised children's tours of Emlen Physick Estate for ages 6–12. Admission is $1 for children, $4 adults.

From the end of June to Labor Day, the Cape May Civic Affairs Department (tel. 609/884–9565) hosts **dances for children and adults,** every Wednesday, Friday, and Saturday at 8:30 PM, and **teen dances** every Thursday night at 8:30 PM (Beach Dr. at Howard St.).

Off the Beaten Track

Higbee Beach, a wild, untamed stretch of Delaware Bay beachfront that is only a 10-minute car ride from Cape May, has become notorious over the past decade as one of two unofficial (and unsanctioned) nude beaches on the Jersey Shore. (The other is the northeastern edge of Sandy Hook.) Nudity at Higbee Beach makes little sense—the brambles teem with insects and several times each day the Cape May–Lewes Ferry chugs past the beach, where bathers, clothed or otherwise, are in full view of the passengers. Go to Higbee, however, for a rare chance to see a stretch of undeveloped coastline. You can reach Higbee Beach either by walking a mile north of Sunset Beach or by driving (or biking) on Sunset Boulevard (Route 606) toward Cape May Point. Turn right (north) at South Bay Shore Road (Route 607). Follow Bay Shore Road north for 1¾ miles. Turn left (west) on New England Road (Route 641) for another mile. The road ends at the beach.

Shopping

Cape May has two shopping districts: **Washington Mall,** on Washington Street between Perry and Ocean streets, and **Beach Drive.** The mall is a mixed bag of high-quality goods, restaurants, ice-cream and candy shops, gift shops, and tourist souvenirs. Clothing shops are plentiful. **Pinebrook** (510 Washington Mall, tel. 609/884–0442) is a very good men's sportswear boutique, especially for sales. The **Keltie News Agency** (518 Washington Mall, tel. 609/884–7797) has a wide assortment of newspapers, magazines, and a reasonably good selection of books, though many of the hardback and quality paperback books are wrapped in plastic so you can't open them. **For the Birds** (324 Beach Drive, tel. 609/884–7152) is for avian fanciers and is stocked with field guides, antique decoys, books, feeders, binoculars, and bird-design T-shirts. Two blocks beyond the mall, **Patricia Jackson** (414 Bank St., tel. 609/884–0323) makes high-quality custom jewelry. Follow Bank Street to Jackson Street for **Mariah's** (225 Jackson St., tel. 609/884–7917), a gift shop that stocks Victoriana.

A block north of the Washington Mall, past the Victorian Towers rest home, is Washington Square. One of the shops there, **Bailywicke** (656 Washington St., tel. 609/884–2761), sells expensive, high-quality, handmade leather goods.

Cape May's second shopping district, which follows **Beach Drive** from Perry Street to Jefferson Street, offers find mostly souvenir items and food shops.

Because Cape May so reverently adores its past, you may find yourself smitten with antique fever. Shops are scattered all over town, around the mall, and beyond.

Cape May is home of the East Coast's third-largest commercial seaport, and fresh seafood, Cape May's best buy, is available at the docks where it's brought in. Buy a large cooler at the Acme between Washington and Lafayette streets. The fish markets will give you a good supply of ice and wrap your fish for your trip home. Fish markets are located at the Fisherman's Wharf area (adjacent to the Lobster House restaurant) and on the Ocean Drive causeway between Cape May and Wildwood.

Sports and Outdoor Activities

Beaches For general information on ocean water quality and beach conditions, contact the **Cape May County Health Department** (Crest Haven Complex at the Garden State Pkwy., Cape May Court House 08210, tel. 609/465–1221). The **Cape May Beach Quality Hotline** (tel. 609/465–2422) supplies information about Cape May County beaches during the swimming season.

Cape May's swimming beaches begin at Gurney Street and Beach Drive and continue south to the end of the Promenade. Public rest rooms are located at Convention Hall. From June 15 through Labor Day, admission to these beaches, as well as to those in the residential sections of Cape May Point, requires the purchase of a beach badge. Most B&Bs and hotels offer beach badges to guests free or for a nominal charge. If no beach badges are available, you can purchase them at the Information Booth at City Hall or on the beach from beach inspectors. Badge fees are $2 for one day, $6 for one week, and $10 for the whole season. For information, call 609/884–9525.

Cape May Point's beach serves the residential community south of Cape May Point State Park. You must purchase a badge to use this beach between June 15 and Labor Day. For fees, call 609/884–2159.

The Cape May Department of Civic Affairs (tel. 609/884–9565) can provide information about the **Cape May International Clam Shell Pitching Tournament,** one of the more hilarious Shore events. It takes place Labor Day weekend on Steger Beach, at Beach Drive and Jackson Street. Participants, who come from Europe and Canada, compete with Americans to demonstrate their skill at skimming a common quahog clamshell into a hole dug into the sand. Civic Affairs also has information about several running races held each year.

Bird-watching This is a serious sport and pastime in Cape May. In the fall the Audubon Society hosts the **World Series of Birding** at the Cape May Point Bird Observatory, located on Sunset Boulevard in Cape May Point. The Audubon Society announces migratory bird activity on the Cape May birding hotline (tel. 609/884–2626). For general information, contact the Cape May Bird Observatory (Box 3, 707 E. Lake Dr., Cape May Point, NJ 08212, tel. 609/884–2626).

Fishing and Boating You can go surf fishing off the jetty at the end of Beach Drive or off the bunker in Cape May Point. More than 60 party and charter boats set sail from the Fisherman's Wharf area or from marinas along the Cape May harbor and canal. The **Cape May Fishing & Sightseeing Center,** on the west side of Lafayette Street opposite Fisherman's Wharf (tel. 609/898–0055 or 729–0320), offers sightseeing and whale-watching cruises from the end of April through October. Call for prices and departure times.

Golf There is a handful of miniature golf courses along Beach Drive. For information on the full-size variety, *see* Chapter 7, Cape May County.

Health Clubs The health spa at **The Grand Hotels** is open to the public for $6 per person, per visit. Facilities include a Universal gym, stationary bikes, rowers, free weights, a sauna, steam cabinets, whirlpool baths, and heated indoor and outdoor pools. Children are admitted with supervising adults. *Beach Dr. and Philadelphia Ave., tel. 609/884–5611. Open weekdays noon–10, weekends and holidays 10–10.*

Body Mechanix (130 Park Ave., West Cape May, tel. 609/884–0777) offers daily aerobics classes for adults and children, taught by certified instructors. There is a child-care facility on the premises.

Sailing Every summer, usually in June, Cape May hosts the annual **Northeastern Regional Championship Hobie Cat Regatta.** The three-day sailing competition is a colorful offshore event. For dates and information, call the Cape May Department of Civic Affairs (tel. 609/884–9565). The only yacht club in Cape May is the **Corinthian** (Delaware Ave., tel. 609/884–8000).

Tennis The **William J. Moore Tennis Center,** just behind the Emlen Physick Estate, has 13 open-air clay courts. *1048 Washington St., tel. 609/884–8986. No reservations. $5 per hour, per person. Open Memorial Day–Oct. 14, weekdays 9–noon and 2–6, weekends 8–6; weekends only in Apr. and Oct. 14–Thanksgiving.*

Dining

The restaurant list was compiled with the assistance of Elaine Tait, food critic of the Philadelphia Inquirer; *Ed Hitzel, food critic of the* Atlantic City Press; *and J. M. Lang, food critic of the* New Jersey Monthly.

Cape May has the single best restaurant district on the Jersey Shore, though most places are café-style—small, informal, and expensive. The food is an eclectic mix of international and traditional Continental cuisines, with an emphasis on fresh seafood, most of which comes from nearby commercial docks. Most are not air-conditioned, discourage smoking, and are open weekends in April, May, and October, and daily June–September. Many do not serve liquor or wine, though stores selling packaged beverages are conveniently located on or near the Washington Mall.

For price ranges, consult the dining price chart in Chapter 1, Essential Information. Highly recommended restaurants are indicated with a star ★.

Expensive– Very Expensive ★ **Alexander's.** For that long, leisurely, gluttonously romantic, diet-destroying French feast, Alexander's, which features some table-side cooking, is the place. Service is classic French, almost deliberately slow, with a degree of hauteur that highlights the dining room's dignified, Victorian surroundings. The five-course Sunday brunch is a killer. *653 Washington St., tel. 609/884–2555. Reservations advised. Jacket suggested. Lim-*

ited off-street parking. *AE, DC, MC, V. BYOB. Open Apr.,
May, and Sept., weekends; June–Aug., Wed.–Mon., closed
Tues.*

★ **410 Bank Street.** The cuisine at Cape May's best restaurant is
an odd blend of Louisiana Cajun and Creole, with Caribbean
dishes and mesquite-grilled seafood as well. You can doodle on
the white paper tablecloth with crayons until the food comes.
On a balmy night, ask for a table in the garden. *410 Bank St.,
tel. 609/884–2127. Reservations advised. Dress: informal. AE,
MC, V. Open Apr., May, and Oct., weekends; June–Sept, daily. Closed for lunch.*

Expensive **A & J's Blue Claw.** Located in the center of Cape May's commercial seaport, this traditional seafood restaurant gets its flounder, tuna, bluefish, and mako shark directly from the boats and
serves them in a nautical setting. They offer gourmet take-out
as well, and there's a fresh fish market near the restaurant. *991
Ocean Dr., on the causeway between Cape May and Wildwood
Crest, tel. 609/884–5878. Reservations advised. Dress: casual.
Free parking. MC, V. Dinner only. Closed Oct.–Apr.*

★ **Frescoes.** Italian restaurants are a cliché at the Jersey Shore,
especially in Atlantic City and Wildwood. Frescoes's inventive
nuovo Milano style blows the others away. You'll find pâtés,
calamari in corn batter, unusual seafood entrées, luscious po-
lenta, homemade ravioli in a Gorgonzola cheese sauce, and extraordinary desserts. *412 Bank St., tel. 609/884–0366. Reservations advised in summer. Dress: casual. MC, V. BYOB. Dinner only. Closed Nov.–Mar. and weekdays Apr., May, and
Oct.*

★ **Maureen.** Even if the Continental nouvelle cuisine menu weren't
top-notch, Maureen's (named for Maureen Horn, wife of chef
Steve Horn) gracious, shirt-sleeve informality is so blissfully
relaxing that you might want to go just for the ambience. The
ocean view, overlooking a busy corner of Ocean Drive, is among
the city's best. The "Mediterranean" Italian restaurant downstairs, *Es Ta Ti* (a blend of the best of trendy northern, and basic red-sauce southern Italian cuisines), has a pleasant, bistro
ambience, with excellent veal and pasta dishes. *Beach Dr. and
Decatur St., Maureen: tel. 609/884–3774. Es Ta Ti: tel. 609/
884–3504. Reservations required. Dress: informal. AE, MC,
V. Closed Jan.–Mar. and weekdays Apr., May, and Oct.–Dec.*
The Washington Inn. Fresh seafood, veal, chicken, and fresh
vegetables with rich Continental sauces are served in a festive
Victorian dining room. The Washington Inn has fireplaces, a
garden room, porch and patio dining, and a lovely wicker porch
and bar. The homemade desserts are wonderful. *801 Washington St., tel. 609/884–5697. Reservations advised. Dress:
casual. AE, DC, MC, V. Dinner only. Closed Jan. and weekdays Feb.–May and mid-Oct.–Dec.*

Moderate– **The Bayberry Inn.** Tucked into the back of Congress Hall, the
Expensive Bayberry serves grilled seafood, duck, beef, and chicken dishes
with Continental and piquant Oriental influences. The walls of
the dining room are decorated with Victorian paintings and il-
lustrations. *Congress Pl. and Perry St., tel. 609/884–8406. AE,
MC, V. BYOB. Dinner only. Closed Nov.–Mar. and weekdays
Apr., May, and Oct.*

★ **Lobster House.** The city's biggest and busiest traditional seafood restaurant boasts its own fish market and raw bar. There's
also a cocktail lounge on an ocean schooner. You can imagine
how fresh the fish is—the Lobster House loads much of it off its

own boats. Yes, lobster, the huge Maine variety, is available, but consider flounder, bluefish, or ocean scallops. There's a small menu of chicken and beef, a children's menu, and early-bird specials in summer. *Fisherman's Wharf, tel. 609/884–8296. Reservations advised in summer. Free parking. AE, MC, V. Open daily for dinner.*

The Mad Batter. On the ground floor of the 1882 Carroll Villa Hotel, this is one of Cape May's best restaurants. If you opt to have lunch on the porch, you'll have a distant view of the ocean. The menu is dependably good, if a bit eccentric, combining Chinese, Thai, American, French, Italian, and Mexican cuisines. No alcoholic beverages are served, and there is a small charge for glasses if you bring your own liquor. *19 Jackson St., tel. 609/884–5970. Reservations advised for dinner. Dress: informal. MC, V. Closed Apr.–May, weekdays, and Oct.*

Peaches Cafe. This tiny, intimate café with peach-colored walls and fresh flowers is a quiet retreat from the bustle of Washington Mall. The menu has a smattering of Continental and Thai dishes, as well as traditional seafood such as feather-light Maryland crab cakes and luscious New England clam chowder. In summer you can sit outside and watch the meter maids ticket the Mercedeses. *322 Carpenters La., 1 block south of the Washington Mall, tel. 609/884–1511. Reservations advised. Dress: casual. MC, V. BYOB. Dinner and Sun. brunch. Closed Nov.–Mar. and weekdays Apr., May, and Oct.*

Water's Edge. A surprisingly good "American nouvelle" restaurant (located up Beach Drive adjacent to La Mer Motel) that from the outside resembles a motel coffee shop. Inside, the settings are elegant, the mood is very posh, and the menu emphasizes regional American cuisine. *Beach Dr. and Pittsburgh Ave., tel. 609/884–1717. Reservations advised. Dress: casual. AE, MC, V. Dinner only. Closed Jan.–Apr. and weekdays May and Oct.–Dec.*

Watson's Merion Inn. Cape May's oldest restaurant has been serving dinner and drinks since 1885. The menu is American—Jersey Shore surf and turf with some early-bird specials. *106 Decatur St., tel. 609/884–8363. Reservations accepted. Dress: informal, no shorts. Limited off-street parking. MC, V. Closed Nov.–Mar. and weekdays Apr., May, and Oct.*

Moderate
★ **The Chalfonte Hotel.** The Southern-style—and we mean Deep South—fixed-price dinners are rich and filling, built around baked Virginia ham, roast turkey, fried chicken, spoon bread, and fresh biscuits. Alcoholic beverages are served, though a 15% service charge is added to beverage checks. Children under age 6 can dine in a separate, supervised dining room. *301 Howard St., tel. 609/884–8409. Reservations advised. Jackets required. MC, V. Closed Nov.–May.*

La Toque. Satisfying French bistro cuisine is served in an unlikely place—what was once Cape May's post office. The omelets make a filling breakfast, lunches are quick, and there is an occasional early-bird special. *210 Ocean St., near the Washington Mall, tel. 609/884–1511. Dinner reservations advised. Dress: casual. AE, MC, V. Closed Nov.–Mar. and weekdays Apr., May, and Oct.*

★ **Louisa's Cafe.** If it weren't for the summer crowds waiting outside, you'd miss this tiny place. The dining room barely holds a dozen tables, but the quality ingredients and care of preparation make the wait worth it. Though many seafood, beef, and duck dishes are prepared, Louisa's heart seems to be in the zingy fresh herbs in the sauces, the al dente pastas, and the vegetables. Louisa's is a smoke-free zone and serves no alcohol. *104 Jackson St., just off the Washington Mall, tel. 609/884– 8406. No reservations. Dress: casual. No credit cards. Closed Nov.–Apr. and weekdays May, Sept., and Oct.*

★ **The Globe.** The Globe proves that casual family-style dining need not be dull. The international menu includes offbeat samples of Chinese, Italian, French, Mexican cuisines, and also good old American surf and turf, well prepared with good presentation. A great early-bird special: Children under age 5 get a free meal if they order before 6 PM. *Broadway and Sunset Blvd., tel. 609/884–2429. Reservations advised. Dress: casual. Street parking. AE, MC, V. Dinner only. Closed mid-Oct.– Apr. and weekdays May and early Oct.*

Inexpensive– Moderate **The Filling Station.** Dependable American dishes and a salad bar are served family style in what was once a gas station. Early-bird and all-you-can-eat chicken and catfish specials are featured. *615 Lafayette St., across from the Acme parking lot, tel. 609/884–2111. No reservations. Dress: casual. Limited off-street parking. AE, MC, V. BYOB. Closed Mon. and Oct.– Mar.*

Lodging

Seasoned travelers know that small inns, as charming as they can be, are not necessarily for everyone. Most forbid smoking anywhere inside. Handicapped persons should note that most small inns do not offer convenient access and cannot add ramps or elevators because of strict historical guidelines governing the appearance of their structures.

Cape May inns are not especially suited to small children, who may inadvertently injure themselves or damage antiques. Families with children should stay in inns that welcome children or consider motels or hotels with a swimming pool, where children can amuse themselves.

Room rates used to rank accommodations are for the peak summer season, June through August, for a standard double room. Expect to pay more for a suite or a room with an ocean view. Rates drop significantly in the cooler shoulder seasons of spring and autumn and are at their lowest in winter. Ask for weekend, midweek, and full-week package rates.

All rooms in hotels and motels have a private bath, unless noted. Many small hotels, B&Bs, and guest houses (a private house, but no breakfast is served) have shared baths. All motels face the ocean unless indicated otherwise.

For price ranges, consult the lodging chart in Chapter 1, Essential Information. Highly recommended lodgings are indicated with a star ★ .

Bed-and-Breakfasts

Very Expensive **Angel of the Sea.** The most expensive B&B in town—$250 in high season—is about a mile from the historic district. The symmetrical Second Empire–style mansion was built in 1850 and moved three times before coming to rest on the Trenton Avenue beach block. Barbara and John Girton have decorated the inn with bright wallpaper and Victorian or white wicker furnishings. All rooms in the large guest house and adjoining cottage are heated and have ceiling fans; eight rooms have whirlpools, and most rooms have porch access. *5–7 Trenton Ave., 08204, tel. 609/884–3369 or 800/848–3369. 27 rooms with private bath. Full hot breakfast, afternoon tea and cakes. Facilities: cable TV, VCRs, free beach tags, beach chairs, beach towels, use of bicycles. Smoking permitted on porches only. 2-night minimum stay on weekends, 3-night minimum stay on holiday weekends. AE, MC, V.*

Expensive– Very Expensive **Colvmns by the Sea.** An eccentric doctor's very eccentric summer retreat is a get-away-from-it-all B&B. Located almost at the northeastern end of Beach Drive, more than a mile from the historic district, Colvmns is named for the bizarre fluted Italianate columns supporting the massive colonial second floor over a wraparound porch. There are incredible views of the crashing surf from the third-floor rooms. Swimming is not allowed on this beach because heavy seas have eroded the beach. The master bedroom has a Renaissance Revival mixed-wood, marble-topped bedroom set. *1513 Beach Dr., 08204, tel. 609/884–2228. 11 rooms with private bath. Full hot breakfast, afternoon tea and sherry. Facilities: bicycles, beach tags. Smoking on porch only. 3- to 4-night minimum stay in summer and on weekends. Off-street parking. No credit cards. Closed Nov.–Mar.*

Humphrey Hughes House. A grand, shingle-style residence named for the ship captain who settled in Cape May in 1692, this house, built in 1903 for a wealthy Philadelphian, is crammed with beautiful period antiques, some of them original to the house. The guest rooms are large, and all feature air-conditioning, TV, and ocean views. In the parlor is an antique (1870) square grand piano. *29 Ocean St., 08204, tel. 609/884–4428. 10 rooms with private bath. Full hot breakfast, afternoon tea. Free use of beach tags and beach towels. Smoking on veranda or sun porch only. 2-night minimum stay weekends, 3-night minimum summer weekends and holidays. Off-site parking. MC, V.*

★ **The Mainstay.** One of Cape May's best B&Bs, the former Jackson's Clubhouse, an 1870 gambling and men's social club, is one of America's first restored B&Bs and a magnificent example of how to do it right. The high ceilings, oversize guest rooms, harmoniously arranged museum-quality antiques, and lavish plantings give the feel of another era. Tom and Sue Carroll view the inn as their stage and their role as innkeepers as a beguiling performance. The hammock on the veranda, which can be seen by passersby on Columbia Avenue, is the city's most ostentatious spot for doing nothing. You can see the ocean from the cupola. *635 Columbia Ave., 08204, tel. 609/884–8690. 12 rooms with private bath in main house and adjacent cottage. Hot breakfast in colder months, Continental breakfast in summer, afternoon tea. Facilities: piano, game room, small garden with fountain. 3-night minimum stay summer weekends. No credit cards. Closed Jan.–mid-Mar.*

★ **The Manor House.** Thanks to innkeeper Tom Snyder's love of comedy and jokes, this B&B has a sense of humor—what the Victorians would call "levity." His morning "reading of the day" is both an introduction and a send-up of the city's attractions and distractions. Rooms have a harmonious mix of antiques and quality modern furniture—not quite the museum quality of The Mainstay or The Abbey, but enough to lend atmosphere and charm. The Snyders are serious about cuisine: Breakfast is five huge courses with fresh ingredients. You can relax in the antique barber's chair in the den or enjoy the player piano. The Manor House is located on Cape May's prettiest street. *612 Hughes St., 08204, tel. 609/884–4710. 9 rooms, 7 with private bath. Hot breakfast, afternoon tea. Facilities: whirlpool in suite, beach tags and beach towels. 2- to 3-night minimum stay requested. Smoking on porch only. Free parking. No credit cards. Closed Jan.*

★ **The Queen Victoria.** In the center of the historic district and blessed with a genteel air, this 1881 Gothic Revival villa is a living lecture on Victorian architecture presided over by Dane and Joan Wells. Beautiful handmade quilts grace the beds and all rooms have sinks; some baths have whirlpools and TVs. One suite, a ground-floor cottage, is accessible to the handicapped. *102 Ocean St., 08204, tel. 609/884–8702. 17 rooms (13 with bath) and 7 suites. Hot breakfast, afternoon tea. Facilities: bicycles, beach tags and beach towels free to guests, crib available for infants. 2-night minimum stay requested on weekends and holidays; in summer, 3- to 4-night stay requested. Off-street and limited on-site parking. MC, V.*

Wilbraham Mansion & Inn. Perched on the southwestern edge of Cape May, this 1840 private house is the only B&B with its own heated indoor pool, measuring 36 by 18 feet. The Bridal Suite opens onto the pool area. Much of the furniture is original to the house. One large suite has a pedestal tub. All rooms are heated and air-conditioned. Proprietors Pat and Rose Down collect musical instruments. *133 Myrtle Ave., 08204, tel. 609/884–2046. 7 rooms with bath and 2 suites. Hot breakfast, afternoon tea and snacks. Free parking, free use of beach tags, beach towels and bicycles. 2-night minimum stay in summer. MC, V.*

Expensive   **Albert G. Stevens Inn.** Next door to the Wilbraham Mansion, this turreted, Queen Anne–style private house is on the fringe of town within a few blocks of the beach and Washington Mall. Interiors are mixed woods, with a few antiques and reproductions, and there is an outdoor hot tub. *127 Myrtle Ave., 08204, tel. 609/884–4717. 6 rooms (4 with private bath) and 2 suites. Full hot breakfast, afternoon tea. Beach tags provided. No smoking. 2-night minimum stay weekends, 3-night minimum on holidays. Off-street parking. MC, V.*

Captain Mey's Inn. Named for the Dutch discoverer of Cape May, this 1890 house was built for a physician and has been furnished by Carin Feddermann and Millie LaCanfora with a Dutch theme (it features a beautiful collection of Delft porcelain). Three Tiffany-style stained-glass windows grace the foyer. The inn is near the Washington Mall. *202 Ocean St., 08204, tel. 609/884–7793. 10 rooms, 5 with private bath. Hot breakfast, afternoon tea. Facilities: fireplace, garden. Room service. Free parking. MC, V.*

Columbia House. Barbara and Bob Daggett are the hosts of this 1885 Queen Anne home in the historic district. The house is stocked with carefully researched Victorian antiques. All rooms are heated. Coffee and tea are served in the rooms, smoking is permitted, and children of all ages are welcome. *26 Ocean St., 08204, tel. 609/884–2789. 2 rooms with bath, 3 suites. Facilities: ceiling fans, TV, use of beach tags, towels. 2-*

night minimum stay, 3 nights in summer. Off-street parking. No credit cards.

Fairthorne. Built in 1892 for a whaling captain, the Fairthorne was originally called Hanson House. The house has peach and pink walls, lace curtains, and Victorian period antiques. The Fairthorne is one block from the beach. *111 Ocean St., 08204, tel. 609/884–8791. 7 rooms, 5 with private baths. Full hot breakfast, afternoon tea. Facilities: beach tags, beach towels. Smoking on veranda only. 2- to 3-night minimum stay on summer weekends. Off-site parking. MC, V.*

Summer Cottage Inn. This 1867 Italianate bracketed cottage with a cupola is run by Nancy Rishforth, a popular walking-tour guide. She was a caterer in a former life and makes sumptuous hot breakfasts and elegant afternoon tea. Rooms, which are heated, are furnished in various period styles. The garden suite, with a private entrance and sitting and dressing rooms, is furnished with linens, crystal, and china. *613 Columbia St., 08204, tel. 609/884–4948. 9 rooms, 6 with private bath. Facilities: ceiling fans, fireplace, baby grand piano, game room, porch swing, beach tags provided. 2-night minimum stay weekends, 3 nights summer weekends and holidays. MC, V. Closed weekdays in Jan.–Feb.*

The Wooden Rabbit. Children of all ages and their parents are welcome to this playful Hughes Street inn decorated with motifs and characters taken from Beatrix Potter's storybooks. Greg and Debby Burow have filled the inn with wicker furnishings, brass beds, collectibles, and folk art. Rooms are air-conditioned. *609 Hughes St., 08204, tel. 609/884–7293. 3 rooms with private bath. Hot breakfast, afternoon tea, bedtime chocolates. Facilities: TV, fireplace, beach tags, beach towels. 2-night minimum, 3-night minimum July–Aug. No smoking. Off-street parking. MC, V.*

Moderate– Expensive ★

The Abbey. The 1869 summer home of Philadelphia coal baron John B. McCreary is one of the best examples of the Gothic Revival in Cape May. It is noted for its antiques and the eccentricity of its innkeepers Jay and Marianne Schatz. There's nothing remotely religious associated with the property. A block from the beach and two blocks from the Washington Mall, the Abbey's guest rooms (and the 1873 cottage beside it, which the Schatzes also own) have private baths and period antiques; some also have refrigerators and are air-conditioned. *Columbia Ave. and Gurney St., 08204, tel. 609/884–4506. 14 rooms with private bath. Hot breakfast in spring and autumn, Continental breakfast in summer, afternoon refreshments. Facilities: garden and croquet yard, free beach tags and beach towels. AE, MC, V. Closed Jan.–mid-Mar.*

Abigail Adams' Bed & Breakfast by the Sea. Edward and Donna Misner are the proprietors of this five-room inn, one of architect Stephen Button's Seven Sisters (1889). Breakfast can be served in your room in the spring and fall. One suite with an ocean view has a sitting room. *12 Jackson St., 08204, tel. 609/884–1371. 5 rooms, 3 with private bath. Afternoon tea and beverages. No smoking. MC, V. Closed mid-Nov.–mid-Apr.*

Barnard-Good House. Near the edge of town on Perry Street, this Second Empire cottage has can't-miss-it lavender trim and is famous for serving the Cape's most filling, fanciful, opulent, and altogether outrageous inn breakfast. Don't even think about losing weight, though special diets can be accommodated. The decor is scrupulously Victorian—one bathroom even has a copper tub. Nan and Tom Hawkins are the innkeepers. *238 Perry St., 08204, tel. 609/884–5381. 6 rooms with bath, 1 suite. Facilities: free use of bicycles, beach tags. Smoking on veranda only. 2- and 3-night minimum weekend stay, 4-night minimum for suite. MC, V. Closed mid-Nov.–mid-Mar.*

The Brass Bed. All of the rooms in this 1872 Gothic Revival cottage, replete with extravagant gingerbread carpentry, sport a 19th-century brass bed. John and Donna Dunwoody have used cream and buff colors to offset the shiny beds. The inn is located on one of Cape May's prettiest streets. *719 Columbia Ave., 08204, tel. 609/884–8075. 8 rooms, 6 with private bath. Hot breakfast in fall and winter, Continental breakfast in spring and summer, afternoon tea. MC, V.*

The Duke of Windsor Inn. An 1896 cedar-shingled Queen Anne home built for a Delaware Bay boat pilot, the Duke is near the Physick Estate on Washington Street. The magnificent oak staircase in the foyer leads to two pentagonal tower guest rooms. *817 Washington St., 08204, tel. 609/884–1355. 9 rooms, 8 with private bath. Full hot breakfast spring and fall, cold breakfast in summer (served in formal dining room), afternoon tea, free parking and beach tags. No smoking. MC, V. Closed Jan.*

The Gingerbread House. The best known of the 1869 Stockton Place Row Houses, the Gingerbread's intricate trim is a part-time passion of woodworking innkeeper Fred Echevarria. Fred's mother, Joanne, did most of the watercolors inside. All rooms are heated and have ceiling fans. Some rooms have antiques while others have modern wood pieces. *28 Gurney St., 08204, tel. 609/884–0211. 6 rooms, 3 with private bath. Facilities: Continental buffet breakfast, fireplace, free use of beach tags. 2- and 3-night weekend minimum stay, 4 nights on weekends and holidays June–Aug. No credit cards.*

The Manse. A quiet accommodation on Hughes Street, this comparative youngster was built in 1908 as a parsonage. The furnishings are traditional dark woods with Oriental rugs and some modern pieces in varying styles. The Manse features some elaborate stained-glass windows. *510 Hughes St., 08204, tel. 609/884–0116. 5 rooms with shared baths. Full hot breakfast, afternoon tea. Facilities: beach tags, beach towels, hair dryers, free on-site parking. Smoking on first floor only. 3-night minimum stay July–Sept., and holiday weekends; 2-night minimum other times. No credit cards. Closed Jan.–Feb.*

The Sand Castle. Peg Barradale is the innkeeper of this large 1873 "carpenter-Gothic" cottage a block from the ocean and four blocks from the Washington Mall. It has country Victorian antiques and a large two-bedroom suite with a private sun deck. All rooms are heated and have ceiling fans; some rooms are air-conditioned. *829 Stockton Ave., 08204, tel. 609/884–5451. 7 rooms, 1 with private bath; 3 apartment suites with private baths and kitchens. Continental breakfast, afternoon tea. Free transportation to and from the bus terminal, free use of bicycles, beach tags and beach towels. Smoking on veranda only. 2-night minimum stay in summer, 3 nights on holiday weekends. MC, V.*

The Victorian Rose. Romance and roses go together, and this Gothic Revival house and adjacent cottage are almost engulfed by 150 rosebushes and rose patterns on dishes, wallpaper, bed linens, and in the Victorian detailing in the guest rooms. Innkeeper Bob Mullock, a jovial fellow who leads MAC walking tours, likes Mozart and big-band music. Children of all ages

permitted in cottage. All rooms have ceiling fans; some have
TV and air-conditioning. *715 Columbia Ave., 08204, tel.
609/884–2497. 10 rooms, 5 with private bath, 3 with efficiency-
style kitchens; 3 suites. Hot breakfast. Use of beach tags. 3-
night minimum stay weekends June–Sept. No credit cards.
Closed Jan.–Feb.*

Windward House. This Edwardian, shingle-style house has
three porches, a third-floor sun deck, a fireplace, Victorian
antiques, and a player piano. Two suites have access to a second-floor porch. Innkeepers Owen and Sandy Miller have a collection of vintage clothing. The rooms are heated and air-
conditioned. *24 Jackson St., 08204, tel. 609/884–3368. 8 rooms
with private bath and refrigerator. Continental breakfast in
summer, hot breakfast in cooler months, afternoon tea. Facilities: free use of bicycles, beach tags. Smoking permitted. MC,
V.*

Moderate **Poor Richard's Inn.** This relaxing Second Empire villa (circa
1882), built for the original owner of the adjacent Carroll Villa,
is stocked with rustic and Victorian antiques. It's a block from
the beach and next door to the Mad Batter restaurant. Well-be-
haved children are welcome. All rooms are heated and air-conditioned. *17 Jackson St., 08204, tel. 609/884–3536. 9 rooms, 4
with private bath. No credit cards.*

Woodleigh House. The two cottages in this B&B have some antiques and quilts but are not as fancy as B&Bs closer to the historic district. They offer a more down-home atmosphere than
the museum-style inns. All rooms are heated and have ceiling
fans. *808 Washington St., 08204, tel. 609/884–5329. 8 rooms in 2
cottages, 4 with private bath. Continental breakfast. Facilities:
garden with picnic table, use of refrigerator, bicycles, and
beach tags. Smoking on verandas only. 3-night minimum stay
weekends June–Oct. Off-street parking. No credit cards.*

Guest Houses

Expensive **The Prince Edward.** Subdivided into one- and two-bedroom
suites, this Queen Anne home has antique furnishings and 12
elaborate stained-glass windows, 10 of which are original. All
rooms are heated and have ceiling fans; one suite is air-conditioned. Children of all ages welcome. *38 Jackson St., 08204, tel.
609/884–2131. 3 suites, 1 1-bedroom, 2 2-bedrooms. Facilities:
kitchens, parlor, TV, and private entrances, laundry machines, beach tags, off-street parking. Smoking permitted. 2-
night minimum stay, 1-wk minimum June–Sept. No credit
cards. Closed Jan.–Feb.*

The Victorian Lace. An 1869 house with a covered porch, this
inn is just far enough from the central historic district to encourage rest and relaxation. It features lace curtains and antique and wicker furnishings. All rooms are heated and have
ceiling fans. The large three-room suites have kitchens and can
sleep four to six people; the two-story carriage house has a
kitchen and king-size bed. Suites are rented for the weekend
off-season and by the week in summer. Families with children
preferred. *901 Stockton Ave., 08204, tel. 609/884–1772. 4 3-
room suites with efficiency kitchens, 1 carriage house. Facilities: outdoor grill, picnic table, free beach tags and towels. No
credit cards.*

Moderate– **The Puffin.** Bob and Toni Greene run this 1905 Dutch Colonial
Expensive Revival house with Victorian and seacoast decor. Their pride is

a working Edison phonograph. All suites have kitchens and private baths. The third-floor apartment has a sun deck and an ocean view. *32 Jackson St., 08204, tel. 609/884–2664. 2 studio apartments and 3 1-bedroom apartments. Facilities: beach tags. 1-wk minimum June–Sept. Off-street parking. No credit cards.*

Moderate **Holly House.** This immaculate Jackson Street Seven Sister is notable for its carefully detailed contrasting green-and-red coloring. All rooms are heated and have ceiling fans. Innkeeper Bruce Minnix directs television soap operas in New York (leaving his wife, Corrinne, to run the house). A former mayor of Cape May, Minnix fought for preservation and restoration, helped create the MAC walking tours, and recently produced and directed "Victorian Cape May," a 25-minute video. *20 Jackson St., 08204, tel. 609/884–7365. 6 rooms with shared bath. Facilities: beach tags, free off-site parking. No smoking. MC, V.*

Springside. Another one of Stephen Button's Seven Sisters, this inn has bright modern art and furnishings. All rooms are heated and have ceiling fans. Meryl and Bill Nelson, the innkeepers, have a collection of dollhouses. *18 Jackson St., 08204, tel. 609/884–2654. 4 rooms with shared bath. Facilities: beach tags, off-site parking. Smoking on porch only. MC, V.*

Inexpensive **Belmont Guest House.** This small family house, around the corner from The Chalfonte Hotel on beautiful Columbia Avenue, is a bargain. It has clean, plain rooms without antiques in a delightful part of the historic district. Though breakfast is not included in the room rate, innkeepers Lydia and Robert Magee will be happy to serve a Continental breakfast if you wish. *712 Columbia Ave., 08204, tel. 609/884–7507. 6 rooms, 1 with private bath. Facilities: free use of beach tags, porch, limited off-street parking. No credit cards.*

Hotels

Very Expensive **Best Western Marquis de Lafayette Inn on the Beach.** The beachfront Marquis is a motel that "Victorianized" itself, adding period-style furniture and trim. All rooms face the ocean and have balconies. The rooftop Top of the Marq is a steak house that Cape May's old guard frequents for dining and dancing. Rooftop and poolside restaurants have live entertainment weekends off-season, nightly in summer. *501 Beach Dr., 08204, tel. 609/884–3500 or 800/257–0432. 73 rooms, 43 with kitchens. Facilities: crib available, coin-operated laundry, beach tags, outdoor pool, sauna, valet service, free parking, meeting rooms. Children under age 8 stay free. AE, D, DC, MC, V.*

★ **The Virginia Hotel.** Original porches and a balcony mark the exterior of this superbly restored, first-class hotel (it was built in the late 1880s). The interior is completely modern, done in soft hues of taupe, peach, and green. Two rooms have private porches overlooking Jackson Street. The Virginia, Cape May's best small property for executive retreats, is recommended for those who want a full-service hotel on an intimate scale. The Ebbit Room restaurant serves breakfast, lunch, and dinner. There is live music nightly in the piano bar. *25 Jackson St., 08204, tel. 609/884–5700. 24 rooms with private bath. Facilities: cable TV and VCRs, video rentals, complimentary newspaper, room service 6 AM–10 PM, bathrobes provided, turn-down service, beach tags, beach chair additional $4,* *meeting room with audiovisual, business support services, valet parking. 2-night minimum stay weekends and holidays. AE, MC, V.*

Expensive–Very Expensive **The Grand Hotels.** Three motels merged after extensive renovation to form the Grand Hotels, which is now the largest hotel in Cape May and the best for a small convention. Rooms, all of which are heated and air-conditioned, are furnished in Victorian style or with modern white wicker. Some suites have twin phones, twin bathrooms, and two televisions. The Grand has Cape May's only health spa. Blackbeard's restaurant serves moderately priced breakfast, lunch, and dinner, with early-bird specials and a children's menu. Live music is featured weekends off-season and nightly in the summer. Twitty's Porch serves expensive Cape May eclectic cuisine at the poolside in summer. The Penthouse piano bar overlooks the ocean. *Beach Dr. and Philadelphia Ave., 08204, tel. 609/884–5611, 800/ 257–8550, or 800/582–5991 in NJ. 202 rooms, 93 suites (24 bi-level). Facilities: exercise room, sauna, steam cabinets, indoor and outdoor pools, whirlpool, 2 ballrooms, 13 hospitality suites. AE, DC, MC, V.*

Moderate–Expensive **The Inn of Cape May.** A striking blend of old and new, the 1894 Queen Anne Colonial Hotel had the city's first elevator and electric bell system. It was restored and is now furnished with antiques. The long porch faces the ocean. The inn is also linked to a motel wing, more suitable than the older, Victorian hotel for families with children. Alathea's Restaurant serves moderately priced breakfast and dinner. *Beach Dr. and Ocean Ave., 08204, tel. 609/884–3483, 800/257–0432, or 800/582–5933 in NJ. 124 rooms, 54 with private bath, some without telephones. Facilities: restaurant, bar, pool, meeting rooms. AE, D, DC, MC, V. Closed Nov.–Mar.*

Moderate **The Carroll Villa.** Mark Kulkowitz and Pam Huber operate this restored Victorian hotel a half block from the Washington Mall. Breakfast at the Mad Batter restaurant, which takes up most of the Villa's lower floor, is included. Guests have use of a separate living-room area, garden terrace, and cupola. Warning: Aromas from the Mad Batter kitchen can be fatal to diets. *19 Jackson St., 08204, tel. 609/884–9619. 24 rooms, 17 with private bath. Facilities: beach tags, off-street parking. 2-night minimum stay weekends, 3 nights holiday weekends. No smoking. MC, V.*

The Chalfonte Hotel. A hotel like no other in Cape May—old, creaky, spartan, and proud of it—the Chalfonte, which dates to 1878, is one of the town's most significant preserved structures. Furnishings are simple to the point of being drab. Most of the guest rooms share bathrooms, and there are no locks on doors, no room service, and no air-conditioning or heat. Rates include breakfast and Southern-style dinner (*see* Dining, above). During the novel Work Weekends (held in the spring and fall), guests who do restoration work receive a discount. Piano music is performed nightly in the King Edward Bar, and concerts, workshops, and films are scheduled most weeks. *301 Howard St., 08204, tel. 609/884–8409. 72 rooms, a few with private bath. Additional rooms, some with private bath, in 3 cottages near the hotel. Facilities: meeting areas, cot or child's crib available. Children stay free in parents' room, with charges for meals and gratuities, ranging from $3 to $26, de-*

pending on age. No smoking. No pets. MC, V. Closed mid-Oct.–May.

Motels

Very Expensive

La Mer. Somewhat out of the way on Beach Drive, La Mer is blessed with the excellent Water's Edge restaurant (*see* Dining, above). You'll have to walk (or bicycle) a few blocks to beaches, shopping, and the historic district, but miniature golf and bicycle rentals are nearby. All rooms are heated and air-conditioned. *Beach Dr. and Pittsburgh Ave., near Christian Admiral Hotel, 08204, tel. 609/884–2200. 68 rooms, 18 with kitchens. Facilities: pool, wading pool, coin-operated laundry. AE, D, DC, MC, V. Closed Nov.–Apr.*

Summer Station. This beachfront condo hotel, named for a railroad station that stood at this site, is suitable for families. It has modern one- to three-bedroom apartments and is close to the historic district and shopping. Most rooms have beach views and balconies, and all rooms have a kitchen with a dishwasher, washing machines, and a TV and are heated and air-conditioned. *217 Beach Dr., 08204, tel. 609/884–8800 or 800/248–8801. 45 suites. Facilities: pool, sun deck, maid service, baby-sitting. 2-night minimum stay in summer, 3-night minimum on summer weekends. AE, MC.*

Expensive

Atlas Motor Inn. Tucked along Beach Drive's eastern motel row, the Atlas is across from the beach, a few blocks from the Washington Mall and the historic district. All rooms are heated and air-conditioned. *1035 Beach Dr., 08204, tel. 609/884–7000, 800/257–8513, or 800/642–3766 in NJ. 100 rooms, 50 suites with kitchens. Facilities: TV, pool, sauna, restaurant, bar with live entertainment in summer, champagne Sunday brunch. Free parking. CB, DC, MC, V.*

Coachman's Motor Inn. This motel is family-owned and only a few blocks from Washington Mall. The motel's Rusty Nail restaurant has a bar with live entertainment. The rooms are heated and air-conditioned. *205 Beach Dr., 08204, tel. 609/884–8463. 65 rooms, 45 with kitchens, most with ocean views. Facilities: TV, pool and wading pool, tennis, shuffleboard, cribs available, free parking. AE, MC, V.*

Periwinkle Inn. Most rooms at this small, beachfront courtyard motel with "Victorianized" details face the pool; others have ocean views. The rooms are heated and air-conditioned. *1039 Beach Dr., 08204, tel. 609/884–9200. 52 rooms, 14 with kitchens. Facilities: refrigerators, TVs in rooms, cribs, outdoor pool, wading pool, shuffleboard, baby-sitting service, free parking. No credit cards.*

Moderate–Expensive

Montreal Inn. This family-operated motel, a few blocks from the historic district, faces the ocean. Rooms are heated and air-conditioned. *Beach Dr. and Madison Ave., 08204, tel. 609/884–7011. 70 rooms, 42 with kitchens. Facilities: TV, heated pool, sauna, restaurant, lounge and packaged-goods store, cribs, coin-operated laundry, valet service, free parking. AE, MC, V.*

The Arts and Nightlife

For news and entertainment listings, consult the daily *Press,* known locally as the *Atlantic City Press.* Among free publications, the *Cape May Herald Dispatch* and the *Star & Wave,* published weekly, have more local news and entertainment listings. Events sponsored by the Mid-Atlantic Center for the Arts (MAC) are listed in **"This Week in Cape May,"** a free pamphlet available at many shops and bed-and-breakfasts, and also at the MAC offices at the Emlen Physick Estate (1048 Washington St.).

The Arts

Concerts
Concerts by Candlelight. The Chalfonte Hotel (301 Howard St., tel. 609/884–8409) has classical and chamber music June–September on Thursday evenings.

The **Sunday Concert Series** takes place during July and August in Convention Hall (Beach Dr. and Howard St., tel. 609/884–9565) every Sunday at 9 PM. Other regularly scheduled summer-season Convention Hall activities include the Boardwalk Revue, a song-and-dance show, every Tuesday at 8:15 PM.

Free concerts are held in the **Rotary Bandshell** in July and August on Wednesday and Saturday evenings at 8 PM. The bandshell is located just west of the Washington Mall between the Mall and Lafayette Street.

Theater
Mid-Atlantic Stage. A varying program of revived Broadway musicals and plays is sponsored by the Mid-Atlantic Center for the Arts in July and August. *Cape May Welcome Center, 405 Lafayette St., tel. 609/884–9562 or 884–2787. Admission: $10 adults, $8 children.*

Victorian Dinner Theater. Period plays, mysteries, melodramas, and farces are performed at the Winchester Inn. *513 Lafayette St., tel. 609/884–4358. Dinner and show Apr., May, Sept., and Oct., Thurs., Fri., and Sat. evening; June, July, and Aug., Tues.–Sun. Dinner seatings at 6:30 PM; show only, 7:45 PM. Fixed-price dinner and show, $30; show only, $12. Reservations required. MC, V.*

Movies
MAC shows classic films—on a real screen with a real movie projector (none of that VCR stuff!)—Monday nights in July and August at **The Chalfonte Hotel** (301 Howard St., tel. 609/884–8409).

First-run movies are shown weekends in spring and fall and daily in summer at the **Beach Twin Theater** (tel. 609/884–4403), on Beach Drive between Queen and Jefferson streets.

Nightlife

Bars, Lounges, Nightclubs
Carney's is the closest thing in Cape May to a Jersey Shore rock-and-roll bar, with live rock bands in summer. *411 Beach Dr., tel. 609/884–4424. Open Mar.–mid-Apr., weekends; mid-Apr.–mid-Oct., daily. AE, MC, V.*

Carney's Other Room, just next door, has much quieter Irish folk music and piano bar sing-alongs in a pub-style setting. *413 Beach Dr., tel. 609/884–4424. Open weekends in May and September, daily in summer. AE, MC, V.*

C-View Inn. Catering to a fishermen and Coast Guard clientele, this unpretentious roadside bar is known for its low prices. *Washington St. and Texas Ave., just before the Cold Spring Inlet bridge, tel. 609/884–4712. Open daily. No credit cards.*

Jackson Mountain Cafe. Live rock and pop bands alternate with comedy nights in this rather new bar decorated with brass and ferns. The café sits on Cape May's highest natural elevation, which is still just a few feet above sea level. The menu features inexpensive lunches and moderate dinners. *Washington Mall and Jackson St., tel. 609/884–5648. Open daily. MC, V.*

King Edward Bar. This relaxing, out-of-the-way piano bar in The Chalfonte Hotel presents folk music, swing, or bluegrass Sunday evenings in the summer. *301 Howard St., tel. 609/ 884–8409. Closed Nov.–May. MC, V.*

The **Rusty Nail**, at the Coachman's Motor Inn (205 Beach Dr., tel. 609/884–0220), **Blackbeard's** at The Grand Hotels (Beach Dr. and Philadelphia Ave., tel. 609/884–5611), and the **Top of the Marq,** the rooftop restaurant in the Best Western Marquis de Lafayette (501 Beach Dr., tel. 609/884–3431) are for dining and dancing (the Top of the Marq gets an older, more affluent crowd). The Rusty Nail and Blackbeard's tend to feature light pop bands. At all three places music starts at 8:30 nightly in summer, weekends spring and fall.

The Shire presents live jazz, pop, and folk music in an unpretentious setting. The menu has inexpensive sandwiches and Mexican noshes. *Washington Mall, tel. 609/884–4700. Music nightly in summer, weekends in April, May, and Sept. AE, DC, MC, V.*

The Ugly Mug. Locals love this informal place that handles the Washington Mall tourist traffic with aplomb. On the ceiling hang hundreds of beer mugs of all shapes and varieties. Folk music is performed occasionally on summer weekends. The menu is mostly inexpensive sandwiches and platters. *Washington Mall and Decatur St., tel. 609/884–3459. Open Mon.–Sat. 11 AM–2 AM, Sun. noon–2 AM. MC, V.*

Appendix: Vacation Rentals

Throughout this guide, we've reviewed many hotels, motels, bed-and-breakfasts, and campgrounds for visitors to the Jersey Shore. Renting a house or apartment is also a popular alternative, especially for families. Therefore, we've provided below a list of realtors that handle vacation rentals in various communities along the shore. Fodor's does not necessarily recommend these realtors or the properties they handle, so you may also want to ask for referrals or recommendations from friends who've rented along the Shore in the past, or, failing that, from hotel owners, innkeepers, or restaurateurs in the communities you're interested in.

It is not unusual to find adjacent rental properties, one in excellent condition, the other run-down, available at rates that bear no relation to the quality of the housing. Rental rates are market driven, averaging $500–$1,000 per week for a two- to four-bedroom apartment with kitchen, dining room, and one–two bathrooms. The rates for houses can be more or less, depending on location.

Inspect the property you plan to rent **before** you sign any lease or agreement. The traditional time for inspections is in January or February. Make sure to ask what comes with the property. A kitchen advertised as fully equipped may not be so, and unless these items are itemized in your lease agreement, you have no way of being sure that the shining pots and pans, nicely polished furniture, television set, or cleaning supplies you see in February will be there when you arrive in July.

Some things to consider when evaluating a rental:

1) Parking. What appears to be a deserted street in the off-season may be filled with vehicles when the weather warms, especially near the beaches. If you will be arriving by car, be sure to ask if a private parking space is included with your rental. Be sure to look at the space to see if you can access it easily.

2) What utilities will be included, especially telephone, electricity, and cable broadcast service for the telephone. If you're renting in the off-season, ask if the property is heated.

3) Extermination. Insects are a perennial problem at the New Jersey Shore, so reach an understanding with your landlord about how to hire an exterminator if pests appear.

4) Proximity to supermarkets, convenience stores, hardware stores, coin-operated laundries, public transportation.

5) Children. If you're traveling with children, consider your proximity to heavily trafficked streets, undesirable taverns, noisy areas, libraries and facilities for rainy-day activity.

6) Senior citizens, handicapped travelers, people with special needs: Proximity to medical care, pharmacies, emergency services, easy access from the property to the street.

If you decide to rent the property, sign a lease agreement (examine the lease carefully before signing) and put down your deposit, usually a portion of your fee. You will pay the balance, plus an amount to be held in security by the landlord to cover incidental damage, when you pick up your keys when you arrive. The security deposit usually is returned immediately when you leave.

Properties

Atlantic County

Absecon **Stewart M Realty** (3 Bayview Dr., 08201, tel. 609/645–0802).

Atlantic City **Atlantic Vacation Center** (122 Delancey, 08201, tel. 609/345–9198).

Longport **Downbeach Real Estate, Inc.** (2401 Atlantic Ave., 08403, tel. 609/822–2835).

Northfield **Lightfoot Properties** (Northfield Area, 08225, tel. 609/272–1649).

Cape May County

Avalon and Stone Harbor **Avalon Real Estate Agency** (30th St. and Dune Dr., Box M, Avalon 08202, tel. 609/967–3001; 376 96th St., Stone Harbor 08247, tel. 609/368–1140).
Diller and Fisher Co., Inc. (3101 Dune Dr., Avalon 08202, tel. 609/967–3311; 9614 3rd Ave., Stone Harbor 08247, tel. 609/368–3311).
Ferguson-Dechert Real Estate, Inc. (2789 Dune Dr., Avalon 08202, tel. 609/967–4200).
Holiday Realty of Avalon (2150 Dune Dr., Avalon 08202, tel. 609/967–7571).
Newbold Real Estate Co., Inc. (68th St. and Ocean Dr., Box 1, Avalon 08202, tel. 609/967–8300).
Stone Harbor Realty Co., Inc. (30th St. and Dune Dr., Avalon 08202, tel. 609/967–7701; 9600 3rd Ave., Stone Harbor 08247, tel. 609/368–1440).

Cape May **E. M. Hanscomb** (917 Madison Ave., 08204, tel. 609/884–3330).
Jersey Cape Realty (739 Washington St., 08204, tel. 609/884–5800).
Kopp & Co. Century 21 (1382 Lafayette St., 08204, tel. 609/884–1800 or 800/648–5558).
Sol Needles Real Estate (Coldwell Banker, 512 Washington Mall, 08204, tel. 609/884–8428).
Roth's (510 Bank St., 08204, tel. 609/884–2806 or 800/227–3639).
Tolz (Box 498, 1001 Lafayette St., 08204, tel. 609/884–7001 or 800/444–7001).

Ocean City **French Real Estate** (1 Atlantic Ave., 08226, tel. 609/399–5454).
Hager Real Estate (111 Atlantic Ave., 08226, tel. 609/399–1856).
Monihan Realty (3201 32nd Ave./Central Ave., 08226, tel. 609/399–0998).
Richards Agency (1717 Asbury Ave., 08226, tel. 609/399–0998).

Sea Isle City **First Eastern Realty** (JFK Blvd. and Landis Ave., 08243, tel. 609/263–1171).

Freda Real Estate (6216 Landis Ave., 08243, tel. 609/263–2271).
Lamanna Agency (4400 Landis Ave., 08243, tel. 609/263–2233).
Laricks Agency (4110 Landis Ave., 08243, tel. 609/263–8300).
McCann and Sons (21 44th St., 08243, tel. 609/263–7422).
Realty Co. (5020 Landis Ave., 08243, tel. 609/263–2267).
Pleasure Realty Co. (23 38th St., 08243, tel. 609/263–6909).
Sea Isle Realty (106 W. Jersey Ave., 08243, tel. 800/223–1916).
Sofroney Realty (4201 Landis Ave., 08243, tel. 609/263–2206).
Townsends Inlet Realty, Inc. (8605 Landis Ave., 08243, tel. 609/263–7200).
Tracey Real Estate Agency (4100 Promenade, 08243, tel. 609/263–1411).

Wildwood   **Parson Realty** (2600 Atlantic Ave., 08260, tel. 609/522–3463).
Ranalli Realty (6th Ave. and New Jersey Ave., North Wildwood 08260, tel. 609/729–1100).
Wildwoods Realty (2101 New Jersey Ave., North Wildwood 08260, tel. 609/729–1701).
Wheaton Agency (300 New Jersey Ave., North Wildwood 08260, tel. 609/522–1486).

Monmouth County

Aberdeen Township   **Weichert Real Estate** (208 State Hwy., No. 34, 08402, tel. 908/583–5400).

Asbury Park   **Burns-Bradshaw, Inc.** (1508 Main, 07712, tel. 908/776–6844).

Bradley Beach   **McNeely Agency** (624 Main St., 08723, tel. 908/775–0208).

Freehold   **Meba, Inc.** (55 Rose Ct., 07728, tel. 908/780–3877).

Ocean County

Barnegat Peninsula   **Childers Real Estate** (Grand Central Ave., Lavalette 08735, tel. 908/830–2700).

Long Beach Island   **G. Anderson Agency** (12001 Long Beach Blvd., Haven Beach 08008, tel. 609/492–1277 or 800/999–1944; 295 Rte. 72 East, Manahawkin 08050, tel. 609/597–8507 or 800/444–8507).
Beach Associates (400 Long Beach Blvd., Surf City 08008, tel. 609/494–3646).
Inman Realty (17th St. and Central Ave., Barnegat Light 08006, tel. 609/494–2776).
Lackey Realty (79th St. and Long Beach Blvd., Harvey Cedars 08008, tel. 609/494–8500; 3rd St. and Bay Ave., Beach Haven 08008, tel. 609/492–7000; Box 115, Ship Bottom 08008, tel. 609/494–4511 or 609/597–3332).
Perk's Realty (6332 Long Beach Blvd., Harvey Cedars 08008, tel. 609/494–1130; 209 Long Beach Blvd., Surf City 08008, tel. 609/494–8280; 7200 Long Beach Blvd., Brant Beach 08008, tel. 609/494–3800; 377 Rte. 72, Manahawkin 08050, tel. 609/597–5600).
Sunset Harbor Realty (formerly Duffy Realty) (2 Susan Ave., Beach Haven 08008, tel. 609/492–5700).
Zachariae Realty (29th St. and Long Beach Blvd., Beach Haven 08008, tel. 609/492–7277 or 800/633–1146; 29th St. and Central Ave., Barnegat Light 08006, tel. 609/494–1776 or 800/633–1143; 11th St. and Long Beach Blvd., Ship Bottom 08008, tel. 609/494–7272 or 800/633–1140; 2709 Asbury Ave., Ocean City 08226, tel. 609/391–1800).

Index

Personal Itinerary

Departure *Date*

Time

Transportation

Arrival *Date*   *Time*

Departure *Date*   *Time*

Transportation

Accommodations

Arrival *Date*   *Time*

Departure *Date*   *Time*

Transportation

Accommodations

Arrival *Date*   *Time*

Departure *Date*   *Time*

Transportation

Accommodations

Personal Itinerary

Arrival *Date*   *Time*

Departure *Date*   *Time*

Transportation

Accommodations

Arrival *Date*   *Time*

Departure *Date*   *Time*

Transportation

Accommodations

Arrival *Date*   *Time*

Departure *Date*   *Time*

Transportation

Accommodations

Arrival *Date*   *Time*

Departure *Date*   *Time*

Transportation

Accommodations

Addresses

Name	*Name*
Address	*Address*
Telephone	*Telephone*
Name	*Name*
Address	*Address*
Telephone	*Telephone*
Name	*Name*
Address	*Address*
Telephone	*Telephone*
Name	*Name*
Address	*Address*
Telephone	*Telephone*
Name	*Name*
Address	*Address*
Telephone	*Telephone*
Name	*Name*
Address	*Address*
Telephone	*Telephone*
Name	*Name*
Address	*Address*
Telephone	*Telephone*
Name	*Name*
Address	*Address*
Telephone	*Telephone*

Addresses

Name _____

Address _____

_____

Telephone _____

Name _____

Address _____

_____

Telephone _____

Name _____

Address _____

_____

Telephone _____

Name _____

Address _____

_____

Telephone _____

Name _____

Address _____

_____

Telephone _____

Name _____

Address _____

_____

Telephone _____

Name _____

Address _____

_____

Telephone _____

Name _____

Address _____

_____

Telephone _____

Name _____

Address _____

_____

Telephone _____

Name _____

Address _____

_____

Telephone _____

Name _____

Address _____

_____

Telephone _____

Name _____

Address _____

_____

Telephone _____

Name _____

Address _____

_____

Telephone _____

Name _____

Address _____

_____

Telephone _____

Name _____

Address _____

_____

Telephone _____

Name _____

Address _____

_____

Telephone _____

Fodor's Travel Guides

U.S. Guides

Alaska
Arizona
Boston
California
Cape Cod
The Carolinas & the
 Georgia Coast
The Chesapeake
 Region
Chicago
Colorado
Disney World & the
 Orlando Area

Florida
Hawaii
Las Vegas
Los Angeles
Maui
Miami & the
 Keys
New England
New Mexico
New Orleans
New York City
New York City
 (Pocket Guide)

Pacific North Coast
Philadelphia & the
 Pennsylvania
 Dutch Country
Puerto Rico
 (Pocket Guide)
The Rockies
San Diego
San Francisco
San Francisco
 (Pocket Guide)
The South
Texas

USA
The Upper Great
 Lakes Region
Vacations in
 New York State
Vacations on the
 Jersey Shore
Virgin Islands
Virginia & Maryland
Waikiki
Washington, D.C.

Foreign Guides

Acapulco
Amsterdam
Australia
Austria
The Bahamas
The Bahamas
 (Pocket Guide)
Baja & the Pacific
 Coast Resorts
Barbados
Belgium &
 Luxembourg
Bermuda
Brazil
Budget Europe
Canada
Canada's Atlantic
 Provinces
Cancun, Cozumel,
 Yucatan Peninsula
Caribbean

Central America
China
Eastern Europe
Egypt
Europe
Europe's Great Cities
France
Germany
Great Britain
Greece
The Himalayan
 Countries
Holland
Hong Kong
India
Ireland
Israel
Italy
Italy 's Great Cities
Jamaica
Japan

Kenya, Tanzania,
 Seychelles
Korea
Lisbon
London
London Companion
London
 (Pocket Guide)
Madrid & Barcelona
Mexico
Mexico City
Montreal &
 Quebec City
Morocco
Munich
New Zealand
Paris
Paris (Pocket Guide)
Portugal
Rio de Janeiro
Rome

Saint Martin/
 Sint Maarten
Scandinavia
Scandinavian Cities
Scotland
Singapore
South America
South Pacific
Southeast Asia
Soviet Union
Spain
Sweden
Switzerland
Sydney
Thailand
Tokyo
Toronto
Turkey
Vienna & the
 Danube Valley
Yugoslavia

Wall Street Journal Guides to Business Travel

Europe

International Cities

The Pacific Rim

USA & Canada

Special-Interest Guides

Cruises and Ports
 of Call
Healthy Escapes

Fodor's Flashmaps
 New York
Fodor's Flashmaps
 Washington, D.C.

Shopping in Europe
Skiing in North
 America

Smart Shopper's
 Guide to London
Sunday in New York
Touring Europe